grief
is a
sneaky
bitch

grief
is a
sneaky
bitch

AN UNCENSORED GUIDE
TO NAVIGATING LOSS

lisa keefauver

Much of the introduction comes from Lisa Keefauver's 2023 TEDx Talk,
'Why Knowing More about Grief Can Make it Suck Less.'

First published in the USA in 2024 by University of Texas Press, Austin

First published in Great Britain in 2024 by Headline Home
an imprint of Headline Publishing Group

1

Cataloguing in Publication Data is available from the British Library

Trade paperback ISBN 978 1035 42643 0
eISBN 978 1035 42642 3

The names and identifying details of people associated with events described
in this book have been changed to protect their identity.

Book design by Endpaper Studio
Offset in 10.61/14.42pt Macklin Text by Jouve (UK), Milton Keynes

Printed and bound in Great Britain by Clays Ltd, Elcograf S.p.A.

Headline's policy is to use papers that are natural, renewable and recyclable
products and made from wood grown in well-managed forests and other
controlled sources. The logging and manufacturing processes are expected
to conform to the environmental regulations of the country of origin.

HEADLINE PUBLISHING GROUP
An Hachette UK Company
Carmelite House
50 Victoria Embankment
London EC4Y 0DZ

www.headline.co.uk
www.hachette.co.uk

Our lives are built by the stories we tell of our experiences. A death, a traumatic event, or some other devastating loss (of relationship, ability, homeland, dream) is akin to the manuscript of our lives being torn to shreds and handed back to us without instructions on how to rewrite or live our lives. Grief is the journey we're on as we rewrite and live our emerging story.

May this book serve as a guide as you rewrite and live the emerging story of your life in the wake of loss.

A BRIEF NOTE ABOUT THE TITLE

I admit the title of this book is bold—and yet self-evident. Grief *is* a sneaky bitch. Since the launch of my podcast of the same name four years ago, hundreds of thousands of listeners have validated this truth, declaring statements such as, "Yes, yes, yes! It absolutely is! That's so true!" You may have had a similar visceral reaction.

I'm also aware that some of you may have had an adverse response. After all, the phrase "sneaky bitch" has been used in our culture in a gendered way to oppress people who identify as women, reinforcing harmful beliefs and causing great and unnecessary suffering.

I assure you, as a woman, I have purposely, proudly, and unapologetically reclaimed this phrase in a non-gendered way to expand our narratives of grief and to create a safe space for all to navigate loss in a meaningful and supported way. The goal with this title, the contents of this book, and all the work I do as a grief activist is to ensure that everyone who experiences grief (which is 100 percent of us) can feel seen, held, and honored in all phases of their journey.

Later in this book, you'll read about "yes, and"—the idea that more than one thing can be true at the same time. Not everything is black and white; situations and feelings can be complex. It is in this spirit that I invite you to join me in acknowledging that, *yes*, grief is a sneaky bitch, *and* we can navigate loss together.

topic index

Grief is messy, disorienting, nonlinear—and a sneaky bitch, of course. Grief makes it hard to concentrate on, process, and recall information, especially in the weeks or months after a loss. Truthfully, you can feel disoriented even if the loss happened long ago. Although I've written this book so that every chapter builds on the prior one, each chapter contains its own dose of grief support.

Since focus can be a challenge, instead of a typical table of contents, I created a topic index. It's grouped by themes, making it easier to jump to the sections and topics that are most on your mind and in your heart. Because everyone's grief is unique, there's no right order in which to read this book, just like there's no one right way to grieve. Still, I suggest starting with the preface and introduction to orient you to me and what this book has to offer.

inviting you to start here

orienting you to the who, what, where, when, and why of grief

preface

life lessons learned at the bottom of the ocean

Dig, if you will, this picture: me as a twelve-year-old basking in the sun, turning my mousy brown, short-cropped hair a particular shade of orange thanks to the copious amounts of Sun-In I sprayed in my hair over the previous few days. (Shout out to the '80s for the look and Prince for the lyrical reference.)

I was sitting poolside on vacation with my dad, having whatever twelve-year-old preteen angst one has. I was probably thinking something like, "Am I getting fat? Do I need a bra yet? Are people noticing my acne? Why doesn't Paul notice me in class?"

Out of nowhere, a scuba dive instructor interrupted my angst and asked if I wanted to go diving with my dad that day. *Me?* He couldn't possibly be talking to me. But he was, and before my brain could process his invitation, I heard myself say, "Yes."

Wait. What the fuck?

Yes, I did have a potty mouth as a twelve-year-old.

Why did I say "Yes"? I wasn't a "Yes, I'm in" kind of kid. But there you have it: my first memory of myself as a yes person (and someone who loves a good swear word).

The scuba lesson lasted only an hour. One hour! I remember the awkward feeling of squeezing myself into a wet suit. The struggle of pulling on a mask and fins for the first time. As I put on the buoyancy control vest and tank for the first time, I remember wondering if I would land flat on my back from the weight of it all. Thankfully, I didn't.

I swam some laps in the pool with all the gear on to prove to them (and to myself) that I was fit enough to dive. Then I sank to the bottom of the pool and took my first breath underwater. It was both terrifying and exhilarating. Kind of like life. That was the moment I experienced something truly remarkable. Breathing underwater made me feel as if I could do the impossible. This embodied memory would serve me so many times in the next four decades of my life.

Within two hours, my dad and I were on a boat in the magnificently blue Pacific Ocean. The dive instructor told me to flip off the side of the boat. Backward. "Don't worry," he said. "It's easy. Just dive in and breathe deep." To my surprise, that's exactly what I did. And somehow, he was right—sort of.

Diving felt awkward, but it was easier than I thought. What I discovered on that first dive into the deep is that life doesn't come with an itinerary, timetable, or even an instruction manual. But I learned two important lessons that day: dive in and breathe deeply.

As far as I can tell, these two actions cover just about everything you need to know to not only survive in this world, but also to thrive.

Well. Almost everything.

Making the choice to say "Yes"—to dive in and breathe deeply—has brought me so many incredible moments of unadulterated joy, love, and laughter in my life so far. It has led me to make some invaluable relationships and friendships, taught me skills I never imagined gaining, and led to some really rewarding (and sometimes crazy) adventures around the globe.

What I hadn't yet realized in my young life, sitting on the edge of a boat in the middle of the Pacific, is that it's one thing to dive in and breathe deeply regarding an event of your choosing—when something holds the possibility of joy, adventure, and happiness. (As I discovered that day, it's almost easy.) But what about when it's not your choice to dive? What about when, instead of a promising adventure, you're shoved into deep waters and what awaits you is pain, suffering, fear, and maybe even trauma? These moments challenge the capacity of those life rules to sustain us. These moments require a critical third rule. It's a rule my scuba instructor taught me on that first dive, though I'd forgotten about it because I didn't need it that day. The third and most important rule of diving (and of life) is that when you're running out of air, it's vital to buddy-breathe.

In fact, these running-out-of-air moments are the type of life experiences that I call AFGO (another fucking growth opportunity). I've had my fair share of them. Perhaps it was all those AFGOs that happened since that first scuba trip that prepared me to dive in, breathe deeply, and buddy-breathe amid the most painful experience I've faced yet: the love of my life dying in my arms.

One of those joyful dive-in moments was when I fell in love with Eric Keefauver. He quickly became my best friend, travel companion, husband, and father to our daughter. His smile lit up my heart and every room he walked into. He was genuinely interested in learning, exploring, connecting, and growing. He was good at everything—which, to be honest, was really annoying sometimes. Like when he took up skiing in his thirties (something I'd done since age five) and was better than me by the end of the first season.

He also had a memory like no one I'd ever known (thank goodness, because that's not my strong suit). He would talk about the height of a mountain featured in a documentary we watched six months prior as if everyone remembered. I was proud if I remembered the title of the film.

Eric lived his life with curiosity and enthusiasm, and he loved with his whole heart.

All these attributes started to disappear within the course of a year, and neither he nor I knew why. He became a stranger to himself, to me, and to our daughter. His personality, memory, and body became unrecognizable over the course of months. Navigating the health care system was frustrating, full of dismissals and misdiagnoses—with no testing along the way.

Even with another adult in the home, I was parenting alone most days and then serving my clients and staff as the clinical director of a nonprofit. It was a living nightmare at home. Both of us were in individual therapy. When Eric's behavior became threatening, I made safety plans. Every single day was hell. I wondered what happened to the warm, generous, compassionate man and father I loved. My mind was on overdrive 24/7, trying to find an explanation for how we ended up in this horror film. I just wanted my husband back.

Then one day in late summer 2011, Eric summoned me to a hospital emergency room. I nearly ignored his call because tensions were so high between us. Thirty minutes later, I stood in a cold exam room, Eric staring at me, then both of us staring at a neurologist. We watched the doctor—his mouth agape—point to an image of Eric's brain. There it was. The answer we had been searching for but were in no way prepared to hear. Eric had a grapefruit-sized tumor that had shifted his brain stem. The doctor was shocked that Eric was even walking or talking.

On August 8, 2011, just nine days after learning about the tumor and four days after our nine-year wedding anniversary, Eric underwent a fourteen-hour surgery to remove as much of the tumor as possible. I spent the day in the hospital waiting room, sitting, pacing, wailing, and screaming, surrounded by friends and family who were taking turns buddy-breathing with me. Late that night, the nurses let me see him in post-op. His head was bandaged, the area around his eyes was black and blue, and his whole face was swollen nearly beyond recognition. I spoke to him and heard his voice. We told each other "I love you," and he told me how much he loved our seven-year-old daughter, Lily.

I'm forever grateful for that exchange, because after going home for just a few hours to check on Lily, I returned to find a roomful of doctors and nurses surrounding Eric's bed. He had slipped into a coma. I collapsed on the floor. Eventually, I called in my people. Together with them, and sometimes alone, I sat by Eric's bedside for the next six days, begging him to wake up. It's hard to breathe when your brain is taken over by information too horrible to process. The natural process of breathing seemed impossible. This was a time where I needed my friends and family to buddy-breathe with me.

For six days and nights, I willed him to wake up. After another twelve-hour surgery and additional scans and testing, the doctors told me that Eric had experienced a series of catastrophic strokes and would never regain consciousness. I stopped breathing for a moment, maybe longer. My dad and father-in-law were there, and I think they stopped breathing too. But eventually we helped one another breathe again.

I made the heart-wrenching decision to take Eric off life support, a choice made a little less painful because we had discussed his wishes before surgery. Next, I decided (the first of a lifetime of parenting decisions I would now make alone) to bring our daughter into the hospital to say goodbye to her dad. After his friends and family said their goodbyes, after nurses removed most of the wires, tubes, and monitors, I crawled into bed with Eric. I curled up next to him for nearly nine hours, soaking his sheets with my tears, reliving the stories and adventures of our twelve years together, and telling him how grateful I was that he taught me what it means to be truly loved. At 6:06 a.m. on August 16, 2011, with my arms wrapped around him, Eric took his last breath.

And somehow, I took my first breath without him. Eventually, my friend Susan came and peeled me away from his side, practically carried me to the car, all the while sharing her oxygen with me, reminding me to breathe. Hours, days, weeks, and even months were a blur after his death. Each minute, then eventually each hour, then each day, I had to remind myself to breathe deeply—to just breathe at all.

I had to learn how to ask others for help. I'm not going to lie; that's been hard. But what I've realized is that we all need help sometimes. This time I was the one out of oxygen. Friends kept reminding me that when they were running out of air, I was always there to buddy-breathe with them. "It's OK," they said. "It's our turn now."

And here I am in 2024, having passed the twelve-year anniversary of Eric's death. I have the honor of doing incredibly meaningful work with individuals, communities, and organizations. The boundaries of this work seem limitless as I reach people across the globe through my podcast *Grief is a Sneaky Bitch*, lectures, and speeches, including a TEDx Talk.

I've gained some incredible new friendships and cherished and savored some old ones too. I'm a full-time single parent to Lily, who's now twenty years old and in college. How did that happen? In her young life, she has already faced some incredible challenges and tragedies that I didn't have to endure. As her mom, this absolutely breaks my heart. But just like I did at age twelve, Lily became a scuba diver. To some, scuba diving may be just a sport or hobby. But I know it's more than that. She's learning the incredible instructions she will need to survive and thrive in this world: dive in, breathe deeply, and buddy-breathe when necessary.

I hope by the end of this book you too will come to know and practice these instructions.

introduction

a guide to reading this book

Hello friend and fellow griever,

While I hope you found comfort in being called my friend just now, I imagine what you didn't love so much is the "fellow griever" part. It's not a title you ever wanted. Me either. Yet here we are, together.

Please know that I see you and I'm holding you in my heart. I recognize the amount of courage it took to crack open a book on grief. I know the strength it takes to show up for yourself and to be with your grief as you turn these pages.

Yes, it's true: Grief is a sneaky bitch. But don't worry, I've got your back. I'm honored to be your guide and companion along the way. Grief's sneakiness is some of what we will explore together throughout this book. My hope is that seeing grief's stealthy nature will help you shed the idea that there's one simple path you're meant to follow, that you should intuitively know how to do it "right" or "better," or that you shouldn't stumble and fall along the way. Just like the guidelines for how to read this book, there's no one right way to navigate loss.

The sneakiness isn't all natural, though. Some of the shifty and devious ways grief shows up in our lives are not inherent to grief. They're artificially created and incredibly harmful too. Implicitly and explicitly, we've collectively consumed a problematic and narrow story of grief based on a harmful set of beliefs that make this painful and messy journey even more unbearable and disorienting.

That's why before you set off and stumble upon whichever chapters call to your heart and mind, I invite you to start here. I want to help you recognize and identify our collective beliefs and the stories we tell ourselves and others about grief. We all hold these beliefs. What I hope you'll come to see is that finding our way forward in grief means that we have so much to learn and unlearn about these grief beliefs first.

GRIEF BELIEFS AND THE STORIES WE TELL

"What we focus on becomes our reality." Yes, that saying is tattooed on my body and, no, I'm not telling you, "Just choose to be happy." Gross. I would never do that to you. The expression comes from my training in Narrative Therapy more than twenty years ago. It means that the language we use to describe events isn't neutral. It doesn't communicate facts. It shapes how we feel and reinforces what we believe.

Belief is defined as "an acceptance that something is true or that something exists." Whether conscious or unconscious, we carry beliefs about all manner of things, including grief. Those are what I call "grief beliefs," and they dictate our assumptions about how we're supposed to feel, think, and behave in our grief. Remember, those ideas aren't facts, and they're certainly not neutral. In fact, many of the grief beliefs we hold can and do have disastrous consequences for all of us.

The more we give voice to these grief beliefs (whether to ourselves or out loud to others), the more we believe them to be true with a capital T. These false but now familiar stories shape how we feel and experience ourselves in grief. Inevitably, we build a story that seems so true that we end up judging ourselves for it.

The problem with the unexamined grief beliefs in our stories is that we're unknowingly and unnecessarily burdening ourselves with toxic and harmful ideas. As we explore in more detail in "Access Denied," the consequences of not examining our grief beliefs don't affect just us. It has real consequences for the people we unknowingly pass them on to.

THE STORY IS INCOMPLETE AND INACCURATE

In the West, individually and collectively we've consumed a very narrow, misguided, and incomplete story of grief. As a result, we judge ourselves and others against a story that goes something like this:

Grief happens when someone you're close to dies. You feel sad, occasionally angry (but only in moderation). Those feelings can last for a while, maybe months (if you were close to the person who died). You mostly keep it to yourself. If you must, you see a therapist or find a group of other grievers like you so that you don't get your grief on other people. You keep busy, get back to work—you know, because it's "good for you." Then, as soon as possible, you move in a neat and orderly fashion through the five stages of grief like some sort of to-do list. And voilà. If you're good enough, tried hard enough, and are strong enough, in about a year, you're done. And now you can move on.

Since you're reading this book, you know that is a load of bullshit. I have a hunch you also know that, deep down, this is the story you and others measure yourself against. The central purpose of my work is to expand the narratives of grief.

I've long valued the wisdom of author Chimamanda Ngozi Adichie's brilliant work. In particular, I've been spellbound by her top-rated TED Talk "The Danger of a Single Story," about the perils of the single story when it comes to racial and cultural stereotyping. In part, she said, "The single story creates stereotypes, and the problem with stereotypes is not that they are untrue, but that they are incomplete. They make one story become the only story."

I've come to see that this truth also applies to the harm our narrow collective grief story has on all of us. The limited narratives we consume about grief cause us to feel unseen and unworthy in our very valid, messy, and varied experiences of grief. It also invites us to deny or discount the differing grief sources and experiences of others. In my professional career as a social worker and in my personal grief, I've come to see that this narrow story of grief is likely the single biggest contributor to our unnecessary suffering in the wake of loss.

STORY ORIGINS

You might be wondering how we got here. You might be asking yourself questions such as, "How did we end up with this narrow, harmful, singular story of grief?" and "Where did these grief beliefs come from and why has no one ever talked about them?" "Why," you might have wondered, "has no one asked me to consider if I wanted to keep them?"

Many years after Eric's death, I carried these questions in my heart. I slowly realized that we all carry these harmful grief beliefs, and I began to see the enormous damage they were causing.

As the wise Maya Angelou said, "If you don't know where you've come from, you don't know where you're going." So let's get some answers. While we each have our own unique assortment of grief beliefs, they come from some common sources and include some themes that many of us share.

Cultural Influences

Culture is the air we breathe. It's the values we absorb from the laws and policies of formal institutions, from the content of our educational systems, and from the media we consume. In the US and much of the Western world, there are five particularly harmful grief beliefs that in our lifetimes have found their way into our psyches.

1. Productivity over process The number of social media hashtags and software apps that exist is proof of how obsessed we are with productivity in our culture. We idolize and celebrate "hustles" and "side gigs." We proudly say things such as, "I'll sleep when I'm dead," and write "#goals." You know you're carrying around this belief in your grief if you've found yourself saying things such as, "I should be able to do all this better, faster, more efficiently." "What's wrong with me?" "Why is it taking me so long to get there?" This productivity obsession, combined with the myth that grief is simply a goal that can be achieved and that we can just move on from, makes it more complicated for us grievers.

2. Simplicity over complexity We love a "X Steps To" formula for just about everything in our modern world. Of course we do, because these formulas are often useful ways to learn some practical skills. And yet the proliferation of clickbait online posts and top five news headlines lead us to believe and expect that nothing needs to be complicated. All we need to be is smart enough to figure out how to distill the plan down to easy, step-by-step instructions and then follow them. You know this belief has infiltrated your grief if you find yourself saying things such as, "I just need to figure out how to get over this. There's something wrong with me because I feel relieved and deeply sad all at once."

3. Destinations over journeys Though we say things such as, "It's not about the destination; it's about the journey," that's not what our culture celebrates. Instead, our media is full of short clips or articles about the result—and maybe for good measure a few highlight reels of the mini-achievement moments along the way. We rarely get a glimpse of all the stumbles, missteps, and stagnations involved in any journey. We collectively miss seeing the value in or realities of what it took to get to the end. We're further deceived because as the news cycle moves on, we don't hear stories of the inevitable stumble backward after having met the goal. Every time you say something to yourself such as, "Why am I feeling this way all over again? I thought I was past this. I just need to get over this. Why can't I move on?" it's a sign that you're carrying this belief in your grief.

4. Stoicism over vulnerability Though not factual, the dominant story told in most schools of how the US became a great nation is rooted in people who "pulled themselves up by their bootstraps." We make heroes out of people who appear unfazed by injuries or obstacles, and we aspire to be unaffected by criticism. Admitting uncertainty and requesting help are considered signs of weakness, judged with pity instead of praise. You've incorporated this belief into your grief if you say things such as, "I can't ask for help because I should know how to do this on my own," or, "I don't want anyone to know I've been crying again."

5. IQ over EQ We admit students into college based on test scores. We promote people at work based on their ability to write a report, give a speech, or manage a spreadsheet. We equate value with a person's ability to use intellectual intelligence (IQ) to navigate the world, while labeling emotional intelligence (EQ) as a soft skill—a nice quality to have. When we're struggling with grief brain and find ourselves saying things such as, "I'm so stupid. Why can't I figure this out? I should be able to figure this out," we're likely prioritizing intellectual over emotional intelligence.

Family of Origin

"What is your earliest memory of loss in your childhood?"

"How did the adults in your life model grief, either explicitly or implicitly?"

"What do you think taught you about what grief should or shouldn't look like?"

I ask these questions of my guests at the opening of each podcast and of my individual clients and workshop attendees during the first session. I even ask the undergraduate students in my Loss and Grief course to consider how they would answer.

Our families are our most informative and influential teachers on all the values we hold, including what grief is and isn't. We learn grief beliefs from the explicit messages we get from our family. ("He's a mess. I can't believe he cried in public.") The implicit messages we take in, such as changing the subject every time the loss is mentioned, teach us about what is and isn't acceptable. We know we've inherited these beliefs when we find ourselves saying things such as, "Well, we just didn't do that in my family," or "It's not OK because my parents used to punish me when I cried."

Spiritual or Religious Communities

Whether we're atheist, agnostic, hold a spiritual practice, or are part of a formal religious community, we're exposed to beliefs about life, death, our purpose, and the meaning we're meant to make from experiences such as loss. As with families, these values surrounding appropriate expressions of mourning are sometimes explicitly stated. At other times, they're implied. These values often come with expectations but no guidance regarding how to follow them. For example, "You shouldn't question why it happened; it was God's will."

EXPANDING OUR NARRATIVES

You might be starting to see how neatly the values and beliefs we learned support the continuation of this incomplete story of grief. Yet instead of us questioning our collective values, culture, and systems, we question ourselves. What that looked like for me was exhaustion, self-judgment, and loathing for not being at the top of my game when I was required to return to work just two weeks after my husband's death.

The unreasonable pressure we put on ourselves in the wake of loss comes at a very steep cost to all of us—to our mental, physical, and collective health and well-being. Not only are we suffering unnecessarily, but we're also inflicting that suffering on those around us at the individual and institutional level by the misguided policies and systems we build and uphold.

Relying on the wisdom of my fifth-grade teacher, Mrs. Davis, I have expanded our stories of grief by breaking them down to the most important components: who, what, where, when, and why, or what I call the Five Ws of Grief.

Who

The first W is "who": Who experiences grief? Every single one of us. To be human is to tell a story of our lives that involve people, places, abilities, hopes, and dreams. To be alive means some of those things will end and some will never begin.

As for who we grieve, the truth is it can be anyone or anything. Of course, we grieve those people we loved who died. But we can also grieve the death of people we were estranged from, people or relationships that are no longer in our day-to-day lives, the versions of ourselves that we were before the loss, and even the version of ourselves that we didn't get a chance to become. The most important thing for you to remember is that you can grieve anyone at any phase of life or death, including versions of yourself.

What

The second W is "what": What do we grieve? We grieve the known, the certain, the connection, and the meaning we've attached to our stories. Grief insists that we come to terms with what no longer is, never was, or never will be.

Grief takes on various forms, from the anticipatory grief we experience in the wake of a loved one's terminal diagnosis to the ambiguous losses we experience when someone is physically present but psychologically distant, as in the case of those who suffer from Alzheimer's disease and addiction. Then there is the person who is physically distant but present in our hearts and minds, as when someone has gone missing, is imprisoned, or has been deployed in the military. Truthfully, the full list of grief types fills the alphabet, including complex, compounded, disenfranchised, and traumatic grief. We will touch on many of these grief types throughout this book. Regardless of what caused the grief, remember, it's a normal response to loss.

Where

The third W is "where." Where has two parts: where grief comes from (the source) and where grief goes (the effect). While death loss is the most obvious source, grief can come from many types of losses. Grief can come from the maturational phases of our lives (leaving home for the first time or retirement) to unexpected accidents and upheavals (catastrophic injury, chronic illness, or another life-limiting event).

Other often-missed sources of grief include things we had a reason to expect to have but that never came to be, such as a nurturing relationship with a parent or a feeling of safety in the world, perhaps destroyed by neglect, abuse, or trauma.

But we also need to understand the impact of grief, that is, where it goes. We all know grief affects our emotional well-being, even if we try to limit that to a small range of feelings. But grief goes well beyond our emotions. It impacts our whole selves, including our physical, cognitive, spiritual, and relational well-being. Remember, wherever your grief comes from, it will affect all aspects of your life.

When

The fourth W is "when," as in "When do we grieve?," and the question I'm asked most, "When will grief end?" Since we experience losses multiple ways and multiple times, we grieve across our lifespan. As the stories of our lives inevitably shift, we grieve. We can also grieve old losses as new again. Sometimes we begin grieving months or years after the loss because we weren't ready to face it before, didn't have the support, or maybe hadn't recognized it as grief until now.

And when does grief end? Contrary to the myths of our limited grief story, it doesn't end, per se. Grief transforms and we are transformed by it. As we explore throughout this book, the most important thing to remember is that grief becomes a part of your story, but isn't your whole story, even though I know it can feel that way in the beginning.

And when does grief end? Contrary to the myths of our limited grief story, it doesn't end, per se. Grief transforms and we are transformed by it. As we explore throughout this book, the most important thing to remember is that grief becomes a part of your story, but isn't your whole story, even though I know it can feel that way in the beginning.

Why

Our final W is "why": why we experience grief. Though we explore some of the scientific reasons later, at the heart of the answer is the fact that we humans are storytellers. This is deeply rooted in our neurobiology. We need story to feel safe and connected, to make meaning of our lives, and to thrive.

Our lives are built by the stories we tell of our experiences. A death, a traumatic event, or some other devastating loss (of relationship, ability, homeland, dream) is akin to the manuscript of our lives being torn to shreds and handed back to us without instructions on how to rewrite or live our lives. Grief is the journey we're on as we rewrite and live our emerging story.

So why do we grieve? Because a fundamental part of our manuscript has been shredded.

CHECKING IN

That was a lot. Grief is a lot. How are you doing?

I imagine these days you're scared and anxious, deeply sad, periodically angry, and somehow numb all at once. Whatever you're feeling is perfectly OK. That's true even if you're experiencing emotions that you've never felt before, or you're just feeling them with a greater intensity. It's even true if it's a feeling you think you *shouldn't* be feeling.

Somewhere down the road, chapters from now, I'll remind you that emotions are information, not facts. I'll reassure you that no feeling lasts forever. Not even the ones we wish would linger, such as joy and delight. Dang it. The ones we wish would go away are sneaky and manipulative and threaten to unpack their bags and move in for good. They're lying. They're just visitors.

My friend, your heart is so precious. I assure you that you have what you need and there is no rushing this journey. You deserve patience and gentleness from yourself and others as you mend and discover a new way of living your emerging story. I am so happy to be a companion along the way, and my hope is that my experience and wisdom provide hope and guidance. But remember, don't compare your grief journey to anyone else's. Yours is unique and beautiful, just like you.

WHAT TO EXPECT

When you finish this book, I hope you will feel seen and held in your grief. My wish is for you to feel accompanied and reassured that, although it's a scary path sometimes, you have the wisdom you need to navigate this journey. To support you, I've created a book that includes:

- *An honest exploration* of the realities of grief that will hopefully offer some relief, help you feel "normal," and cause you to say things such as, "OMG, yes, that happens to me too."
- *Busting the grief myths* getting in your way and offering strategies to ditch the tripping hazards littering your path.
- *Vulnerable stories, mistakes (a.k.a. learning opportunities), and lessons I've learned* so that maybe you don't have to figure them out yourself.
- *Lifting up* the wisdom and insights from those who have guided me along the way.
- *A sprinkling of humor throughout,* because sometimes we need respite from the heaviness of grief.

• *A judicious use of cussing*, because although I don't have the quantitative data to prove it (yet), sometimes profanity is therapeutic.

• *Some improv-style language*, which means in place of "but," you'll find a lot of sentences with "yes and."

• *Metaphors, poems, analogies, acronyms, and other literary devices*, because the best way to explore complex ideas and reach the depth of a soul isn't through straightforward language.

• *Suggestions and gentle reminders* rather than commands or must-do checklists, because, remember, there's no right or wrong way to grieve.

• *Invitations to practice and reflect*, purposeful places for you to pause, digest, and rest.

HOW TO READ THIS BOOK

Each of you is at a different place in your unique grief. So in case you were wondering, "Is there a right way to read this book?," the answer is, "Absolutely not." Feel free to reread one chapter repeatedly, because, as the wise and talented actress and social media personality Tabitha Brown says, "That's your business."

Pick and choose the topics that call to you at the moment. Listen to what you need, not what you think you *should* need. Skim through this book until you find what resonates. You can also pace yourself. Read at a slow pace, maybe one chapter a week, because these days, grief-induced brain fog has taken over and you can't absorb too much. I say, "Been there, done that, no rush. I'll be here."

If reading at a turtle's pace or the hop/skip around approach is stressful, then read it straight through. I say, "You do you, Boo." Start at the beginning and march on. You may even want to read this book twice, coming back to it a year later as your grief changes over time (and it will, I promise).

Grab a highlighter, pen, or pencil and mark it up. Highlight paragraph after paragraph or write notes in the margins. I left plenty of white space for that reason. That's generally how I read books like this. The bonus is that no one will want to borrow your marked up copy.

I invite you to read this book in whatever way makes you feel the best. That is the not-so-secret recipe for grief. Find your way and discover the things, people, practices, ideas, and resources that make you feel better—or at least in the beginning, the ones that make things suck just a little bit less.

WAIT, BEFORE YOU GO, ARRIVE HERE

Before you dive into the book, I invite you to arrive here.

In case you're thinking "Um, WTF, Lisa, I'm here already!" I know, but hear me out.

In our busy modern lives, we switch from task to task, one video meeting to the next, or physically move between places. Constantly. Often, we arrive only with our bodies. We've left our awareness stuck somewhere in the past or allowed it to time-travel to an imagined (often fearful) future. That means we're straddling two places, which, by the way, is impossible. Like me, you've likely bragged about being a great multitasker. You're not. Neither am I. That's bullshit.

For now, I invite you to rest your eyes and take some deep breaths: inhaling through your nose, allowing your breath to expand your chest and move deep into your belly, then exhaling slowly and deeply out of your mouth, letting it all go, noticing the sensation of expansion with each breath in and the way your chest softens as you exhale. Next, take some time to be curious. Pay attention to how it feels to have your body supported. Notice the sensation of wherever your body is being held and met by the couch, the seat, or the ground beneath you. Again, just be curious. There's no right thing to discover. Breathe deeply for a few rounds or a few minutes, whatever serves you. I'll be waiting for you when you're done.

OK, go.

time in grief

*discovering how and why
time feels so different*

the world's still spinning

WHEN THE WORLD STOPPED MAKING SENSE

Grief is difficult. It's not your fault. You're not crazy. For a time, the world won't make sense.

Your loss may have happened unexpectedly. Or it may have been a slow realization, decline, or resignation. Whether the loss came fast or slow, instantly or over months and years, we've all arrived at a version of this horrendous moment when the world stopped making sense.

For me, it was a single moment.

I was lying in the hospital bed with Eric, memorizing every freckle, every hair, every wrinkle, and the sensation of his nearly lifeless hand in mine. I was retelling the stories of our life together. I was doing everything I could to be fully present in that moment. But I also had the sensation that I was floating above us, watching myself do all these things. I was there, but not. I think my mind-body was protecting me from fully taking in what was happening—that my previously healthy, loving, young husband was slowly dying in my arms.

And when he took his last breath, I didn't understand how I was still breathing. How the lights in the hospital were still working. Why the nurses were able to talk in the hallways about this or that. I couldn't believe I could still speak or know how to use the phone (which I did to call my friend to take me home).

I didn't understand how the elevators still worked. Or how my friend could drive her car. I genuinely remember wondering how and why the key still unlocked our front door, even though Eric would never walk through the door again.

Maybe you felt this same confusion? Were you also baffled and wondered how the hell the world was still spinning?

A SOFTER LANDING

That disbelief, fog, and numbness, though disorienting, protected me in the early days of grief. They were (or maybe still are) protecting you too. Maybe in the early days you felt (or still feel) afraid, as if you can't think straight. You're having some physical side effects, such as headaches. You're oddly exhausted. You're "all over the place," and maybe even feeling like (and acting like) someone else. That's emotional shock. That autopilot feeling is your body's way of keeping you from having to process the loss and experience the full pain all at once. (See "This Is Your Brain on Grief.")

I know how weird, unwelcome, even scary it feels when the world is in slow motion and making no sense. It won't last forever, I promise. So instead of spending energy judging yourself or worrying that this phase is permanent, take a moment to honor the gift this response is giving you: a softer landing. Take it slow, stay low, be gentle, and allow yourself the space and time you need to absorb what's happened.

LIVING IN A PARALLEL UNIVERSE

When I arrived in the "after" (the time after the loss), some of the daily thoughts I had were:

- How on earth could that woman be complaining that her husband didn't remember to take out the trash?
- Why the hell is that mom whining about all the activities she must take her children to?
- Who the hell cares that the grocery store doesn't have your favorite items in stock or that a star player's injury is "ruining the team's chances" in the big game this weekend?

Do you ever feel as if you're an alien dropped onto Earth and you're trying to figure out how this planet works? Like when Mork (Robin Williams's fictional character from the '70s sitcom *Mork & Mindy*) arrived on this planet? No? How about a more contemporary reference, such as the fictional Harry Potter when he first arrived at Hogwarts School of Witchcraft and Wizardry. (OK not so contemporary, but in the past two decades at least.)

Early grief can feel like living on another planet or at the very least inhabiting a parallel universe. Besides the brain fog and shock, these early days can make the language, values, customs, and day-to-day rhythm of the world unrecognizable. Do you ever feel as if you're looking through an invisible shield that still allows you to see everything going on, but you can't comprehend any of it?

This stage is unfathomable to anyone who hasn't been in it. But I'm guessing you likely know what I'm talking about. Welcome to the other world. It will take some time to acclimate. Be patient with yourself. Just like Harry Potter, you're going to get knocked off your broomstick more than once. But you'll be OK. You'll dust yourself off and hop back on.

It's so jarring to be asked a question that forces you to recognize that your answer is forever changed.

DON'T TALK TO ME (BUT ALSO PAY ATTENTION TO ME)

I sometimes wish I had a name tag, or better yet a T-shirt, that said, "Fuck off, don't talk to me, but also pay attention to me, but also don't fucking look at me with those pity eyes." How about you?

Fortunately, or unfortunately, we don't wear our loss on our sleeve, as was common years ago when those in mourning wore a black armband. (Maybe we should bring that back?) This is true whether we experienced a death loss or are grieving something else. That means we're frequently bombarded with innocent questions, both by people we know and by strangers. It's so jarring to be asked a question that forces you to recognize that your answer is forever changed.

Plus, since my grief brain was in charge, I thought others should know the answer already. I was honestly puzzled at times, wondering why people asked me questions when they knew the answers would break my heart all over again. Does that happen to you?

THE ROOT CANAL WASN'T THE HARDEST PART

The first time I was asked the dreaded question haunts me to this day. Three days after Eric died, I was in a dentist's office needing an emergency root canal. Because really, universe?

I saw a new dentist (of course mine was away), so I had to fill out a new-patient form. First up, the marital status question. Ugh. For the first of what now feels like a thousand times since then, I had to check the "widow" box. I sat in the waiting room, sobbing uncontrollably. Strangers looking at me with a mix of irritation, confusion, and pity. I composed myself and got in the dentist's chair (in excruciating physical pain and now with puffy eyes). In a chipper tone, the dentist asked me, "How's your week going?" yada, yada, yada.

So if you've burst into tears, flown into a rage, or shut down at an innocent question or the callous-seeming remark coming from that parallel universe, remember, you're not alone. It happens to all of us. Afterward, you might think something like, "That's not like me." It probably isn't. But you're not like you right now, and that's OK. Have some compassion for yourself. If you have extra compassion to spare, have some for the person who asked the question too. If you don't yet, that's OK too.

⊰ AN INVITATION FOR YOU ⊱

humbly bow to grief's spinning nature

One of the challenges we face in times of questioning how the world's still spinning is that we often insist on standing upright and bracing against the power of its spinning force.

Some of that is instinctual and some of that is the byproduct of a culture so obsessed with productivity, grit, and taking charge that even in the depths of deep pain there's no permission for softness, humility, or rest. Author Elizabeth Gilbert, one of my many grief guides, offers wisdom on this. She reminds us that we suffer unnecessarily when we hold tight and brace for impact. She invites us to bow with humility and let grief spin us until it comes to rest, which it always does.

[Grief] has its own timeframe, it has its own itinerary with you, it has its own power over you, and it will come when it comes. And when it comes, it's a bow-down. The posture that you take is you hit your knees in absolute humility and you let it rock you until it is done with you. And it will be done with you, eventually. And when it is done, it will leave. But to stiffen, to resist, and to fight it is to hurt yourself.
—Elizabeth Gilbert

I invite you to offer yourself one of these affirmations when these moments arrive. I also invite you to create an affirmation of your own.

---

affirmations

"I give myself permission to bow in humility to the force of this grief wave."

"I will let my tears flow as a way to find my bearings in a spinning world."

"I offer myself grace and compassion for the confusion I feel in this new world."

start close in

HOW DO I EVEN START?

"I can't do this."

"I don't want to do this."

"I don't know how to do this."

"I don't even know where to begin."

Just after my husband died, and in more moments than I can count since that first day, I've screamed these words to the sky. I've said them to a friend while sobbing uncontrollably, and silently to myself in bed as tears streamed down my face. And to be honest, the words were filled with a lot more expletives.

I'm wondering if you've said or felt something similar.

YOU ALREADY STARTED

I know how much this beginning place feels daunting, overwhelming, terrifying, and even impossible. To be plain, it fucking sucks.

Yet here you are. You've already started, even though you didn't want to and likely would have done anything to not be in this beginning spot in the first place.

You're reading this book and that means you've already taken some steps into this new chapter, into this life in the "after." After the loss. Whether it's been weeks or months later or some time down the road,

I hope in some small way the news that you've already begun feels like a bit of relief. Now you can tell yourself you already have experience with starting. And that's something.

While you're the only person who can walk in your shoes, I've been at the start too. A few times. I've also walked alongside countless people when they started. I'm here to walk alongside you as you begin and offer some guidance along the way.

IN THE DARKNESS

We start in the dark. That's what makes the early season of grief feel so daunting. We're stumbling around in the dark, hands reaching for anything to guide us, feet tentatively stepping to avoid any obstacles that will bring us to our knees. That's where we all start. It seems impossible but it's from that dark place that we lean on hope.

START CLOSE IN

"To begin" simply refers to the first part. The first step, the first action, the first intention. Not the perfect one, not the right one, not the one someone else took, just the first. So each time you begin feeling overwhelmed with what to do next or how you should feel at any given moment in your grief, remember that you don't have to have it all figured out.

Instead, I invite you to start close in. As poet and grief guide David Whyte reminds us, "Start close in, don't take the second step or the third, start with the first thing close in, the step you don't want to take."

I've found that starting close in can be helpful because it:

Illuminates what you already know You've lived on this earth for some time now, which means you've already learned some things about beginnings. You've tried, practiced, stumbled, adjusted, and discovered some things that help you when you're in the beginning of something new. Starting close in helps you remember that you have experience and knowledge that can serve you. It gets you in touch with the wisdom and skills you've already developed. It helps you illuminate what you already know.

Shifts your gaze This new terrain of early grief can tempt you to focus all your energy somewhere far down the road. I call that "horizon time"—a segment of time so far off that you can't be present (tomorrow, next week, next year, your elder years). Our human need to have a fully fleshed-out story means we're often trying to figure out how it will all turn out. The truth is we just can't know that. By the way, that's true in life, not just in grief.

Instead, the invitation to start close in is a reminder to cast your gaze at the ground beneath you, now. That close-in gaze is crucial to identifying the next best step.

Some days feel so filled with your loved one's absence that you find it hard to concentrate on anything else. On those days, remind yourself that your only job in that moment is to breathe. And sometimes, that's all you will do. And that will be enough.

Identifies the next best step (not perfect or right) We're living in an expert-obsessed culture, making us believe there's a perfect or right way to do just about everything, including how to grieve. Think about it. There's a Top 10 List for this and a 5 Ways to Do X for that. There's a blog/TikTok/article on how to be or do everything the best way. This expert culture spills over into how we expect ourselves and others to know how to grieve "well," pressuring us into believing that there's a best possible way.

Starting close in helps you recall what you already know, shift your gaze back to the present moment, and ask yourself, "What's the next best thing I can do for myself?" Not the perfect thing. Not the right thing. (News flash: Neither of these things exist.) Just the next best thing. At the risk of repeating myself, the answer to that question may include steps that appear as inaction but can be equally beneficial. They might include:

1. Sleeping
2. Sitting still
3. Crying
4. Yelling
5. Canceling plans
6. Looking through a photo album or other cherished items
7. Breathing

OLD KNOWING IN A NEW WORLD

It's easy to connect with your inner knowing (the wise, Yoda-like voice in your mind) when the world around you is familiar. It's simple to do when you've walked those roads before, been in those places, faced similar obstacles. Why? Because you've practiced. You've built up a sort of muscle memory, intuitively knowing when and how to enact the skills, resources, and responses needed under similar circumstances.

In grief, you're walking roads you've never been on before, entering spaces you've never been in, and facing obstacles you never could have imagined (nor would have wanted to). This is true even if you've grieved before. Because you've never been this version of yourself before while grieving this loss.

And yet you might be expecting yourself to know how to do it. You might be frustrated with yourself when the breath work, meditation, exercise, journaling, body movement, therapy, sleep, medication, or whatever you use to serve you doesn't seem to be working. Or you might not even have the energy or interest in trying those things right now. I get that too.

The truth is that the tools and actions that soothed you in the past might no longer work. Or they might not work right now. Or they might require practice in this new environment. Perhaps they might need a bit of tweaking.

THE LESSONS OF OLD KNOWING

Instead of judging yourself for not wanting to try to use old skills or for trying and feeling as if they don't work, I offer you a different way to think about these first steps you take.

There have been hundreds if not thousands of things you've begun over the course of your life: subjects in school, athletics, relationships, foreign languages, jobs, technology. At the start of each venture, you couldn't even conceive all that you didn't know. You couldn't imagine that someday what was once unknown would feel so familiar, so easy, and barely even require your focus and attention.

At first, you likely had no clue where to begin. So you tried, stumbled, adjusted, tweaked, practiced, practiced, practiced, adjusted, and practiced some more. Each action might not have looked like much or felt like much. Sometimes it may have even left your ego bruised and deflated. But it wasn't all for nothing. Some attempts taught you how not to do things. "Oops, that didn't work." Other actions seemed vaguely right but not easy at first—or second or fifth. Regardless, each step offered you information.

Over time, things that felt unknown and impossible became familiar, reflexive, embedded in your muscle memory. You worked hard each time to learn and develop new vocabulary, new skills, new ways of being in the world. I offer you this as a reminder that if you've done it before, you can do it again.

LEARNING WITH PATIENCE AND COMPASSION

Have you ever watched a child take first steps? Ride a bike or try to swim for the first time (or second time or even the tenth time)? What did you think when the child stumbled, fell, or even refused to try? Did you respond with judgment and disappointment? Likely not. Instead, you were likely patient, understanding, compassionate, and even proud of the child's willingness to try.

Let's say for a minute that you criticize the child for not doing something right or for being imperfect. Would the child be motivated and confident to keep trying or curl up and give up? I know you know the answer.

So as you take these steps into this new life, I invite you to be gentle with yourself. Remember that you've already started. You already have some old ways of knowing available to you. You already know what it feels like to start new, and that it takes practice, practice, practice.

You've experienced that practice makes progress, not perfection (because perfection is an illusion).

Offer yourself wide-open patience, abundant self-compassion, and sweet encouragement for every single step you take, no matter how big or small—remembering that sometimes you will stumble backward, and that's OK.

Offer yourself wide-open patience, abundant compassion, and sweet encouragement for every single step you take, no matter how big or small—remembering that sometimes you will stumble backward, and that's OK.

⚑ AN INVITATION FOR YOU ⚑

practice starting close in

It's easy to get lost in horizon time when we're desperately trying to discover a place or time when we won't feel this bad. In this early place of desperation and confusion, many of us feel overwhelmed as we figure out what to do next. Remember, you've already started this journey, and throughout your life, you've gained skills needed for starting and learning. Still, you might feel stuck or lost because, like many of us, you're expecting too much of yourself now while casting your gaze too far into the future. So I offer you a few ways to practice starting close in.

The next time you're feeling overwhelmed with where to begin or what comes next, ask yourself:

"Am I focusing on horizon time or the present?"

If the answer is horizon time, ask yourself:

"What is the next best thing I can do for myself right now?"

The answer might not come right away. Just be still and listen.

The next time you hear the inner critic telling you that you're "not doing this right or well," try reminding yourself:

"This grief is still new and unknown. I will offer myself wide-open patience, abundant self-compassion, and sweet encouragement as I do my best to make my way through the day."

You might even turn this into a daily mantra for a while, perhaps saying it out loud over your morning coffee or tea.

The next time you take an action (which can look like inaction, such as taking a nap) that makes you feel better, or at least makes your grief suck less, open your journal and explore these writing prompts:

What action/inaction did I take?

How did the action/inaction make my mind feel?

How did the action/inaction make my body feel?

What circumstances were in place that helped make the action/ inaction easy (or easier) to do?

How can I recreate these circumstances more regularly?

the messy middle

AFTER THE BEGINNING

I recently stumbled upon the phrase "the messy middle." Mind you, I found it in the context of the business world and, no surprise, it's been used to encourage people to get creative and power through to complete a project, achieve an outcome, launch a product, and all around be more productive. Still, I think there are some notions and lessons that might help you find more compassion and grace in this phase of your grief.

We experience the messy middle when the acuteness of grief starts to soften a bit but is not that far off in the rearview mirror. It's a time of extraordinary volatility. A period full of uncertainty, struggles, ups, and downs. Yes, in this messy middle part there are ups. And that can feel messy too.

ROUTINES AND EFFORTS ARE BRINGING YOU UP

In the messy middle, our daily routines are changed from the early days of grief. They're likely significantly different than before the loss. Yet they're becoming more familiar. We've moved beyond the early days, the firsts, the initial period of starting, practicing, falling, and getting back up. Hopefully by this time, we've started caring for more aspects of our whole selves, including our cognitive, physical, and emotional well-being. That includes getting rest, eating nutritious meals, and staying hydrated. It might mean we've participated in support groups or maybe even signed up for therapy.

It might even be a period in which we're managing to have some good days—or at least not horrible days. We might not be excited and enthusiastic about the future, but we're building a more coherent story about what life is now and we're open to the possibilities of what's to come. These new routines and efforts are helping. Sometimes.

AND THEN COME THE DOWNS

Even though it's normal and even necessary for this middle passage to be full of ups and downs, we struggle to accept that fact. We find ourselves having days when it sucks more than it used to, or the same, or who can even tell anymore, and we're reminded that we're not at the end. We're still in the messy middle.

The challenge for most of us is that we've bought into the idea that there's always an easy solution: A or B. This potion or that daily routine. There must be a straight line from here to there where we can bypass all the crap in the middle. So we're stuck thinking that there should be a clear and simple path, a bridge that carries us across the Middle Sea and into the place of ease. Many of us listen for that familiar voice to confirm our doubt. This is often when our self-critic gets very loud.

WHEN YOU'RE NOT "GOOD AT IT"—YET

Historically (OK, and still from time to time like at points along the way as I write this book for you), I'm uncomfortable with not being "good at" something. I work consistently to quiet the very loud, judgmental, and bossy inner critic who thinks I should magically excel at something after an unreasonably short amount of time and effort. My name for that voice is Lucille, as in the fictional Lucille Bluth from the TV show *Arrested Development*. If I'm not effortlessly at ease with something after a short while, Lucille tries to tell me:

- "Why bother? You'll never be good at it."
- "You're a loser and should be embarrassed."
- "Other people figure it out easily. There's something wrong with you."

- "You should just copy what other people are doing."
- Repeat the above on an endless loop.

Does your inner critic say mean stuff like that to you too? Have you named it? As I mention in "*Should* Is a Dirty Word (and Not the Swearing Kind)," it helps to give the critic a name. Our inner critic seems to get even louder as we travel in this middle passage. My inner critic has shown up across so many learning phases of my life, arriving somewhere just past the starting line, immediately judging me for stumbling and falling.

Lucille has been there when I tried to learn the guitar (haven't succeeded yet) and trained for my first half-marathon (now done five of them—very slowly). She's shown up a month or so into every single job I've had. She was mouthy as hell when I was only two episodes into producing my podcast. Hell, Lucille showed up when my then-eleven-year-old daughter mastered solving the Rubik's Cube and was confused by why I couldn't learn it. "It's just algorithms, Mom." Fast forward: My daughter's record for solving the whole thing is 5.4 seconds. Yes, I said seconds. I still can't solve even one side, and I'm OK with that.

What I've learned (OK, continue to learn) is that discomfort, frustration, even doubt are normal responses to this middle part. Though a shitty and uncomfortable way to feel at times, the messy middle invites us to be open to new possibilities, new ways of talking to ourselves, new approaches to try to be mediocre at things. It's a door to experimentation and curiosity.

What I've learned (OK, continue to learn) is that discomfort, frustration, even doubt are normal responses to this middle part. Though a shitty and uncomfortable way to feel at times, the messy middle invites us to be open to new possibilities, new ways of talking to ourselves, new approaches to try to be mediocre at things. It's a door to experimentation and curiosity.

THE SECONDS AND THIRDS

One of the many surprising things about grief is that the firsts aren't always the hardest milestones to cross. It seems so cruel and unfair. You've put in the time. You've crossed the firsts (birthday, holiday, anniversary of the death). Besides the original loss, these firsts are the second scariest times of them all. So why on earth can the seconds or thirds feel just as hard or sometimes harder than the firsts?

The answer is messy and mixed (no surprise there). In part, it's because the shock has worn off. Remember that numbness you felt when you couldn't understand how the world was still spinning? By the time the seconds and thirds come around, you feel the pressure to resume daily activities in large part because of the cultural pressure to be "normal."

It might feel harder too because the early attention, support, and compassion you might have felt after the loss has receded or even disappeared. It's also partly because the sheer distance from that moment, even the acute pain of that moment, can make you feel farther away, and that's scary and hard too.

YOU'RE MESSY AND SO AM I

Between you and me, we're all a little bit messy. All the time. That's not a sign of our weakness or brokenness. It's a reflection of life being messy. Some seasons of our lives, we're full-toddler messy, covered in permanent marker and glitter glue and wearing a loaded, pull-up diaper. Sometimes we're just a little "spilled coffee on our white shirt" messy. The reality is that our "having it togetherness" is pretty much an illusion. It's more accurate to think of messiness and togetherness as a spectrum, not a place that we arrive and stay.

That's true even in the seasons of our lives when we're not actively grieving. It's for dang sure true when we're grieving, including this place of the messy middle. There are loads of benefits to giving yourself permission to be messy here in this middle part. Some include:

- When you release the striving energy to be "put together" in your grief, you not only save wasted energy by not trying to meet

unrealistic standards, but you also help show others that the myths are harmful to them too.
- It's in embracing the messy that we make discoveries, from the unexpected joy we're able to feel in moments to the unmet needs of our physical, emotional, or spiritual selves.
- Messiness is also the domain of creatives. Neurobiologically speaking, when we can allow ourselves to be playful and cre-ative (a.k.a. messy), we send a signal to our nervous system that we're safe.

TIME HEALS ALL WOUNDS (NOT!)

I'm going to go with a hard pass that the phrase "time heals all wounds" has ever been useful or appropriate or comforting. If you're anything like me, when someone says it, you have a somewhat violent impulse to tell them to fuck off (or "bugger off," as my British friends would say).

And even though time doesn't heal all wounds (and no one should ever say that ever again), time does play a role. As we explore through-out this book, grieving is not something that can be completely done, and certainly not in a hurry. It's not something we can complete by checking off a to-do list. Damn it. Wish it were.

Here's how I think about the role of time in grief. Time—lots of time—gives us the space we need to grieve. Time gives us the space for:

- Feeling and falling apart and feeling some more.
- Resting.
- Receiving loving compassion from others.
- Trying new things, so many new things, and mostly hating the newness of it all.
- Learning and sitting in the deep discomfort that happens there.
- Not knowing what's next.
- Practicing curiosity and letting go of judgment and expectation again and again.
- Reflecting and shifting perspectives.
- Asking for help and being willing to receive it.
- Breathing. Lots of breathing. Even when it's hard. Even when we don't feel like doing it.

- Stumbling forward and backward, standing still, sitting down, and getting back up.
- Feeling some more at depths and levels of intensity we didn't think possible.
- Practicing self-compassion, even when we don't know what that looks or feels like.
- Rediscovering joy, feeling weird about feeling it, and eventually, in fits and starts, accepting that grief and joy can coexist.

Only time—again, lots of time—can give us the space to do all that. But as we explore throughout this book, time is a necessary but insufficient ingredient to healing. Simply letting time pass isn't enough. During that time, we need to attend to our cognitive, emotional, physical, spiritual, and relational well-being.

WHEN FEELING BETTER FEELS BAD

Another sign that you're in the messy middle is that you've started feeling better, whatever that means for you. There might be days without tears or a few nights in a row of good sleep. Increased energy, interest in going out, or looking forward to new things might indicate that you're feeling better. Remember, feeling better isn't meant to denote a permanent state. It doesn't mean you'll always be moving in an upward direction from here on out. It's just somewhere along the continuum past absolute shit and before absolute bliss. These better periods might last hours or days. You're noticing that you're able to string more of these moments together than in the early days of grief.

Remember, feeling better isn't meant to denote a permanent state. It doesn't mean you'll always be moving in an upward direction from here on out. It's just somewhere along the continuum past absolute shit and before absolute bliss.

But there's often a catch to feeling better in grief that we don't talk about enough. Ugh, of course there's a catch, because the middle is, well, messy. The catch is that sometimes feeling better feels bad, like surprisingly and devastatingly bad. I know it doesn't make sense on the surface, but perhaps deep down you already know what I'm talking about. Grief is weird. We're desperate for the pain and intensity of it to fade away, but when it does, we can feel bad that it's happening.

I've never had a grieving client who, somewhere in the messy middle, hasn't expressed sadness or guilt for feeling better. The client acknowledges that somehow, over time, love, pain, and grief have gotten all jumbled together. It feels as if the pain of grief is the only expression of love left—the only remaining link of the life the client and the loved one shared.

Sometimes we conflate feeling bad with the best way to honor our loved ones. You may feel a deep sadness, believing that feeling better represents a growing distance from them. If you're somewhere in this messy middle, maybe you've felt this way. If it's any consolation, I've felt all these things too. And as convincing as this feeling is, I promise it's not true. Your love and memories are a part of you and will allow you to continue the bond you shared. (See "Memories for Safekeeping.")

⚘ AN INVITATION FOR YOU ⚘

embrace the mess

Messiness gets a bad reputation. The good news about messiness is that it reminds us that things aren't set in stone. Messiness means that we have space to change and grow in directions we might have missed if we followed the rules. Remember, messy people are often more spontaneous, flexible, and creative. They can be better problem-solvers, they don't sweat the small stuff, and they're able to be in the moment. As we explore throughout this book, you'll see that these are all qualities that benefit us in our grief.

We're often less of a hot mess than we think. We hold ourselves to impossible standards and are our own worst critics. Embracing messiness is a way to free us from harmful and unrealistic expectations we often have. In other words, it helps us ditch the "shoulds" of grief. So here's a wild card, an important invitation for you to embrace the mess.

---

try one or more of these activities to embrace the mess

1. Do something novel, messy, and playful that has no purpose.

Put on your favorite music jams and have a solo dance party. Skip down the road. Let your toddler put a full face of makeup on you. Get out an old instrument you have lying around. If it's raining, go for a walk in the rain or jump in a mud puddle.

2. Write and reflect on five things at which you used to be a hot mess.

Write down five activities or skills you were once shitty or at best mediocre at when you began. See if you can feel self-compassion for the mess you made of it back then. Maybe you can even find humor about what a mess you were. Take some time to think about how many hours or years it took you to feel competent.

(continues next page)

(continued from previous page)

3. Exchange the mess.

Whether it's your therapist, best friend, sibling, or hairdresser, find those you trust and tell them that you're feeling like a mess about some aspects of your grief. Make sure to tell them you're not looking for suggestions, just recognition. Then ask them to share something they're feeling a mess about. Being reminded that we're all messy sometimes helps us have more self-compassion.

4. Choose your own adventure.

What came to your mind when I invited you to embrace your messiness? Write it down in your journal and then make a plan to go do it.

wait.
am I still grieving?

LOCATING YOUR PLACE

There may come a time when you ask, "Wait. Am I still grieving?" If you're early in your grief, you're probably not even reading this chapter. You likely saw the title and said, "Next." I get that.

If someone would have told me—even two years after my husband died—that I might be asking myself, "Wait. Am I still grieving?" I would have told them that they were crazy. To be honest, my response would have sounded more like "Fuck off." (Well, at least in my mind.) So in case you stumbled upon this chapter out of curiosity or because you like to read books in order, stay around for a bit. You may not relate to this part right now, but it might offer some insight that you can tuck away for somewhere down the road.

ANSWERS WITH QUALIFIERS

For many of you, the answer to the question "Wait. Am I still grieving?" is "Yes, absolutely." It might be your answer for one year, ten years, or forever. And as I share throughout this book, that's OK. Our goal is not to move on from grief, but to move *forward* with it.

In some shape or form, this question will likely arise for you, and when it does, it's a signal that your relationship with grief is changing. You'll likely notice that your answer to this question shifts over time to include some qualifiers that represent a qualitative change to the meaning of your "yes."

"YES, SOMEWHAT, I MEAN KIND OF, YES"

It may be hard to imagine, but someday you might find yourself answering the "Wait. Am I still grieving?" question with something like "Yes, I'm still grieving. Well, kind of, but I guess it's not a daily thing or on my mind as often as it was." If you're in this place, I see you.

Like many people, you also might have a lot of complicated feelings about this answer. One of those feelings might be guilt. To you, this answer might signify that you're a bad partner, parent, sibling, or friend. You may also feel a longing. Longing for a time when you were grieving more actively because it made sense, felt familiar, or even helped you feel connected to your person.

You might feel relief or something akin to happiness when you recognize that this is your answer. And having that feeling might trigger one of the feelings previously mentioned. See what I mean? Complicated. If this is you, it's OK. I offer you this reminder: It's normal for your answers to shift, and that doesn't signify anything negative about you as a person or about your commitment to the love you have for your person.

"WEIRDLY, NO" (OR "HELL NO")

You might be one of the many people who's been wondering if it's normal that your answer is, "Weirdly, no," or even, "Hell no." Yes, it's perfectly normal and valid that the answer to this question might be some version of "No." That might be an answer you come to very soon after a loss or perhaps years or decades down the road. Regardless of the timing, it's perfectly OK.

There are several relationships, circumstances, and experiences in which, over time, the grief is essentially gone. This might include short-lived relationships that ended or the grief over losing a job or a home. This might be your answer regarding the death of someone with whom you had a complicated or nonexistent relationship, or perhaps the death of a childhood pet. It might even be the state you're in a de-

> ### *caution/invitation to the "no" answer*
> *I do have one caution or invitation if you have a definitive "No"*
> *answer. I invite you to say "No"—out loud—and then check*
> *inward, noticing what comes up in your body. Does your body*
> *stiffen? Jaw or chest tighten? Do you feel an impulse to run or*
> *physically move away? Pay attention to what far-off thoughts*
> *or feelings come up. Are there gnawing emotions or thoughts*
> *cropping up that you haven't addressed?*

cade or so after the death of someone you loved. If you've faced your grief (versus suppressed it) and you feel this way, it's OK!

For lots of valid reasons, many of us never learned how to give ourselves permission (or got from others) to grieve certain losses. (See "Access Denied.") If you do the exercise above and something comes up for you, this might be a time to explore what's been preventing you from grieving and seek external support, such as a therapist, to help you process it.

Remember, grief isn't something you can just wish away. It needs to be seen, felt, and acknowledged. Hiding it away or running from it isn't really an option. It finds a way, and ends up affecting you cognitively, physically, emotionally, spiritually, and relationally.

STUG HAPPENS

A third, more confusing (but also common) scenario is that at one point in your life, you answered the question, "Wait. Am I still grieving?" with "No, I'm not," or some other qualified answer, and then—BAM! Months or even years later you feel knocked down by a wave of grief over that loss you thought you'd left behind and you're scream-crying "Yes, absolutely!" all over again.

While we commonly refer to this occurrence as the "waves of grief," grief theorists call it Sudden Temporary Upsurge of Grief, or STUG. Who doesn't love a good acronym? You've felt a STUG before, haven't you? I've had many just while writing this book. I had one recently when my now-grown daughter sent me a video clip of her dad filming her as a baby. The sound of his voice broke me open for a few hours. It can happen out of nowhere. (But it doesn't really, right?) It happens in response to a memory, an object, a scent, a song, the sight of a certain person, a movie, an occasion, the way the sun looks just so. The list is endless.

Rest assured, we all experience STUGs and they aren't signs of backward progress. It's just the nature of grief—nonlinear and more like waves crashing on the shore or the dust cloud that follows around the Peanuts cartoon character Pigpen. Even though STUG is common, it can feel like a betrayal to the answers above. It might have you reassess and ask again, "Wait. Am I still grieving?" Remember, there's no right answer. It isn't a bad mark on your character, a demerit on your grief progress or even a red flag. Consider questions like these as an invitation to get more information to determine what action is needed.

AND THEN THERE'S RE-GRIEF

Yes, I said "re-grief."

"Re-grief? WTF? I didn't want to feel grief in the first place, let alone redo it." Is that what you were thinking? Fair. To ease your mind, re-grief isn't starting grief all over. In essence, the term refers to the times and ways we newly process an old loss when we arrive at a significant developmental milestone or profound life event.

Re-grief is common in processing profound losses faced in childhood. Children experience significant cognitive and emotional development stages through young adulthood. For example, if a child was five years old at the time of the original loss, each new phase of language acquisition or social and emotional development, each new milestone such as the first boyfriend/girlfriend, prom, or graduation may invite that person to reprocess—make new sense of and attach new meaning to an old loss.

And it's not just for children.

Regardless of our age, we're in a relationship with grief for the rest of our lives. That means the intensity, frequency, and intimacy ebbs and flows. And yet there are certain milestones as adults that might elicit this more profound relationship shift known as re-grief. These moments might include marriage, parenthood, retirement, or a certain milestone birthday. For example, adoptees often experience re-grief after the birth of their first child, recognizing in a new way the profound loss of not being raised by their biological parents.

NEW RELATIONSHIPS AND OLD GRIEF

Speaking of relationships, whether it's new friendships, romantic partners, children, or even new pets, the arrival of new relationships can be one of the surprising phases of your life, during which you find yourself back to answering "Wait. Am I still grieving?" with "Somewhat, kind of, yes." Don't be surprised if new relationships are an unwelcome source of STUGs. In fact, it makes total sense that new connections bring up the ones you've lost.

If this all sounds familiar and you're experiencing these STUGs in the wake of a new relationship, hear me out. If you find yourself thinking things such as, "Maybe this means I'm not ready for this," "This is embarrassing. I didn't want them to see me upset," "I'm worried I'm making my new _____ feel bad," or anything like that, let me stop you right there.

Remember a few key things I've already shared with you about grief: There's no timeline, no expectation to forget your person altogether, and there's no benefit in suppressing your pain or sorrow for the comfort of someone else.

OK, I'll stop there.

Well, just one more reminder. You can be ready for love or parenthood or pet ownership *and* experience waves of grief. The people in your life now are here for all of you, including the parts of you that experience waves of grief. Instead of seeing these waves as warning signs and running away or shutting them down, remind yourself that this is perfectly normal in grief.

⚶ AN INVITATION FOR YOU ⚶

have compassion for the changing answer

Even though we intellectually know better, many of us internalize the pressure to "move on" in grief. We believe in the myth that insists we can only feel one way or another, not both/and. We carry the burden that our answer to the question "Wait. Am I still grieving?" on any given day must remain so forever after.

I invite you to write a note to yourself. Take some time to reflect on my reminder that it's perfectly normal for the intensity and presence of your grief to ebb and flow. With that in mind, what will you want your future self to remember when struggling with the burden of the move-on myth? What words of compassion can you offer yourself when you notice your answer today is different than last month? Grab your journal and begin with "Dear Me . . ."

what the hell is happening to me?

helping you see the 360-degree impact of grief (no, it's not just all in your head)

everything sucks (and other negative thoughts)

IT REALLY DOES SUCK SO MUCH

Why are people so insistent on trying to convince us that grief doesn't suck so much? I'm guessing I'm not alone in feeling occasionally enraged by the expressions people say to our face or in the cards they send because they are mostly not-so-subtle attempts to talk you out of feeling sad. As Megan Devine's book title so aptly puts it, "It's OK that you're not OK!"

Many years ago, my frustration led me to action: designing and launching a line of empathy cards. Yes, I said empathy, not sympathy, because no one wants to be pitied. One of the first cards I released (and the most popular) says, "There's nothing I can say except this is fucking bullshit and it sucks so much." Why?

Because it *is* bullshit, and it *does* suck so much, and all we desperately want is at least one person to see the world as we see it. Someone who isn't trying to rush us out of the dark, pessimistic, and deeply negative place we are rightly in.

NEGATIVITY IS NORMAL

Feeling negative is a perfectly normal response to loss. In fact, did you know we're wired to feel negative sometimes? It's true!

We're evolutionarily designed with a negativity bias, which "is our tendency not only to register negative stimuli more readily but also to dwell on these events" (Kendra Cherry). I won't nerd out on you about the science of why, but it's how our species has managed to stay safe and survive across time. So remember, feeling negative sometimes is an essential and normal part of the human condition.

There's nothing I can say except this is fucking bullshit and it sucks so much.

The reason I bring you this fun science fact is that there's so much pressure to be positive, especially in Western culture. All the dang time. Have you felt that? Even in your grief? Toxic positivity, as researcher Susan David calls it, perpetuates the myth that a positive attitude is the only human state that is normal. That can make us feel wrong or as if we're failing if we're anything but sunny and filled with positive thoughts. But I promise, you're not wrong for feeling negative.

The death of someone you loved, the life-limiting or terminal diagnosis you received, or whatever loss you've faced is justifiably categorized as negative by your brain. Of course you're seeing the world in a negative light. Of course you're having negative thoughts. It also means that, for a while at least, it's normal that you're particularly primed to be on the lookout for other potential negative things.

NEGATIVITY BIAS CAN BE STICKY (AND SNEAKY)

Being on the lookout for potential negativity is also where things can get sticky. Yes, negativity is normal and even useful. Yes, awareness of our negativity bias is important. It gives us space to be more self-compassionate and find more grace for ourselves as we navigate this truly hard thing. And we also need to be aware of negativity's sneaky and sticky spiderweb-like qualities because when we accidently get stuck in its web, the usefulness of that bias is diminished, while the potential for harm increases.

Not surprisingly, there's no timeline for the benefits of negativity's presence in grief. And, like grief, it's not all or nothing, here or completely gone. It can be sneaky and seem to appear out of nowhere. It can be sticky and show up more often in certain domains of your life. Honestly, it happens to all of us.

ASSESSING ITS VALUE

Some places to assess whether your negativity bias has overstayed its welcome include your relationships, decision-making process, and your perceptions of people. While a healthy level of pessimism or suspicion is important for our overall emotional safety, taken too far it can damage the trust critical to healthy relationships.

Another warning sign is being overly attuned to negative comments or criticism. You may miss seeing the value of the supportive gestures offered by well-meaning grief supporters. This can lead to unnecessarily or prematurely cutting off relationships that are otherwise beneficial. I'm guilty of this one. In the words of Taylor Swift, "It's me, hi, I'm the problem, it's me." Ugh, I hate it when she calls me on my stuff. Really, I've been there, done this.

Our negativity bias means that the risk of loss naturally looms larger in our imagination than the possibility of gains. And while decision-making is complicated for a lot of valid reasons in the wake of loss (see "This Is Your Brain on Grief"), grievers have a heightened aversion to experiencing more loss with the wrong decision. You might notice that it's gotten extra sticky if you're consistently frozen and unable to make even little decisions. Been here, felt this too.

THE CONSEQUENCES OF REPETITION

Yes, it is absolutely valid to want to feel seen and heard while navigating our justifiable pain. And one of the consequences of speaking internally or externally about the negative too often is that the negativity gets amplified. Even worse, it casts a shadow and distorts our view of the positive, or at least the neutral.

When we are complaining, we are increasing our view that the locus of control is external. If we reframe, we can help ourselves see that we have agency. In an episode of the podcast *Hidden Brain*, guest Mike Baer shared that his research revealed that "the extent of complaining was a strong predictor of the increase in anger and a decrease in hope."

Sigh. Yet another both/and in grief. On the one hand, it's valid to feel negative about our loss and the secondary losses that follow. We also know that finding someone to hold space for the truth of our experience, our pain, our sense of brokenness is also helpful. And now we learn that continued repetition with no offer to reframe (both our own efforts or that of the listener) increases our suffering by amplifying anger and diminishing hope.

WHEN NEGATIVITY GETS STUCK

So if acknowledging and honoring negativity is helpful until it's not, what do we do if it's gotten sticky?

Notice It The first thing is to practice noticing that it's happening. Seems simple, but because it's so natural or instinctual, we often miss it. Noticing requires us to practice being more mindful, a skill that's useful in every aspect of grief and life. Essentially, you're invited to notice the thoughts and sensations in your body in the present moment, without judgment. Be curious about how these thoughts make you feel. (See "What Do You Notice?")

Switch It Up Like tracks in the snow, our negative thought patterns create tracks that we easily slide into. Switching things up is a helpful tool for getting unstuck. This might include something as simple as getting up and going to another room, or even a new location (I like all things nature). As weird as it may sound, smiling works too. It triggers oxytocin, that free, feel-good chemical in our brain. If smiling is not an option, switching it up might look like listening to upbeat music or calling a friend. It's just about interrupting the automated thinking loop you're in.

Assess and Reframe Once we've noticed the negativity loop, the next step is to assess and reframe. Maybe this is a valid or helpful negative thought, such as, "I really don't like these people because they've consistently said hurtful things even after I've told them the harm it causes me emotionally." Ask yourself, "Is that true? If so, what action does that invite me to take? Maybe cutting off that relationship is valid."

Often, these thoughts aren't true or helpful. They might sound something like "I can't trust anyone to be supportive in my grief. Nobody gets me." One sign that negativity has become harmful is all-or-nothing thinking. You might ask yourself, "Is it true that everyone is useless?" You may notice the absoluteness of your thought and offer yourself a reframe. Something such as, "Interacting with people who do X makes me feel worse. I do notice I feel more supported around people who do Y and Z." This gives you direction to take helpful action, such as making plans with people who do Y and Z.

Practice Gratitude I promise I'm not trying to lure you into the toxic positivity trap. Cultivating a gratitude practice doesn't require you to give up the negative thoughts you're having. That's the either/or and all-or-nothing thinking sneaking up again. Taking a mindful approach by taking time to appreciate small and big things—through affirmations, random acts of kindness, even by saying thank you with specific details of what you're thankful for—can interrupt the stickiness of negative thought loops.

⚜ AN INVITATION FOR YOU ⚜

reframe out loud

In my experience, talking out loud helps me organize thinking, remove distractions, improve memory, and reinforce the message. Talking out loud, whether to yourself or to others, can be so helpful. It reinforces the message that you're trying to communicate.

What happens if the only things we're saying out loud are expressions of anger, hopelessness, frustration, absence, and all that we're lacking? Those feelings are valid and likely what we're experiencing. Are they the only things? No, not likely. Yet the act of giving voice to those experiences not only reinforces the truth of that message, but also makes it harder to recall or connect with the neutral or positive experiences in our lives. It also shapes what we see as possible—and what isn't.

That's why I talk out loud to myself, every day. For years now, I've been speaking my mantras out loud the minute my feet hit the floor in the morning. Throughout the day, I speak out loud to myself about all manner of things. When I have a spark of an idea that I want to hold on to, I say it out loud—sometimes repeating it several times. When I notice that I'm sliding into all-or-nothing thinking, I offer myself a both/and alternative out loud so that I can shift the message I'm reinforcing.

If you notice negativity is dominating your discourse, I invite you to think of alternative messages, ones that might include neutral or even positive or hopeful statements. Get out your journal and write down the messages you might want to incorporate into conversations with supportive people in your life or, like me, ones that you want to start saying out loud to yourself throughout the day.

this is your brain
on grief

BRAIN, BODY, AND TRAUMA

Over these next three chapters I will separate the topics of our brain, our body, and trauma to make the information more digestible. But the truth is our brain and body are really one entity and we experience trauma in and through both. Many of us (including me) struggle to separate these topics because much of our suffering results from our collective misunderstanding of their interconnectedness.

WHEN YOUR BRAIN FEELS FRIED

This is your brain. This is your brain on ~~drugs~~ grief. Any questions?

If you're in your forties, fifties, or older, you likely just chuckled out loud at the quote above. You probably also know where I'm going with this metaphor. If not, hang on for the ride, kids. In the '80s, there was a drug-prevention TV ad featuring an egg. The camera pans to a plain egg. The narrator says, "This is your brain." Then he cracks the egg into a hot frying pan. Next you see an egg frying in a pan with this voice-over: "This is your brain on drugs. Any questions?"

Don't worry, I'm not here to lecture you on drug use. It's just that, like drugs, grief takes a toll on your brain (and body, as we'll discover in "Your Body Knows"). The effects of grief on the brain can linger for weeks, months, maybe longer. What are the effects? For starters, things such as brain fog, confusion, forgetfulness, memory lapses, and anxiety. Sound familiar? So yeah, your brain is fried like an egg. Or a more vegan-friendly way to describe the toll is simply "grief brain."

This chapter is metaphor-dense to help make this incomprehensible concept more comprehensible. Even if we had a complete scientific explanation of grief brain, which we don't, I offer you different ways to understand what's happening to you so that you can ditch the unrealistic expectations and judgment you have of yourself about how you're *supposed* to be thinking and feeling. You'll also learn why caring for your brain health is important in grief.

THE GRIEVING BRAIN

While there's still a lot of unknowns about how and why our brains and body suffer in grief, researcher Mary-Frances O'Connor is helping us know more. In our podcast conversation and in her fascinating book *The Grieving Brain*, she explained how she and other researchers are using tools such as fMRI machines and other scientific approaches to help us understand what's happening in the brain of grievers.

Some of the many insights and explanations we're discovering is that grieving is learning, as if we're being faced with a puzzle. This explains why it feels as if our minds are playing tricks on us. Though I didn't have the science behind it, this insight aligns so beautifully with the shredded manuscript metaphor I've been using all these years.

O'Connor explains, "Grief is a heart-wrenchingly painful problem for the brain to solve, and grieving necessitates learning to live in the world with the absence of someone you love deeply, who is ingrained in your understanding of the world. This means that for the brain, your loved one is simultaneously gone and also everlasting, and you are walking through two worlds at the same time. You are navigating your life despite the fact that they have been stolen from you, a premise that makes no sense, and that is both confusing and upsetting."

LEARNING IS A BRAIN DRAIN

In times of acute grief, which is another way to say early grief (even though there's no specific time limit), we're trying to comprehend the incomprehensible. Take that in for a moment. We're trying to understand or intellectualize something that our mind, heart, and body can't yet process.

It's like the first time a student cracks open a physics textbook or hears a lecture on parallel universes. (OK, I use a lot of science references because it's been my nemesis. Pretty ironic since my father is a well-known space scientist. Honestly, I remember opening a textbook he coauthored, and I couldn't even understand the foreword, let alone the book.)

Learning, even when it's something we're interested in, can be very tiring. When it's something we're *not* interested in, such as how to live with grief, it's downright exhausting. It's a brain drain. That's why it's useful to think of grieving as learning. I know you're thinking, "But I don't want to learn how to do this." I get that. And while you don't have a choice, as I explore in "Start Close In," the good news (sort of) is that you already have a lot of life experience in learning something new.

In the wake of loss, you're learning how to write/edit/rewrite the manuscript of your life. You're discovering new ways to find your place and identity in the world. You're learning new roles, tasks, and responsibilities. Learning these lessons involves a lot of emotional, physical, practical, and intellectual effort, likely more than you've ever exerted.

Yet we expect ourselves and others to know how to live this new life. To be good at it. To be fully functioning. To have unlimited energy for it. Oh, and to be rational. In grief, especially early on, we're anything but these things. I say screw these false expectations. It's OK to be none of these things. It's perfectly OK to claim your grief brain.

PLAYING TRICKS ON YOU

Have you ever walked into the house expecting your loved one to be there? Maybe you've picked up the phone to call your person with some exciting news. I'd be surprised if you haven't. I'm not sure I've met any grievers who haven't wondered if they were losing their mind because they thought, for a moment, that their loved one was some-how still alive.

If those we love are missing, we assume that they are just far away and will return. When we find ourselves expecting our person to walk through the door, it isn't a sign that we're refusing to accept the fact of the person's death or that we're avoiding the emotional upheaval that comes with the reality. This is simply a function of what O'Connor explains as our brain's "here, now, and far" function.

Our brain is wired to hold people and places like a map so that we can find our way back when we're separated. Whether we were pres-ent for their death or received a phone call, we store that information in something called episodic memory. It can take more than one of these types of memories to override the well-worn path in our brain that makes us expect our person to be in the physical world.

This function of the brain also explains why some losses are harder to comprehend and process than others. The ambiguity of some losses, such as when people disappear without explanation, makes it difficult to overwrite the expectation of their return. Millions of people experi-enced this kind of ambiguity amid the COVID-19 pandemic, when they couldn't be present in the hospital to witness their loved one's illness or death. The lack of memories of the loss, or the reasons for it, makes this process challenging too. (See "Ambiguity S-U-C-K-S.")

LOSING IT, TEMPORARILY

Have you ever thought or said out loud, "I've lost it"? I have, and so has pretty much every grieving person I've ever met. As we also explore in "Secondary Losses: The Sneakiest Bitches of Them All," grief brain can cause us to experience mild to sometimes significant diminished brain functions and abilities. So, yes, we have lost it, but I promise it's only temporary.

"Focus where? Concentrate on what?"

"What did they just say?"

"Why can't I do this? I just read the instructions."

"What just happened in the show? I guess I'll have to re-wind. Again."

Ever have any of these thoughts? Again, you're not alone. In *A Grief Observed*, C. S. Lewis explains the experience of grief brain so perfectly: "At other times it [grief] feels like being mildly drunk or concussed." Exactly, C. S. That's exactly how it feels.

At other times it [grief] feels like being mildly drunk or concussed.
—*C. S. Lewis*, A Grief Observed

I was a voracious reader before Eric died. That's why I was really disturbed the first time I picked up a book a few months later. I'm not exaggerating when I tell you that I had to reread the first page four times. FOUR TIMES. I couldn't focus well enough to understand or remember what I'd just read. I chucked that book across the room after the fourth try. Also not an exaggeration. Dramatic I know, but it was so freaking concerning. Nearly a year after my temper tantrum, I retrieved the thrown book and eased my way back into the world of reading for the first time. (Thanks to comedian Tina Fey for writing a funny and easy-to-read memoir.)

The reason I made this book into short, digestible chapters with a lot of white space on the pages is that reading can feel nearly impossible in early grief. Remember, if you can only handle a chapter, page, or even paragraph at a time, you're not alone. If you need to reread things, that's OK. If you need to throw the book across the room, you have my permission. When you're ready, pick up the book, dust it off, and try again. Your focus and concentration will improve over time. Meanwhile, be patient with yourself.

Grief Time Recently a client hesitantly admitted that time feels so weird. She described time as "moving like fast and slow and standing still all at once." I told her I get it and explained that it's what I call "grief time." Sometimes time in grief feels as if someone hit the 2x fast-forward button on a video. Other times it's as if the person hit pause. Still other times it feels as if someone pushed the dreaded "start from the beginning" button.

I assured her, and I'm assuring you, that time really is weird, but it won't feel this weird forever. When it's happening, and you feel out of sorts, try to remind yourself, "Oh, this is grief time. It won't always feel like this." While time can certainly be disorienting, there are some positive things that come out of our changed relationship with it, such as our ability to be present and savor the small things more often.

Confusion Whether it's trying to complete tasks you've done a million times before or understanding instructions you're receiving for the first time, being easily confused and overwhelmed is very common in early grief. Remember, your brain is working in overdrive to comprehend the incomprehensible after a significant and profound event. This can leave little space to recall some of the simple and mundane information and skills you need for day-to-day living.

Decision Fatigue Oh, the irony. At the same time our brain turns to mush, we're asked to make a lot of decisions. More decisions than we usually must make, and some of which are huge and consequential. During early grief, we're often forced to make medical decisions, funeral arrangements, financial decisions, housing arrangements, and so much more. Even little decisions can feel overwhelming, insignificant, or both at once. For me, one of those early, seemingly small but overwhelming decisions centered around what pictures we should use at Eric's memorial. What did I do? I invited input from friends and family, delegated the task of gathering the photos and then gave final approval. I think. Did I? Who remembers?

Forgetfulness Are you forgetting things? More than usual? I didn't notice this at first because Eric was my memory keeper. Even before becoming a widow, my memory recall was average at best. As time went on, I noticed I struggled to remember what I did or said an hour earlier. I missed appointments I had just made the day before and I'm sure I missed more than one friend's birthday celebration.

Then I noticed I couldn't remember other things from the past, such as details of our courtship. That forgetfulness sent me into a panic, and I often felt overwhelmed because he wasn't there to fill in the blanks like he always had before. Has something like this happened to you? I'm sorry. I hate how it feels. Again, it won't last. It's why later we'll discuss how journals, sticky notes, and even the notes app on your phone will be a savior.

ANXIETY

Whether it was an unexpected or traumatic death or the anticipatory grief you experienced in the wake of a terminal diagnosis, feeling anxious is common. In the wake of loss, we feel particularly out of control and lack safety and certainty. Our body-mind is doing its job, in a way, by keeping us alert to the possible risks and dangers out there. (Cue the superhero who has remained in character too long.) If this sounds like you, it's important to let go of the inner critic that says you shouldn't be experiencing this and instead tune into learning from it and determining how to ease the intensity.

Sometimes anxiety in grief arises because we're afraid of and avoiding certain emotions or memories. Though we often associate anxiety with persistent worry, it can also show up as irritability and shutting down. Safe spaces, both emotional and physical, are necessary to address and alleviate anxious feelings. (See "Your Body Knows.")

DEPRESSION OR SHUTTING DOWN

While depression and grief aren't the same thing, they share many common symptoms. Additionally, being in a prolonged stress state can initiate or worsen an existing history of depression. Both grief and depression can involve intense sadness and withdrawal. Generally, in grief, waves allow moments of reprieve, or even fond memories or feelings, whereas depression is prolonged and consistent without a break. If you have a history of depression or are concerned that there are no moments of relief, I invite you to seek a qualified mental health professional, not just your general physician.

DREAMS AND NIGHTMARES

Grief dreams can happen prior to loss (the anticipatory grief phase) and afterward. There's still relatively little known about the cause of these dreams, but as researcher and podcast host Joshua Black explains, there are common themes:

1. Dreams that don't involve the person, just some feelings of grief.
2. Dreams in which the person is mentioned, but not seen.
3. Dreams in which the person is present in some form.

Years ago, I shared one of my recurring dreams on Black's podcast *Grief Dreams*. The exact details varied, but the dream went something like this: I would bump into Eric somewhere in the world. We'd run into each other's arms, talk about how it's all been a terrible mistake and tell each other "I love you." But then, we'd both realize that he is dead, and I'd be standing there alone, recognizing that I'd been imagining this conversation.

Then I'd wake up in real life and realize he is dead all over again. I had versions of this dream so many times in the first year after his death. In more recent years, he has visited me on only rare occasions but now we both know he's dead, and he wants to show me something, tell me something, or just remind me of how much he loved me.

If you haven't dreamt of your person, that's OK. I've had so many clients over the years express feelings of guilt for not having dreams. They're concerned that not having specific dreams where their person is present must mean they don't care enough. Though there is growing research on dreams, the truth is we really don't know why we dream, and we certainly don't have control over when, what, or how we do it.

So I invite you to set down any sense of responsibility you have about dreaming or not dreaming. For those of you who desperately want to see your loved in a dream and never do, I acknowledge the pain and anguish you feel. For some of you, that pain is almost unbearable.

THINKING ISN'T ENOUGH

Where are my fellow intellectualizers, academics, and researchers? Oh, how I've wished I could use my intellectual knowledge to "hurry through the pain." After all, I was a clinical social worker and director of a family services nonprofit at the time of Eric's death. Surely, I concluded, I can figure this out and "grieve well." I had a lot of false beliefs that "because I know things," I should be able to think it through. Sorry. You can't think your way through grief. Trust me. I've tried.

Sorry. You can't think your way through grief.

Yes, learning about grief, including the science behind how your brain and body are affected, is useful. It gives you context for what you're experiencing. It can even help you set down, repeatedly, the myths and unrealistic expectations you have about your overall functioning. It can also help you think about incorporating some of the tools you need to support your brain and nervous system. But investing in learning at the expense of wading through grief can just delay the journey. Learning doesn't replace the need for "sitting in the suck," as podcast guest Amber Emily Smith so aptly describes it.

RESOURCES FOR YOUR GRIEVING BRAIN

First, I want you to pause for a minute and see if you can hold compassion for your grieving brain. Reflect on all the energy it's expending 24/7 to try to solve this complex puzzle of loss.

Now let's focus on some small but important steps you can take to nourish your brain as you move through grief. Just as I suggest in "Your Body Knows," start with the steps that feel most accessible first. Remember, part of your brain's reaction to this scary and out of control thing that happened to you may be to retreat. That means it's going to take some practice and may require pushing yourself out of your comfort zone to try some of these resources.

Stop Expecting It To Work the Way It Did

The first thing you can do for your grieving brain is to let go. Let go of the expectation that your brain should be functioning like it did before. The immense self-judgment and criticism that come from that unrealistic belief can lead us into a stress spiral, which can further diminish our brain function. As I already shared, grief is a drain on your brain. So remember that these losses are temporary and don't expect it to be any different than it is in this moment.

Write Things Down

Write things down. I mean all the things. Remove the expectation and burden that your brain can recall everything during this time. It can't. So have some analog and digital backups. Set timers and reminders for everything on your phone or computer. This might include bill due dates, trash day, school pickup times, even brushing your teeth if needed. I used a lot of journals, pads of paper, sticky notes, and the notes app on my phone for a long time.

Another helpful writing tool is journaling. I know, another "ugh" moment for some of you. However, putting your thoughts and feelings down is therapeutic and can help you release what you're holding on to. Journaling is one tool to help separate yourself from your feelings and thoughts. It can make your unrealistic expectations or harsh self-talk more visible. It can also make space for the clarity you're craving and reduce some of the anxiety you're carrying. Having a log over time also helps you see how things are changing.

Seek Support, Accept Help

As I share in "Your Turn to Buddy-Breathe," every single one of us needs help when we're grieving (and even when we're not). Set down the cape. You don't need to be Wonder Woman or Superman. You don't have to do it all, nor can you. That's a fantasy. Accepting help from friends, neighbors, or colleagues with some complex (or even simple) tasks frees you up to use your currently limited brain energy for healing.

Plus, people are often desperate to feel useful, so letting them do something for you helps them too. Besides the meal-train delivery, friends helped me with things such as organizing and hosting play dates for my daughter. One friend even enrolled her in a camp for me. I know it's hard. Take the help. I'm begging you.

Mindful Reminders

Offering yourself a daily affirmation or reminder that encourages self-compassion and grace for this phase of your grief is a powerful tool for releasing the expectations and strain on your already drained brain.

Say your affirmation out loud in front of the bathroom mirror or quietly to yourself when you first wake up in the morning. Write it in your journal. Whatever method you choose, remember that how we talk to ourselves influences how we see ourselves, our capacity to heal, and the actions we believe we're capable of taking. Maybe it sounds something like, "I deserve compassion and grace as my brain heals from this loss. I'm doing the best I can today, and that's enough."

---

*I deserve compassion and grace as my brain heals from this loss.
I'm doing the best I can today, and that's enough.*

Rest and Respite

Though rest in moderation feels impossible in grief, the science is clear: Lack of rest equals poor brain function. Not what our already overwhelmed brain needs. So find it where you can get it. While sleep is one way to get physical rest, sometimes it's hard in grief. Remember, sleep isn't the only way to rest. Yoga, stretching, and massage count too.

It's not just physical. Did you know that there are seven types of rest our bodies need? In her TED Talk, Dr. Sandra Daulton-Smith explained that beyond our physical need for rest, we also need mental, sensory, creative, emotional, and spiritual rest. Spend time with a friend talking about something other than grief. Listen to music or dance to a favorite song. Take a drive somewhere scenic. Pick up an old creative endeavor—or try a new one. Practice savoring each bite of a delicious meal.

Eat Well and Drink Water

Speaking of eating, nourish your body with healthful food and drink plenty of water. More obvious and important reminders, I know. You also may be thinking, "Who has the energy for that? Or the appetite?" Since people are likely to bring you food either way, maybe ask for some options that make your body feel good or request a meal delivery service for a while. Eating food with protein, vitamins, and minerals that your body needs will aid in your digestion and heart health—all of which impacts your brain function.

Oh, and drink up, my friends. Dehydration can lead to headaches and more brain drain. This doesn't apply to alcohol, sadly. Alcohol serves as a depressant to the body-mind you're trying to nourish and restore. So keep that to a minimum.

Move Your Body

I promise, you don't have to run a marathon or a 5k, or even run at all. But a little consistent movement can go a long way. More annoying science: Moving your body has a positive effect on your overall brain health. Movement releases some fun things such as endorphins, dopamine, and serotonin, which can help alleviate anxiety and depression.

A simple thirty-minute walk a few times per week can reduce brain drain. If you're using a wheelchair or if walking is difficult, find any movement that feels right for your body. All movement increases blood flow, which also benefits the brain. If you have access to the outdoors and can get some vitamin D, bonus points. Movement can be a form of mindful meditation, as J'aime Morrison (podcast guest, surfer, and creator of the short experimental film *Upwell*) shares in "Your Body Knows."

Keep Learning

"Keep learning" seems counterintuitive as a resource when our brains are drained from all the learning we're already doing in grief. And yet keeping our mind actively engaged on something new *and* pleasant can be the creative rest and rejuvenation that our brain needs. Researchers have found that cognitive training can improve memory and thinking. So if you're struggling in these areas, try learning something new. For now, that might be reading this book.

⚚ AN INVITATION FOR YOU ⚚

nourish your grief brain

"My brain is so tired." I said these words so many times early in grief, sometimes to myself, sometimes to a friend, but always with a judgmental or embarrassed tone—in utter defeat. Honestly, when I did say these words to another, it felt good when the person would respond with something like "I bet it is," or, "That makes sense." In case you're feeling defeated and you don't have anyone around to support you, imagine me saying this to you. "Of course your brain is tired, my friend. That's totally understandable. How can I support you to help it feel rested and restored?"

You may also be thinking, "I don't know where to start," or, "I don't even have the energy." I invite you to consider the circumstances you can create to make nourishing your grief brain a little bit easier to do.

---

set your intention
Caring for yourself might feel like the last priority right now. But setting a goal to nourish your brain will make it easier to do. Plus, having a more resourced brain can help you complete the other things you consider a priority.

start small
We love lists in our culture—with big, sweeping gestures and big outcomes. That's not needed or reasonable here. Think of one or two things you can try to do every day for the next seven days. Or just for today.

find a buddy
We've established that your brain isn't operating at max capacity. That's why it's important to ask for support, feedback, or encouragement from someone who cares.

(continues next page)

(continued from previous page)

acknowledge what's working

The outcomes of these practices may not create big aha moments. That's why it's important to pause periodically to see what activities or practices are helping, even just a little bit. It's equally important to evaluate what isn't nourishing you, even if it's a familiar, comfortable habit or an old routine.

adjust as you go

Your brain capacity and needs change over time. Don't forget to use what you learned when you assess what's working and what isn't. Adjust as you go. Maybe revisit weekly in the beginning, then monthly.

your body knows

IT'S NOT ALL IN YOUR HEAD

As I mentioned, the brain and body are broken up into two chapters in this book, essentially to give your reading brain a place to pause. It's a lot of information to absorb. However, your brain isn't an autonomous organ separate from your body. Maybe you've heard this phrase "brain-body connection." Maybe you think it makes sense, but you don't really get what it means. Or honestly, maybe you think it's a bunch of new age BS. It's important to understand how they are connected because it will help you understand how and why your body experiences grief.

It's more accurate to think of the brain and body as points along a complex web of bike lanes, side roads, and highways with traffic moving in both directions, all the time. Instead of cars, these pathways are made up of things such as hormones, chemicals, and neurotransmitters. What's transmitted between the body and brain are the essential components of everyday functions such as digestion and breathing. They also relay information that enables us to move, think, and feel.

The false assumption that our brain and body are separate means that we often ignore the body, prescribing (or not prescribing) interventions for one without seeing the impact on the other. So let's explore the signs that our body knows grief and identify opportunities to nurture and care for our whole selves.

WE HAVE SUPERHERO POWERS

Did you know you have superhero powers? While we can't shape-shift, become invisible, or leap tall buildings in a single bound, we do have the stress response. Fight, Flight, Freeze, and Fawn are our superhero names. Seriously, at just the perception of danger (real or not), our brain and body leap into action like some sort of superhero to the rescue. We don't turn green like the Incredible Hulk, but just as quickly as he does, we experience a cascading set of biological and physiological changes throughout our mind and body that help keep us safe and ready to respond to danger. I mean, that's pretty badass, don't you think?

Our bodies and minds can do incredible things when we don our stress superhero persona. Blood pumps to our heart and muscles are ready for us to battle (or to run, freeze, or appease the enemy). Think of the mother who lifts a car when her child is in danger. Our body is just as heroic in everyday ways too. In grief, that might look like staying up all hours of the night to console our grieving child or navigating the tasks of funeral preparation on zero hours of sleep.

WE CAN'T ALWAYS WEAR THE CAPE

Some of our bodily functions really cramp a superhero's style, so they go offline when we're stressed. Digestion pauses, because we don't want to have to stop to pee when we're on the run. Hormones that make us sleepy can also shut off, because we don't want to fall asleep when danger is lurking around the corner. The impact of this prolonged superhero mode is wide and varied but can include a series of aches, pains, infections, and even serious and chronic illnesses. Signs you might be feeling grief in your body include:

- *Body Pain* Muscles tense in response to stress activation, and this can lead to all kinds of aches and pains throughout your body. Muscle tension can also make it feel harder to breathe sometimes.
- *Clumsiness* Ongoing stress to your nervous system can cause your body to act and react differently, resulting in increased clumsiness.
- *Dissociation/Disembodiment* Extreme or prolonged stress can

cause you to feel disconnected from yourself and the world around you. Almost as if you're detached from your body. This disconnectedness can also be a sign of a trauma response. (See "Too Much Too Soon.")

• *Headaches* You're likely not surprised that stress, including the stress of grief, can trigger new or intensify existing tension and other types of headaches.

• *Heart Issues* Stress hormones make your heart pump faster to reach vital organs. That's why you might experience a pounding heart. Over time, a sustained increased heart rate and high blood pressure could lead to a heart attack.

• *Heartburn* Stress increases production of stomach acid, which can create or exacerbate heartburn symptoms.

• *High Blood Sugar* Stress releases extra sugar into the bloodstream. If this happens over a prolonged period, you increase the risk for type 2 diabetes.

• *Sex Drive, Functioning, and Fertility Issues* Stress interferes with the reproductive system and can lead to fertility issues in both men and women. Stress and the corresponding fatigue that comes with it can take a toll on your libido. Stress in the brain can interfere with a man's ability to get an erection. Stress hormones can also throw a menstrual cycle into chaos, resulting in missed periods or, in extreme cases, no periods at all.

• *Stomachaches and Digestive Issues* Your body's digestive system can be impacted by stress, leading to ailments such as stomachaches and nausea.

• *Weakened Immunity* Stress takes a toll on your immune system's natural defenses, leaving you more vulnerable to infections.

YES, STRESSORS SUCK

Stress is a fact of life. It isn't realistic or even possible to remove all stressors from our lives. They can be "good" stressors, such as starting a new job or school, or "bad" stressors, such as getting a divorce or being fired. And when we're grieving, the volume and intensity of stressors are higher than normal.

For all the reasons we've already explored—from dealing with intense emotions, thoughts, and memories to decision-making and fatigue—our body considers stressors to be threats. Stress is an embodied, automated response, not a rational choice. So seeing our stress as some sort of weakness or moral failure is inaccurate and unhelpful.

GETTING STUCK IS THE PROBLEM

Remember, our response to stressors is meant to be temporary, allowing us to flee to safety quickly. Meaning, when the stress response is activated, we're meant to discharge it when we're no longer in danger. Just like the Hulk needs to return to Bruce Banner to go about his day-to-day life, we need to set down our superhero persona to function well.

The challenge is that our perception of danger is constant. As a result, we stay hulked up, remaining in our Fight, Flight, Freeze, or Fawn character. We perceive the intense thoughts, emotions, and memories as stressors. So often we find ourselves getting stuck in stress, and that's when it becomes a problem.

Our brain and body speak different languages. If we keep thinking, "I'm OK. I just need to calm down. It's just a stressor," our bodies cannot hear our thoughts. We must speak the language of the body. We must do something to send a signal to our body that we're safe.

As Emily and Amelia Nagoski explain in their phenomenal book *Burnout: The Secret to Unlocking the Stress Cycle*, "Dealing with your stress is a separate process from dealing with the thing that causes your stress. To deal with your stress, you have to 'complete the stress cycle.' You have to do something that signals to your body that you are safe or else you'll stay in that state, with neurochemicals and hormones degrading by never shifting into relaxation. Your digestive system, immune system, cardiovascular system, musculoskeletal system, and reproductive system never get the signal that they're safe."

Unlike the days when we ran from the physical danger of the saber-toothed tiger and sought safety in a cave with our tribe, our modern-day stressors are largely cognitive and emotional. This makes discharging stress more of a challenge. That's largely due to our misunderstanding that stress is just "all in our head." That means we're trying to respond to stress with our thinking brain. Thankfully, there's growing recognition that stress is embodied, and that we must respond with the language of the body to release it.

GETTING UNSTUCK

We usually try to use our rational brain to tell our wise bodies to stop protecting us from danger. We admonish ourselves and others for feeling stressed in the first place and then try to solve the problem by saying unhelpful things such as, "Don't be so stressed out. Everything is going to work out." Voilà, problem solved.

Yeah, no, of course that doesn't work. So let's all agree to stop saying stuff like that.

If we can't talk or think our way out of a stress state, what can we do? The good news is that there are a lot of easy and accessible tools we can use—scientifically backed strategies to discharge stress. The challenge we often face is convincing ourselves to use the tools that we so desperately need.

Crying, believe it or not, is one of those tools. Many of us have that one down. What else? Some of my favorite tools include topics we explore in more depth throughout this book such as physical activity, creativity, laughing, meditation (including progressive muscle relaxation), physical affection, and breathing.

This may seem random or odd to you, but I want to share this tool anyway in case it helps you. There's a mindfulness activity I do whenever I'm feeling stuck in stress and then feeling judgmental for being stressed. I take a moment to appreciate the stubbornness of my physiology. I acknowledge the protection I'm being offered. I even place my hand on my heart and say to myself, "Way to have my back, body. I appreciate the concern. I know you're trying to protect me. And, cut it out already. I don't need your help right now. I'm safe in this moment." Then I do one of the activities above. For me, "beauty walks" have become my go-to strategy any time stress shows up. (See "Seeking Creative Resources.")

INTERNAL CALENDAR

Sometimes you don't need the calendar to tell you what day or season it is. You feel it in your body, your heart, and your soul. You know with all your being that this is the anniversary of the time that changed everything.

Maybe you know the feeling I'm talking about. When your body knows before your mind does. Maybe you wake up earlier than normal or can't sleep. Perhaps you're flooded with overwhelming and terrifying fear.

Instead of ignoring these things, maybe get curious about why your body feels so heavy. Observe the tightness in your chest or maybe notice the aching in your body, the extreme fatigue, or the screaming in your head. These kinds of internal calendar alerts happen to various degrees across our grief journey. I promise: They're not setbacks or signs that you're not healing. And I know how scary and overwhelming they can feel.

Sometimes you don't need the calendar to tell you what day or season it is. You feel it in your body, your heart, and your soul. You know with all your being that this is the anniversary of the time that changed everything.

For a few years I didn't understand what was happening to my body and mind every July and August, my season of the calendar that's full of land mines. Headaches, aches, pains, colds, fatigue, clumsiness, you name it. I would ignore my body and search my dreams and memories for what could be bringing on this extreme shift and dismiss the constellation of aches and pains and issues in my body because the feelings weren't happening on the exact *day*.

There can be obvious days and not-so-obvious days. For me, it's the day I got the call that Eric's "MRI results are back and they found . . ." It's the few days after that when we celebrated what turned out to be our last wedding anniversary. The day of his first brain surgery. The next day when I heard his voice for the last time. It was also the day of his second brain surgery and the day he died in my arms. This all takes place over the course of two and a half weeks, but my body typically alerts me that the season is coming prior to the series of anniversaries.

MOVEMENT AND MOURNING

Grief is like a shifting undercurrent of water and mindfulness helps us adapt to it and ride it forward. I love how J'aime Morrison uses her wisdom as a professor of theater and movement to help us understand how movement is a meditation that offers us an embodied way to mourn.

Her insights also come from her experiences as both a widow and a surfer. "I have come to believe," Morrison shared, "that deep grief unmakes us, and that mourning is as much about grieving our lost love as it is about being forced to remake ourselves. Understanding that grief comes in waves, and we must learn to ride them, I have found that movement, as meditation, as a mode of transformation and as a creative force for healing, helps us tune into how grief shows up in our bodies and how to move through it, creatively, from the inside out. Movement won't change the terrain but can help navigate it."

⅔ AN INVITATION FOR YOU ⅔

relax your body

I promise I'm not going to tell you, "Just relax." Our body responds to stress by tensing our muscles. Again, thanks body. The problem is, we often walk around with tense muscles that we're unaware of, which reinforces the message to our body that we're stressed. One of the best ways to interrupt that vicious cycle is with a progressive muscle relaxation exercise. Essentially, it involves bringing your awareness to your body and slowly tensing then relaxing each muscle. It can offer immediate relief, and the more you practice, the more skills you will have to help you relax.

I've created some prompts and instructions (facing page) so that you can guide yourself through a progressive muscle relaxation exercise. If you'd prefer to be guided, I've got you covered. At the bottom of this page you'll find a QR code; scan it with your phone and it will take you to a guided meditation.

If you'd like to practice now, I invite you to get into a position that is most comfortable for your body, where you feel held and supported. You can keep your eyes open or read the prompts and guide yourself from memory. This exercise requires you to pay mindful attention to each muscle, so do your best to remove distractions from the room. You are invited to tense each muscle, but not to the point of strain or pain. In fact, if you have injuries or pain, skip that area of your body. As you move along, pay attention to the sensations you're experiencing: the sensation of the muscle when it's tightened, the sensations of releasing tension in each muscle, and the feeling of relaxation that results.

progressive muscle relaxation

start with mindful breathing

Begin by taking a deep breath in, noticing the sensation of your lungs expanding. Hold your breath for a few seconds and then release it slowly and let the tension release from your body. Pause and repeat. Another slow, deep breath in that fills your lungs and expands your belly, then slowly exhale, noticing the tension leaving your body once more.

progress from bottom of your feet to the top of your head

(example process for feet)

Bring your attention to your feet. Tense and curl your toes and arch then flex your feet. Hold the tension and notice the sensation. Hold for five seconds. Release the tension, paying attention to the feeling of relaxation. Be with that sensation for a few seconds.

Repeat this process as you move up your body. Your calves, upper legs, and pelvis. Move on to your stomach, then chest, repeating the process as you arrive at each muscle group. Next, do the same for your back and then move your way up your arms, starting at your fingers, then forearms, upper arms, and shoulders. Move up to your shoulders, neck, and head and repeat the process.

Tense the muscles in your face, focusing on the muscles around your eyes, mouth, and jaw. Tensing each muscle, notice the sensation of tension, hold for five seconds, then release the tension, savoring the feeling of relaxation after each release.

too much too soon

NO TIME TO PROCESS

Trauma is a word that gets thrown around a lot in our everyday language, especially in relationship to grief. I think the casual and uninformed nature of its use can be problematic, both for normalizing grief (expanding our understanding of grief as a normal response to loss) and to those individuals who suffer from post-traumatic stress disorder (PTSD) because of trauma they experienced.

ALL GRIEF ISN'T TRAUMATIC, BUT ALL TRAUMA INVOLVES GRIEF

My working theory is that not all grief is traumatic, but all trauma involves grief. This means that grief is a normal response to loss and, given time and support, we don't necessarily get stuck in or hijacked by a nervous system in overdrive. On the other hand, all trauma is about loss of control, loss of safety, loss of security, loss of relationship. Therefore, all trauma has a component that requires attention to grief.

DEFINITIONS AND DESCRIPTIONS

Trauma

Trauma is often explained as a response to a distressing event in which we experience "too much too soon," making it nearly impossible to integrate into our bodies and minds, impairing our capacity to adapt and thrive. The result is a disorganized nervous system that remains hypersensitive to threats.

While there are varying definitions of trauma, I prefer this one by world-renowned physician and author Dr. Gabor Maté: "Trauma is not what happens to you, it's what happens inside you because of what happened to you. Trauma is that scarring that makes you less flexible, more rigid, less feeling and more defended."

Big T and Little t Trauma

Essentially the difference between Big T and Little t trauma is the scale or intensity of the external event that caused the traumatic reaction in the individual. Big T is generally related to a life-threatening event or deeply distressing or disturbing situation. It can also be acute psychological trauma from something like repeated abuse: any situation that caused the individual feelings of extreme helplessness, fear, lack of control, and danger.

Little t trauma is also highly distressing but falls outside the above descriptions and can include non-life-threatening injuries, bullying, emotional abuse, death of a pet, or end of a significant relationship. I'll explain more below, but it's important to note that two people can endure the same event and one may not experience it as traumatic.

Traumatic Grief

This isn't a diagnosis, but *traumatic grief* is a term generally used to describe the grief that accompanies unexpected or violent death. It usually describes a grieving person who is experiencing post-trauma survival mechanisms in addition to traditional signs and symptoms of grief.

It can be difficult to differentiate between symptoms of PTSD, grief, and traumatic grief. While fear predominates in PTSD, grief is about the loss. Someone experiencing traumatic grief will have both and an underlying sense of powerlessness.

Is it a useful description or term? I'm not certain, but if it gets someone to seek assessment for possible trauma, it's worthwhile. Trauma-informed intervention is critical in treating a traumatized person. Support without that lens can cause further harm and unnecessary suffering.

WHEN FEAR DOMINATES YOUR GRIEF

One challenge in clarifying trauma versus the "normal" stress in the wake of profound loss is that trauma can show up in the body in many of the same ways as prolonged stress: feeling easily overwhelmed or on edge or having a tight chest, general muscle tension, difficulty sleeping, memory issues, brain fog, anxiety, depression, and dissociation.

If a grieving person experienced a loss as traumatic, they may develop PTSD. This is characterized by physiological and psychological symptoms occurring long after the event. Again, while stress is normal, in PTSD, the body is experiencing a chemical and emotional threat response long after the danger is over. PTSD behaviors or symptoms interfere with regular functioning in life.

A note about the language of *disorder*: Yes, it's useful to have a label to help us see if we're functioning optimally. However, the term ruffles my feathers (and that of many clinicians) because it harbors judgment and criticism of our bodies—the parts of ourselves that are just trying to keep us safe.

Though the list of trauma symptoms is wide and expansive, therapist Suzy Fauria offers four broad categories:

1. Arousal and Reactivity Trauma impacts the body's normal or baseline response to everyday stimuli, triggers, or stressors. For one, it can shrink your "window of tolerance"—the appropriate level of arousal by your nervous system needed to function and thrive daily. In other words, it's that sweet spot where you can handle stressful situations and triggers without becoming completely overwhelmed.

This includes heightened intolerance of distressing situations. It can look like feeling easily overwhelmed to the point of shutting down or flying into extreme fear or rage over what others would describe as nonevents or non-triggers.

Hypervigilance is simply an elevated state of awareness, constantly scanning the landscape and assessing for potential threats. To be honest, this is one that I experience to this day—one of the residual trauma responses that show up if I'm not actively working on regulating my nervous system—even after a lot of trauma therapy.

2. Avoidance Avoidance is another category of trauma responses that we enact, often subconsciously, to protect ourselves. This can include avoiding people, places, activities, thoughts, and feelings that are connected to the trauma.

3. Cognition and Mood Change From self-judgment, guilt, and shame to a loss of interest and negative worldview, the impact of trauma can lead to distorted thinking and mood change long term. It can lead to self-destructive behavior and have a negative impact on maintaining relationships.

4. Reexperiencing Reliving a terrifying moment or experience from the past (e.g., you witnessed a violent death or found the body of the deceased) can be a picture or video in the mind. It can also be more of a feeling of being triggered by certain smells, sounds, and sights (of certain objects or faces) where your body returns to the sensation of helplessness, overwhelm, and lack of safety you felt during the traumatic event.

COMMON MYTHS
All Violent Deaths Result in Traumatic Grief
Because trauma is the internal response to an external event, two people can experience the exact same loss in the exact same way (e.g., murder of a parent) and respond differently. Personal factors, history, and capacities such as coping styles, emotional regulation, cognitive schemas, prior history of trauma, and immediacy of access to support all play a role. While violent, unexpected, or out-of-order deaths are more likely to result in traumatic grief, all types of death losses have the potential to overwhelm the nervous system, resulting in trauma.

Trauma Is a Sign of Weakness
In debunking this myth, I really appreciate the approach of Internal Family Systems—a trauma intervention approach created by Richard Schwartz. In essence, it invites us to look at our trauma-related behaviors and responses as beautiful and necessary parts of ourselves

that acted to keep us safe in the wake of the overwhelming event. The ongoing symptoms we might be experiencing or demonstrating are simply parts that adapted to protect us but that no longer serve us—or even cause us more harm.

There's No Helping Trauma

Healing in the wake of trauma is gradual and takes a lot of time, patience, and hard work. Even though you may always be susceptible to triggers (since the original trauma that evoked the symptoms won't go away), symptoms can be managed.

ATTACHMENT, LOSS, AND FEAR

The relationship between attachment, trauma, and grief is complex. A full discussion of it is beyond the scope of this book. However, as we explore and understand how and when trauma and grief might be overlapping in our lives, we need to briefly explore our primal drive for attachment and the consequences of when it's tampered with or broken.

We are neurobiologically wired to survive, and as infants, we do that by forming attachments to one or more caregivers. In cases where attachment isn't formed or is permanently broken, our bodies treat the lack of attachment as a threat to our safety. As a result, we are often flooded by fear that drives us to act accordingly, to protect ourselves through one of the trauma responses: flight, fight, freeze, appease, or dissociate.

In essence, we see the world as a dangerous place. These broken attachments can come from experiences such as adoption, abuse, and the death or disappearance of a primary parental caregiver. Even inconsistent or unreliable opportunities for attachment can trigger our fear response, keeping us on alert for any signs that the attachment will disappear again. Either way, fear dominates how we see the world, and that costs us.

If, like me, you carry attachment wounds—and have an anxious, disorganized, or avoidant attachment style—you're more likely to respond to the loss of a significant attachment figure (e.g., parent or partner) with fear. This is made more likely if the loss itself was abrupt or violent. As a child of parents who experienced trauma and as a survivor of rape in my teens and other crimes in my early adulthood, I carry a history of trauma and an insecure attachment style. Though I miraculously experienced a secure attachment in my relationship with Eric, the traumatic circumstances of his death meant that those old wounds and responses returned, and fear dominated my grief early on.

Why am I telling you this? Well, as my former therapist recently explained to me, we don't need to have the loss itself or our past experiences be labeled traumatic (or meet the criteria for a PTSD diagnosis) to consider the value of trauma-informed interventions with a griever. Why? Fear is primal and greedy and blocks our ability to experience our grief "cleanly," including the normal and profound sadness that accompanies it. (See "Of Course It's Complicated.")

How do you know if attachment wounds and fear are interfering with your grief? While it looks different for each of us, some telltale signs that fear is in charge include perfectionism, fear of taking risks, postponing, craving control, numbing behavior, trouble with decision-making, suppressing needs, and people pleasing. There are so many great resources on healing trauma out there, including *The Tender Parts: A Guide to Healing Trauma through Internal Family Systems Therapy* by podcast guest Illyse Kennedy, *The Power of Attachment* by Diane Poole Heller, and *The Myth of Normal* by Dr. Gabor Maté.

Finding a wise trauma-informed therapist who specialized in trauma-intervention skills made a tremendous difference in my grieving process. If fear predominates your grief, regardless of the trauma label, I highly recommend you find a trauma-informed provider to support you in your grieving process.

SKILLED SUPPORT

You don't have to (nor should you) diagnose yourself. As in all things related to grief, you don't have to do this alone. Getting help is critical. If you suspect or know that you experienced a traumatic death or have unprocessed past trauma that's affecting your current experience of grief, make sure you see a therapist or other mental health provider who specializes in trauma. It can make a world of difference.

Interventions such as EMDR (eye movement desensitization and reprocessing), Internal Family Systems, and some SSRI (selective serotonin reuptake inhibitor) medications can assist you to recover regulation of your nervous system so that you can tolerate and be with your grief. (There's even new research showing benefits of the controlled use of psychedelics.)

AN INVITATION FOR YOU

*try soothing exercises**

Every person experiencing grief, regardless of a possible trauma diagnosis, feels anxious and overwhelmed. This invitation involves trying two of my favorite techniques that I use regularly, even on the days when I'm relatively calm. Using them frequently has helped the techniques become more instinctual so that when I need them, they're easily accessible. The nice thing about both exercises is that they're effective even if you only have a few minutes.

*Again, if you know you have a history of trauma or trauma related to your grief, please make sure you find a trained professional to support you in developing practices that help soothe your activated nervous system.

legs up the wall

One of the quickest ways to activate that "rest and digest" part of your nervous system is to lie down on the floor and put your legs up on the wall.

Scoot your bottom against the wall and then lift your legs and let them rest on the wall.

Bring you awareness to your head and relax the muscles in your face and neck.

Place your hands on your belly or on the floor beside you.

Notice whether you're holding tension or effort anywhere else in your body and soften if you can.

You can stay there for ten to fifteen minutes or whatever's comfortable for you.

(continues next page)

(continued from previous page)

extended exhales

Another quick way to soothe yourself is to extend your exhalations twice as long as your inhalations.

Find a comfortable position for you. This could be seated or standing.

Take a moment to notice your shoulder position. If they're hunched forward or up by your ears, try to roll them back and down to create openness across your chest, making deep breaths easier.

Soften your gaze. If you feel comfortable, close your eyes.

Bring your awareness to your chest, to your breath as it is.

Next begin to breathe in slowly through your nose, taking your breath into your belly, then feeling your chest expand.

Then begin to slow your exhale, out of your mouth, feeling your chest contract and belly soften.

When you've got the hang of it, begin making your exhale even slower.

That might be inhaling to a count of three and exhaling to a count of six. Or it could be a 2:4 ratio.

Remember, your mind will wander, so when it does, just bring your attention back to your breath. Counting in your mind as you inhale for three and breathe out for six.

You can do this for ten minutes if you'd like, but even a two-minute session can be helpful.

emotions and feelings and moods, oh my!

FEELINGS HAVE A STORY

By now you know that I love a good metaphor, so I'm using one to help you understand the differences between emotions, feelings, and moods. Knowing the nuances between them can be helpful in traversing the emotional landscape of your grieving world.

EMOTIONS ARE RAW DATA

Emotions are automatic. They show up without your permission. Rude! The scientific explanation is that emotions are a neural impulse that moves an organism to action, prompting automatic reactive behavior that has been adapted through evolution as a survival mechanism to meet a survival need. Emotions are information and they exist to protect us, even if we don't want them to. Scientists have discovered that emotions only last ninety seconds—if we don't interfere with them.

FEELINGS ARE DATA WITH STORIES

Feelings are about how we perceive our emotions, arising through an act of interpretation. Our feelings are affected by the stories we tell ourselves and that others tell us about our circumstances. And then there are the stories we've learned about the good or bad labels for each feeling (happiness = good; anger = bad). Because our feelings involve stories, we have a chance to explore how reliable or helpful the narrator is (or not). Unfortunately, we're often the ones acting as the unreliable and unhelpful narrator. After about ninety seconds, what we're experiencing are feelings based on the stories we've attached to the emotions.

MOODS ARE WHAT HAPPENS WHEN THE STORIES TAKE HOLD

Though the definition of *moods* includes the word *temporary*, our everyday use usually implies something longer. How long? I'd say somewhere more than fleeting and less than forever. Moods come about when the stories attached to our feelings become entrenched, developing a rut. Think of the tracks on a muddy road during what they call "mud season" in northern Vermont.

THE WHOLE DANG ALPHABET

The emotions we experience in the wake of loss could fill the alphabet. Yet our collective story of appropriate and permissible grief emotions seems to be stuck in the S section—sadness and sorrow. While those feelings are predominant, this narrow view denies the myriad of very real and valid feelings we might experience in the wake of loss. (By the way, this emotional illiteracy affects us outside grief as well.)

In *Atlas of the Heart*, researcher, social worker, and one of my many grief guides Brené Brown explains that we have eighty-seven emotions and experiences. Eighty-seven! Do you see now how absurd the cultural belief is that in response to the most profound loss in our lives, we're only meant to experience a few?

I won't list all eighty-seven here, but I will say recognizing that there is a wide range of reasonable and appropriate emotional responses to loss has brought me and so many of my clients relief. Just some of the feelings people like you might experience in grief include anger, anguish, anxiety, bittersweetness, confusion, calmness, despair, dread, fear, foreboding joy, frustration, guilt, heartbreak, hurt, jealousy, joy, loneliness, nostalgia, shame, and even relief. We can have them all, feel them all (and more), and we don't need to believe in the limits.

If anyone judges your emotions (even when that's you), channel the wisdom of Hermione Granger (a character from the *Harry Potter* books and films) and reply, "Just because you've got the emotional range of a teaspoon doesn't mean we all have."

FOLLOW THE YELLOW BRICK ROAD

Believe it or not, we have some things in common with the characters in the film *The Wizard of Oz*. As Dorothy and her friends follow the yellow brick road, they become increasingly afraid of lions, and tigers, and bears (oh my!). They spend nearly their entire journey unaware that they had the strength within them all along to encounter, survive, and thrive. The same goes for us as we walk down the path of booby traps that come with confronting the feelings, emotions, and moods surrounding our grief. And yes, sometimes it seems as if freaky flying monkeys are around every corner.

LET IT HAPPEN

Whether you refer to them as emotions or feelings, we need to let them happen. And I mean all of them. This is an especially important (and difficult) reminder for those of us who tend to ignore certain or all emotions. For me, anger is that emotion. I have a lot of harmful stories that I'm trying to unlearn about anger because I recognize they're getting in my way. I remind myself that anger is just a catalyst; it's not good or bad, it's just that holding on to it doesn't let it do its job of moving me to action. For example, when someone I love is grieving and a person says something well-meaning but harmful, my anger for that harm compels me to speak up and interrupt that person and comfort my friend. So for all of us, our first step is to learn to be with our feelings. All of them. I wonder if you know what yours are.

This wisdom comes in part from another grief teacher, the poet Rainer Maria Rilke, who wrote, "Let everything happen to you: beauty and terror. / Just keep going. No feeling is final."

His invitation is so profound and it's so dang hard to do. One of the consequences of our grief-illiterate culture is that because we criticize and sometimes pathologize most feelings (besides happiness), we have very little practice being with our emotions. Lack of practice leads to discomfort with many or most emotions we feel. We then often mistake our discomfort as a further sign that they're wrong or bad feelings to have and that we're bad for having them in the first place.

Our grief avoidance means that many of us inherit these limiting beliefs about what feelings are acceptable or not acceptable in the wake of loss. These beliefs around emotions in grief also come with other vague yet socially enforced rules about how long emotions should last, who should have them, etc.—making the hard work of grief even harder.

It's harder because in addition to experiencing the deep pain of grief, we are often riddled with judgment and anxiety every time an emotion emerges that is not on this pre-approved list. "Relief? Is it OK that I feel relief? Am I a bad person for feeling a moment of joy so soon after my person died?" If you're anything like I was in my early grief, these concerns send you further into feeling isolated and alone. (See the introduction for more on grief beliefs.)

Many of us have beliefs about the appropriateness of having and expressing certain emotions in grief. Some beliefs we've developed are helpful and positive, such as, "It's OK to express sadness and sorrow over the death of my loved one." But many of us carry rules about emotions in grief that are not only unhelpful to our healing, but also often downright harmful, such as, "I don't have the right to feel anything about this death because (fill in the blank)."

While I can't undo years of miseducation with a few sentences—I'm going to try.

You aren't your emotions.
You aren't your emotions.
You aren't your emotions.

Emotions don't have inherent value and therefore neither do you for feeling them. Emotions can be painful and sometimes unbearable to feel, but they don't represent something good or bad. They are simply information. When they come up, be with your emotions. Feel them all. No matter how sticky or painful or uncomfortable they may be.

Do your best to notice your emotions with kindness and compassion. When you feel judgment about them, notice that too. Say to yourself, "Oh, that's the old sneaky grief belief about emotions Lisa warned me about." Noticing them while they're present gives you a chance to learn from them. Trust that they will move through you, as every single emotion you've ever experienced has done.

You aren't your emotions. Emotions don't have inherent value and therefore neither do you for feeling them. Emotions can be painful and sometimes unbearable to feel, but they don't represent something good or bad. They are simply information.

DISCOVERING OUR STORIES

We develop our grief beliefs around emotions throughout our lives. Many of the ones most deeply entrenched in our way of seeing the world developed in childhood. We learned the rules of emotions based on the reactions we got from caregivers when we displayed certain emotions. For example, if you were isolated and punished whenever you expressed anger as a toddler, today you likely have a negative story about anger. You might say, "Anger makes me unlovable or not worthy of being around." Or as a teenager, when a parent told you to "get over it already" only a few days after your first breakup, you might have learned that sadness over losing a partner, for any amount of time, is unacceptable. Caution: Avoid bringing all-or-nothing thinking to this topic; you also likely learned positive or helpful beliefs from your caregivers.

Does this mean you should ignore your feelings because they might be based on unreliable stories or beliefs? Heck no. Yes, you need to make space to feel all your feelings. It's necessary, welcome, and informative. And it's important to not take them as facts. It can be helpful for you to be curious from time to time to discover whether a story has taken hold around a certain recurring emotion that you're experiencing (or the absence of certain emotions you expected to feel). Here are some helpful themes you might look for and questions you might ask yourself.

Binary Does my story include a lot of either-or thinking? How about all-or-nothing thinking?

Duration Do I allow the stories to go on and on and repeat them out loud or to myself? Do they keep me with my feelings even longer? Or do my stories insist that I shut off access to certain emotions? Or both, depending on the emotion?

Tone Are my stories full of compassionate language or judgmental statements?

Ownership Are the stories mine? Do they represent what I believe regarding emotions or are they stories I inherited from somewhere else?

Helpfulness Do the stories I hear internally when I'm feeling big feelings support my healing or are they hurting me?

When I'm feeling sad, lonely, irritated, angry, frustrated, etc., I've learned to listen quietly to the stories rambling around in my head. It's taken some time and a lot of practice. I continue to practice because old habits die hard.

Feelings of loneliness plagued me for a long time after Eric died—understandable at first when the love of my life was dead. I would find myself weeping under the weight of it. Even years after his death, I noticed loneliness hanging around for long stretches. The loneliness might disappear briefly, but it would return often and with the same intensity. When I heard myself saying the same things about my loneliness to a dear friend for the two-hundredth time, that's when I got curious. Well, to be honest, first I got frustrated with myself, then I got curious.

I really tried to be an outside observer. I listened to how I was talking to myself before the loneliness showed up and after it arrived. What I heard was a lot of all-or-nothing thinking, such as, "I'm always going to be alone," "Nobody makes time for me," and, "I'm the only one who ever reaches out." I took a hard look at how much truth there was to these stories. What I noticed was that the more I said those things to myself and to this friend, the more the stories became true and the lonelier I felt.

It took time, but I started to look out for the exceptions and made sure that I noticed them, such as when I spent quality time with family and when friends reached out first. I also challenged my assumption that it was other people's job to reach out first. I didn't deny the feelings I had, but by interrupting the stories when loneliness came up, the intensity diminished, and loneliness became a less frequent visitor. We'll break down that process next.

RECOGNIZING AND SHIFTING YOUR RELATIONSHIP WITH EMOTIONS

These grief beliefs take the shape of stories you develop in your head that can exacerbate your relationship with certain emotions or sever them. The process of shifting your relationship over time with your emotions isn't the same as ignoring or denying your feelings. It's finding a way to get some distance from them so that you can observe them, allow them to move through you, and limit your propensity to get stuck in the stories that don't allow growth or healing.

Any emotion that we feel intensely or causes us discomfort, such as anxiety, can convince us that *we* are the feeling and it's in charge of us. That's not a healthy relationship. Here are the steps I used, based on the experience I shared above, to shift my relationship with emotions and the stories I tell about them:

1. Be With Your Body Remember, emotions are neural impulses that live in our bodies, so it's important to return to the body. Find a way to be with your body, especially when you're experiencing powerful emotions. Being in your body, or being embodied, allows you to become aware of and then move with intention based on what you discover. As one of my grief teachers, Prentis Hemphill, explains, "Embodiment is the awareness of our body's sensations, habits, and the beliefs that inform them. Embodiment requires the ability to feel and allow the body's emotions. This embodied aware- ness is necessary to realign what we do with what we believe."

One avenue to embodiment? Do something grounding that stops the storytelling and brings you out of your worried mind and back to the present: walking, swaying, humming, or deep breathing. Also helpful? Adding upbeat or calming music to invite a more positive state. These things combined can shift your mood.

2. *Externalize the Problem* You are not your thoughts and feelings. But thoughts and feelings are tricky because they go unchecked most of the time. This is what in Narrative Therapy we call external- izing the problem. Imagining your thoughts and feelings as separate from you gives you space to see them as separate and allows you to stop impulsively reacting to them. You're replacing "I am lonely" with "Loneliness is here for a visit" or "I am having the feeling of loneliness."

Whether you do this through mindfully listening to your thoughts or by writing them down for fifteen minutes and then reading what you've written, it's important to learn to be a witness to your thoughts.

3. *Interrupt the Auto Play* For whatever reason, we often get into ruts of telling and retelling our stories in cycles (to ourselves and to anyone who will listen). While we absolutely need and deserve to be seen and held in our grief, repeating the same feelings-ladened stories can keep us stuck in an emotional loop, reinforcing a mood that may not serve us. Interrupting your story is important because your body is experiencing the emotions as if they were happening in the moment.

4. Notice the Exception Stories Noticing if your stories have an all-or-nothing pattern is a useful practice when your relationship with emotions is difficult, either because you struggle to access them or they overstay their welcome. This practice requires you to be curious, compassionate, and discerning, not judgmental.

Is your discomfort with the emotion tied to a grief belief you hold? Are those beliefs unhelpful? Maybe the belief sounds like "Sadness is a sign of weakness, so I shouldn't feel this way. Feeling this way makes me a bad person. It makes me hard to be around and unlovable."

What if an alternate story sounded like "Of course I'm sad. How could it be any other way? This person meant everything to me, and my sadness is a normal response to losing them." How would a shift in your story of sadness shape how long the emotion stays or how you feel about yourself during and afterward?

Noticing the exception to your dominant stories of emotions is also a useful practice when you find yourself enmeshed in an emotion that's likely overstayed its welcome, like loneliness was for me. If you find certain emotions hanging around with the same intensity and frequency or repeatedly returning for long stays, this tool might be useful.

Noticing the exception story in the case of regret might mean you continually hear "I shouldn't have (fill in the action/inaction). If only I had done (that one thing) differently, the outcome would have completely changed. It's all my fault." Next time you hear that story, consider an alternative version, such as, "I made a decision, and at the time, it was the best one with the information I had. If I had known the consequences or outcome, I would have made a different choice."

One metaphor I like to use to find a healthy balance between suppressing my feelings and getting stuck in them is to treat them like visitors over for a cup of coffee. I wrote a poem years ago as an offering for you to consider a different relationship with your feelings.

Stopped by for a Cup of Coffee

While you were busy, your emotions stopped by for a cup
of coffee.
Just visitors seeking a warm and inviting respite,
these travelers arrived with tales and insights at your door.
Journeyers wishing to pass along the wisdom they discovered,
about the path already taken and the terrain that lies ahead.

While you were busy, your emotions stopped by for a cup
of coffee.
Fear knocked nervously, first tapping then banging.
Sadness meandered slowly up your front walk.
Anger arrived unannounced and rang the doorbell repeatedly.
Confusion zigged and zagged until it stumbled onto your
porch.

While you were busy your emotions stopped by for a cup
of coffee.
Joy's radiant light was dimmed by your drawn curtains.
Amazement's gifts of wonder were left unopened on your
front porch.
Delight's bright smile went unseen through your closed door.
Gratitude's comfort faded to unease waiting to be let in.

While you were busy your emotions stopped by for a cup
of coffee.
Those intrepid visitors are still waiting on your doorstep,
simply wanting to feel the warmth of being seen and held
by you.
These wanderers are desperate to share the wisdom from
their travels,
and they won't be on their way until you invite them in for a
cup of coffee.

BITTERSWEET AND OTHER COMBINATIONS

Not only can we easily experience dozens of different emotions in response to profound loss, but oftentimes we can also feel more than one in the same moment. These emotions are not mutually exclusive and they sometimes come in odd and surprising pairings.

Foreboding joy is a great example. It happens when joy is interrupted by the thought "What if something bad happens?" This thought is the way we protect ourselves from being vulnerable—not surprising given that we've just experienced a profound loss and would like to not repeat it again. This is often one of the first ways joy shows up in grief. (See "When Joy Shows Up.")

Sometime after the early phase of my grief, I found bittersweetness, the combination of sadness and happiness. Maybe that's when I knew I had crossed over the imagined threshold into the messy middle. *Bittersweet*, written by grief guide Susan Cain, was revelatory.

Cain defines bittersweetness as "a tendency to states of longing, poignancy, and sorrow; an acute awareness of passing time; and a curiously piercing joy at the beauty of the world. The bittersweet is also about the recognition that light and dark, birth and death—bitter and sweet—are forever paired." She offers us permission, if not encouragement, to hold both/and.

"Smiying" is when you're smiling at something beautiful or good that's happening, and crying because your person isn't here to experience it with you.

Smiying is an emotional term I created years ago after I experienced it too many times. You know I love words and I needed a label to describe what was happening to me. People would see me smiling and crying and be totally confused. I was too the first few times it happened. Smiying is the unique combination of joy or happiness and longing or homesickness. It's the moment when you're smiling at something beautiful or good that's happening and crying because your person isn't here to experience it with you.

According to researcher Naomi Rothman, experiencing mixed emotions (a.k.a. emotional ambivalence) helps us be more adaptable, creative, and receptive to support. Learning to name and label the specific feelings we're having gives us a chance to do some of the activities above, including observing them, discovering what they're trying to teach us, discerning if there are unhelpful stories attached, and deciding what we want to do with them.

DIFFICULT, CHALLENGING, AND MISUNDERSTOOD EMOTIONS

Sadness Versus Anguish

The number of vague and overlapping definitions of sadness, sorrow, and anguish point to the fact that we often struggle to identify the differences when we're experiencing them. Sadness is often defined as a feeling of unhappiness resulting from a loss and can range from mild to extreme. Sorrow is a deep sense of distress, disappointment, or sadness. Anguish is explained as severe mental or physical pain or suffering.

Shame, Regret, and Survivor's Guilt

According to Brené Brown, shame is an "intensely painful feeling or experience of believing that we are flawed and therefore unworthy of love and belonging." Shame is a value judgment against your humanity, with stories that say, "I am bad." Unlike other emotions, shame isn't informational or productive. Shame prevents healing. The conditions that make shame grow, as Brown describes in *Atlas of the Heart*, are secrecy, silence, and judgment. Empathy is the most important quality for interrupting shame.

Still, so many of us feel shame in grief, whether it's around our behavior related to our loved one's life or death. On my podcast, Lizzie Cleary explained how shame often shows up in loss and grief, saying that "shame is something that is often experienced with loss and grief. The shame of wishing that you could have done something different, feeling there would have been some way for you to stop it. Similar, not the same, but similar shame I think is often experienced for trauma survivors. Thinking if you had just done something different, you could have stopped it, you could have avoided it." As Cleary's description shows, we often misname or conflate feelings of shame, regret, and guilt in grief.

Survivor's guilt is a response to an event in which someone else died or experienced a loss and you didn't. Regrets can include feeling disappointed about things we said to or did with our loved ones, often involving things or actions that went unsaid or undone. In our everyday lives, guilt and regret can be useful emotions when used with self-compassion as an assessment tool. These emotions help us discover when we've acted in contradiction to our morals and thereby caused harm to ourselves or others. In these cases, when these emotions are not buried in shame about our value as humans, they can allow us to grow, repair, and experience forgiveness (from ourselves and sometimes others).

NOT SORRY

Though grief expression doesn't always involve tears, for many of us, it's a big part of the way we release our emotions. Somewhere along the way, many of us were taught that crying is something to be done in private, an embarrassing sign of weakness. The message was clear: Tears were a symptom of a problem that we should be embarrassed to have.

I'm not sure I've ever had a client who hasn't apologized for shedding tears during an individual session or even in guided meditations. So I'll say to you what I said to them: There are no apologies needed when you cry. I don't care if you do it at the doctor's office, in the checkout line at the grocery store, at a party, in the middle of a concert. Yes, I admit these are personal examples—just some of the places I've cried deep, heaving, ugly tears.

As we've touched on in previous chapters, crying is one way to complete the stress cycle, making it scientifically proven to be good for us. It activates the parasympathetic nervous system, which can help us relax. It releases those feel-good chemicals including oxytocin, which can help ease emotional and physical pain. It releases endorphins, which as ironic as it seems can improve our overall mood and well-being. Crying can also help us get rid of built-up cortisol.

Again, be curious about the story you have attached to sadness and tears. Don't let the assumptions, judgments, or impatience of others discourage you from traveling your grief journey in your own way. Remember, others' expectations don't change what you need. Repeat after me: "Crying is a beautiful expression of my full humanity, not a sign that I'm weak."

Repeat after me: "Crying is a beautiful expression of my full humanity, not a sign that I'm weak."

⚖ AN INVITATION FOR YOU ⚖

practice RAIN

RAIN is a favorite technique I learned from meditation guide Tara Brach for how to be with my "griefy" feelings. RAIN is an acronym for an easy-to-use mindfulness approach to being with emotional difficulty: recognize, allow, investigate, and nurture.

You can use RAIN as a regular meditation practice or as difficult emotions arise in your grief.

Spend some time noticing what it feels like to be in your body with this awareness. Acknowledge any sensations of peace or softness you've created for yourself. The benefit of this practice is to help you get unstuck or prevent you from overly identifying with a particular feeling or belief.

---

recognize

"What's going on?" This might be a whisper while pausing to identify the feelings present. Again, noticing the sensations in your body might make it easier to identify.

allow

Allow the experience to be there just as it is. Setting down any judgmental thoughts about what you're noticing. Bringing yourself back from wherever your judgmental mind has taken you and returning to present awareness. This might look like giving yourself permission, whispering, "It's okay to feel this way," or, "This makes sense."

investigate

Investigate your experience with interest and care. This involves being kindly curious. Ask yourself something such as, "What does this emotion need me to know?" Be wary of going intellectual. Make sure to connect with the "felt" sense in your body.

(continued from previous page)

nurture

Nurture yourself and your emotions with self-compassion. What does this emotion need from you? Comfort? Reassurance? Forgiveness? Offer what you need in a compassionate whisper. Maybe something such as, "I love you. I'm sorry you're hurting," or, "I'm here and I'm listening." Again, emotions are embodied, so you might find a physical gesture of care helpful, such as placing one or both hands on your heart.

another full-time job

A JOB YOU DIDN'T ASK FOR

I'm sorry to break the news but you have another full-time job that you didn't want. You're now doing grief work. Comedian Michael Palasack tells a joke about parenting that applies to the work of grief: "They say being a parent is a full-time job, but it feels more like a horrible unpaid internship. Like the first five years you bring your boss lunch every day, and he just throws it on the ground half the time."

THE PROBLEM WITH GRIEF WORK

The term "grief work" is a commonly used phrase to describe the energy and effort required to grieve. Honestly, the term has received a lot of mixed responses, I think for good reason. On one hand, the theory and metaphor of grief work is useful when you consider that any type of growth, development, or healing rarely happens on its own. It takes recognizing that you have a goal or somewhere you want to get to. It requires paying attention, putting in the effort, and learning about and using new resources. Also required? Guidance from others who've done the work and reducing sources of interference or harm—obstacles that could get in the way. These activities sound like things we do at work, right?

I also think the grief work metaphor can be problematic, even unintentionally, for those of us who are grieving. Our Western work culture is full of expectations and ideals that are harmful, both for our real-life work and for the ways these values seep into expectations of our own grief work.

As I mentioned in the introduction, our broader culture in the West (including our workplace culture) is obsessed with productivity, destination, simplicity, stoicism, and having a high IQ. Those values don't align well with the realities of grieving. In fact, they're downright contradictory. Grieving is a messy, nonlinear path. It takes a long, indeterminant amount of time. Grieving requires vulnerability, emotional intelligence, and agility. Our intellectual brain (a.k.a. our cognitive functioning) is temporarily compromised. Grieving is incredibly complex, everyone's path is unique, and the results aren't always visible for quite some time.

RULES AND RESPONSIBILITIES

The rules and responsibilities for the job posting of grief work (like most job postings) are inaccurate, unclear, unrealistic, and designed to make you feel as if you're failing when you're not. This chapter is my way of helping you let go of any work-culture beliefs that you're bringing to the "work" of your grieving process. In the plainest terms, the rules of grief are—there are no rules. Your only responsibilities are to focus on your cognitive, physical, emotional, spiritual, and relational well-being.

In the plainest terms, the rules of grief are—there are no rules. Your only responsibilities are to focus on your cognitive, physical, emotional, spiritual, and relational well-being.

ON-THE-JOB TRAINING

As I share in "This Is Your Brain on Grief," grieving is learning. Just as there's no curriculum you could have studied in school to perfectly prepare you for success on the first day in your career, a lot of what you would learn in a classroom wouldn't apply in the real world of grief work.

When you start this job, there's no training program or instruction manual. There's limited guidance or supervision, very few helpful colleagues, and often unwelcome critical performance reviews from people you barely know. Even if you take a class on grief (I teach a Loss and Grief course), nothing fully prepares you for the reality of this job.

The job you have—grieving this loss—is neither a job anyone has done before you nor a job you've done before. So ditch whatever expectations you had at being good at it on the first day, first month, first year. You're learning as you go and that's why you feel overwhelmed, exhausted, and uncertain that you're up for the job. I promise, you have what it takes. It's just going to take time to feel that way.

ON-CALL RESPONSIBILITIES

The demands of grief work make it feel, at least in the early phase, as if you're on call 24/7, including weekends. You take the work home with you. It follows you to the grocery story. It even shows up at your other job, the one you probably had to return to way too soon because of limited to no bereavement leave. You've likely taken this on in addition to the other work you were already doing: your actual paid job(s), parenting, adulting, caregiving, etc.

THE ILLUSION OF WORK/LIFE BALANCE IN GRIEF

While you're burning the candle at both ends, do you find yourself saying, "I'm so lazy," "I haven't gotten anything done for X," or "I'm not paying enough attention to Y"? Yeah, I get it. I've fallen into that trap so many times myself over the years. Here's the thing that you (and I) need to remember: That's trashy, productivity-obsessed, bullshit thinking. Plain and simple.

The truth is that grieving is a grind, especially early on. It's mentally, physically, spiritually, and emotionally exhausting. So the next time you hear yourself uttering, "I'm just so lazy these days," try replacing it with "Grief work is hard, and I've been putting in a lot of effort today. I think I will take a well-deserved rest by (anything you find restorative)."

GRIEF WORK SKILLS

While everyone's job requirement is unique to them, there are some skills that are universally beneficial in grief work. I explore them throughout this book and in-depth in "Your Brain on Grief." Here's a quick summary of some of the most helpful grief work habits you might want to acquire. Note that like all habits, these take practice.

1. Sleep regularly, possibly more than usual.
2. Drink water throughout the day and eat nutritious food.
3. Practice kind self-talk and self-compassion.
4. Be mindful and nonjudgmental about whatever you're experiencing.
5. Move your body in ways that soothe your nervous system.
6. Find people who will encourage your growth.
7. Develop rituals or ceremonies that serve you.
8. Ask for and, more importantly, accept help.

⚜ AN INVITATION FOR YOU ⚜

take a break from the grief job

I invite you to take a break from grief work. Surprised? I know that throughout the book I'm offering you different ways to be with your grief. Reminding you to care for your cognitive, spiritual, physical, and emotional well-being. Saying things such as, "Invite your emotions over for a cup of coffee," and, "Be a should detective." I stand by it. Still, like any job, you need a break from it. What might that look like for you?

Because each of you are at such different places, I won't offer specific break activities (or nonactivities). Instead, I invite you to use the following prompts to help you discover more about the eight skills you likely already have and gain insight into how to put them into practice when you're ready.

**Get out your journal and answer each prompt.
When you're ready, begin practicing.**

I find it easiest to rest when I:

*One way to make drinking water and eating nutritiously
more accessible would be to:*

One loving phrase I will offer myself each day is:

*When I'm having feelings that are hard, I will practice being
mindful of them by:*

Even when I'm tired, I feel better when I move my body by:

*Right now, the person who best helps reflect my growth
back to me is:*

*The three rituals or ceremonies that help me most in my
grief are:*

The last time I accepted help, it gave me a chance to:

relating
to yourself
and others
(or not)

*(re)discovering yourself and
your relationship to others in grief*

everyone is stylish
in their own way

YOU'VE GOT STYLE

You've got style. Truly. Even if it feels as if you've just thrown on sweats and a baseball cap, you have style. We all have a grief style, meaning a way we experience and express our grief. And while we all put our own flair on it, generally our styles can be broken into a few broad categories.

Emotional/Intuitive If you rock this style, you're likely to experience a fuller range of emotions, including being more comfortable with strong ones. You're sensitive to your own feelings and the feelings of others. You're less focused on finding logic, being rational, or intellectualizing the pain. You seek spaces and places to share how you feel and are less prone to hide it from others. This style may appear a little chaotic or disorganized to others.

Creative No, you don't have to be an artist or fashion designer to rock this style. It also doesn't mean you've created a collage or built a physical memorial. Having a creative grief style means you gravitate toward creative outlets to express your experience of grief. Maybe you're less of a talker, but you experience and express your grief by creating something of your own.

You might also like engaging with the creative work of others who best represent how you feel. Think listening to melancholy music lyrics or rewatching old movies. You use these outlets to help you deal with the difficult and strong emotions of grief. This style may seem interesting to others. Some find it hard to grasp.

Rational/Instrumental The rational/instrumental griever is interested in function over style. If you rock this style, you likely experience and express your grief in a more intellectual and maybe even physical manner. You tend to crave information and are always seeking facts. You lean toward completing practical and tactical tasks. Your way of feeling better is to do something and try to create order. You're less comfortable with the intense emotions of grief and you tend to keep busy. This style can make you appear to others as more stoic and even dispassionate about the loss.

Did any of these sound like you? Are you wondering, "Is there a best style to have?" Nope. There isn't a best style or correct style because, like fashion, it's subjective. Sometimes people's styles can clash and some of us like to mix and match our styles.

WHEN YOUR STYLE IS IN DISARRAY

There's a fourth option called dissonant. While not so much a style on its own, dissonance is what happens when what you're rocking on the outside doesn't match how you're feeling on the inside. There is some level of inner conflict between the style that suits you best and your comfort or confidence to express that outwardly.

This may come from lack of confidence. For many of us, it comes from the explicit and implicit pressure we feel from others to change our style. Explicit comments such as, "Boys don't cry," "Don't be so emotional," or "Keep your private business private" may cause you to suppress your natural style. You may be equally influenced by the implicit behaviors and inactions of others, including people not having the person's picture out or changing the subject when the death comes up in conversation. Either way, these messages discourage you from owning your authentic grieving style.

NOT OWNING YOUR STYLE

If the description of dissonant grieving style struck a chord for you, please know you're not alone. Many feel that way to some degree from time to time. If you notice that this happens only occasionally, keep an eye out for it. Work to find more spaces and places where you can freely, and with support, rock your style.

If you realize that you feel dissonant most of or all the time, I see you. Instead of thinking about this information as defeating, I invite you to be curious instead. Ask yourself:

1. Whose expectations and needs am I putting before mine?
2. What assumptions might I be making about what others expect of me in my grief?
3. How can I check these assumptions and who do I need to talk to about them?
4. Who or where might be a safe space for me to explore grieving in a way that comes naturally to me? Is it with a certain set of friends? A grief support group? With a therapist or grief guide?
5. Where in my schedule can I create more time for the rituals and activities that help me grieve my way?

CLASH OF STYLES

Did you have an aha moment above? Did that give you a clue about why you and a family member are in conflict more often since the death of a loved one? Did you notice yourself firmly rocking one style and them another? Maybe one person rocks the '70s vintage concert tees while the other is head-to-toe in luxury fashion. It happens. A lot. I'm not sure I've met a family whose members haven't had differing grieving styles.

Difference isn't inherently a problem. The challenge comes when there are explicit or implicit rules that make you feel bad about your style, or even feel the need to hide it altogether. If this is happening in your family, consider talking directly to the person with the different style about what you're noticing. You might even start by sharing this chapter with them. If that feels impossible, is finding a third-party family member or even a therapist to mediate a conversation an option? If the answer is still no, consider the questions above, including "Where in my schedule can I create more time for the rituals and activities that help me grieve my way?"

STYLES CAN CHANGE

Just like some don't wear skinny jeans anymore (I still do), you may notice you're grieving this loss differently than previous ones. That's normal. The way we grieve one loss may not be how we grieve another. There's a myriad of reasons for that: our developmental age, our relationship with the person who died, the type of loss, our history of other losses, our current support system (or lack of it). The list goes on.

In case you're recognizing (and, more concerningly, judging yourself) that you're grieving one loss differently than another, please cut yourself some slack. It's OK for your style to change. If you think it's a result of one of the reasons above, remind yourself that it's normal and OK. If for some reason you think it's because of some perceived pressure to grieve in a certain way, then revisit owning your style and see if something there resonates.

⚵ AN INVITATION FOR YOU ⚵

try a Marie Kondo approach to your grief style*

Have you heard of Marie Kondo and the KonMari Method? Her philosophy regarding decluttering is to keep only those things that speak to the heart and discard items that no longer spark joy. I mean, doesn't that concept warm your heart?

I know joy may feel so far off to you right now. That's OK. Using the prompts below, get out your journal and reflect on the pieces of your grief style that bring you joy, or at least offer you some level of ease or support. What activities, places, people, and behaviors make you feel more nourished (even if just incrementally or temporarily)?

I also suggest you take inventory of those pieces of your style that aren't serving you, that bring unnecessary pain and suffering or that deplete you even further. You may want to come back to this activity over time. This can even be a useful tool to explore together with your counselor or therapist.

*Gentle reminder: We can grieve even the things we choose to leave or let go of. So if in making your discard list you feel some sort of way about your decision to let go of what is no longer serving you, make sure you offer yourself permission to grieve that too.

---

keep (joy, ease, support, nourish)

activities:

places:

behaviors:

people:

discard (pain, suffering, depletion)

activities:

places:

behaviors:

people:

knowing and honoring your needs

WHAT DO YOU NEED?

What do you need today to make your grief feel lighter or to carry it with more grace? Really. I'm asking you right now. What do you need? Think on that question for a few minutes.

Now, I have a few more questions for you to consider. How did thinking about what you need make you feel? What happened in your body when you read that question? Was there tension somewhere? In your throat, chest, or maybe gut? Did you feel a wave of exhaustion or maybe tears forming? How about your thoughts? What came up? Did they sound something like "I have no clue," "It doesn't matter what I need," "Nothing anyone can help me with," or "A fucking break"?

---

pause again

Before we explore why you may have struggled to answer the previous questions or experienced some visceral reactions, I invite you to pause. Get still, take some full breaths, and bring your awareness to any place in your body you're holding tight. Bring your attention there and see if you can soften those spots in some way. Don't judge what you discover. Instead bring kindness there. Maybe you could even wrap your arms across each other and give yourself a big hug. Spend as much time with this as you need. I'll be here when you return.

Isn't it weird that just thinking about a question can cause all these thoughts, feelings, and sensations to happen? Often, thinking about what you need can bring up levels of frustration, anger, and resentment. That happens because the real answer deep down is "What I need is my person back!" It's important to honor that thought and the feelings that come with it. What's equally important is that we don't get stuck there.

TRYING EVEN WHEN IT'S HARD

It's not just identifying your needs that can be hard. Once we name them, prioritizing and acting on them can be even more of a challenge. Remember, we can do hard things. Doing the hard thing of checking inward and discovering your needs in grief on a more regular basis has a lot of benefits, including:

Rediscovering Yourself The practice of checking inward to discover your needs offers you a chance to see yourself and be with yourself in ways you haven't been for some time. It's a way to feel reconnected, and even discover new parts of yourself that are emerging. That disconnection we feel from ourselves is one of the painful and surprising consequences of loss. (See "Who's Got Your Back?")

Finding Your Agency Feeling as if everything is happening to us and that we're out of control is one of the scariest results of profound loss. We often feel aimless and powerless. One benefit of learning to identify what you need is that it allows you to see what actions you can take to meet those needs. Having that knowledge is important because it allows you to feel capacity, and a sense of agency to make things happen instead of feeling as if it's all happening to you.

Feeling Better Supported We can't do it alone. But sometimes help doesn't feel very helpful. That's often because the grief supporters in our lives don't know what we need, so the help they offer misses the mark. Sometimes they don't even bother to try in the first place. Your best chance for feeling supported in grief is by knowing what you need so that you can communicate it to those people who want to have your back and are asking, "What do you need?"

Practicing Makes It Easier Each time you identify a need and act on meeting it (whether on your own or by asking for support), you experience gains. You feel more connected to yourself and your sense of agency, and you experience some relief as your need is met. Those gains can be hard to come by because we don't take those steps often enough. As annoying as the cliché can be, it really is true: The more you practice, the easier it gets.

But if it's so helpful, why is it so dang hard for a lot of us to do? Because we've learned some lessons along the course of our lives that make it problematic. We've developed some limiting beliefs and never learned skills that would make it easier to do. That's exactly what we'll explore next.

IT'S OK TO HAVE NEEDS

Did you know it's OK to have needs? I'm not being sarcastic here, even though it seems as if I am. On the surface it seems like a ridiculous question. For many of us, thanks to the lessons we've learned from family and our broader culture, we hold a deep-rooted belief that it isn't OK to have or express our needs. Or that only certain needs are acceptable or that our needs should always come last.

Consciously, or subconsciously, many of us equate having needs with being weak. We confuse self-care with selfishness. Sacrifice and burnout are seen as badges of honor. This distorted way of thinking about our needs is why you might have had a negative gut reaction when I asked what you need to address your grief. So the first step in identifying, prioritizing, and acting on your needs is to believe that your needs are valid and worth being met. Please believe me: Your needs are valid.

AND . . . ACTION (OR NOT)

Good news. As you begin to practice listening inward, you'll discover categories of your grief needs that you can meet on your own—benefitting your physical, cognitive, and spiritual well-being. No negotiating, seeking permission, or asking for help from others is required. Really, you've got this.

Interestingly, many of the best ways to meet your needs will include not doing something. This includes not signing up for, volunteering for, or in general saying yes to things that you no longer find beneficial. This is a great option for meeting needs such as taking more time for rest. You can also give yourself permission to drop commitments, temporarily or permanently, that you made before the loss.

I know that might sound hard and make you worry that you're letting others down. Here's the thing: If you maintain all commitments, you're letting yourself down. Remember, your needs matter. There are ways to attend to your well-being that may not require negotiation with others. That might include starting therapy, signing up for a meal delivery program, getting a massage, going for a walk each day, or taking naps.

REQUESTS AND NEGOTIATIONS

Sometimes requests and negotiations are required. If we need more time off from work, many of us will have to negotiate with our boss. If we're parents of young children and need to exercise to feel better, we might need to negotiate with our partner for childcare coverage or hire a babysitter. To get more sleep at night, we might need to ask our snoring partner to sleep in the other room. Negotiating for our needs with others can be challenging because of the beliefs we carry, like our value comes from not being needy.

CLEAR IS KIND (AND EFFECTIVE)

Just as it takes effort to figure out what you need, learning how to communicate those needs effectively will likely require practice too. Clarity and directness in your communication are key, but oh so hard to do.

First, it requires you to believe in the value of your need and your right to negotiate for it or ask for others' support. One you've got that, you'll have to communicate clearly—both by being direct about the importance of the request and by clarifying the details of what you're asking for. Remember, as Brené Brown says, "Clear is kind." I'm not joking when I tell you that I've practiced making requests in front of a mirror or found a trusted friend to role-play with. You can try it too.

USE THE B WORD MORE OFTEN

There are times when what we need to clearly communicate isn't a favor or negotiation for more time. That requires a different kind of action. Sometimes we need the "b word." No, not that one. I mean *boundaries*.

Often, setting a boundary with someone is a way to feel more at ease in our grief. It's a difficult but necessary action. It's a tough one for me. Honestly, I work diligently to put boundary-setting into practice. My rate of use isn't as high as I'd like it to be. But when I do set a compassionate boundary—wow. The return-on-investment (ROI) is 100 percent.

I struggle with setting boundaries because I've swallowed the proverbial Kool-Aid that says it is an act of aggression or confrontation. Is that your experience? Along the way I've also learned that my ability to meet other people's needs, even at the expense of my own, is what makes me valuable. Sound familiar?

I'm working on unlearning this and have found therapist, somatic teacher, and political organizer Prentis Hemphill's thoughts on boundaries extremely valuable. Hemphill says, "Boundaries are the distance at which I can love you and me simultaneously." I've found myself sharing other wisdom by Hemphill with clients, including "Boundaries give us the space to do the work of loving ourselves. They might be, actually, the first and fundamental expression of self-love." How does that sit with you? Does it change your willingness to set more boundaries to meet your needs?

When it comes to setting boundaries to meet your needs as you grieve, some areas you'll want to consider include:

Physical Physical boundary violations can feel like uncomfortable touch (hugs when you don't want them) or being denied your physical needs (being told to stand when you're tired and need to sit down). It might include someone invading your personal space in a way that is uncomfortable. Setting a physical boundary could sound like "I'm not comfortable with hugs. I'd prefer we shake hands from now on when we see each other."

Emotional You might need to set an emotional boundary if you find people overestimating your ability to take in what they're sharing. This might also be a boundary you set for yourself in a way, such as deciding not to share your grief feelings with certain people who have a history of responding poorly. Communicating an emotional boundary might sound like "I'd like you to check with me first before you talk about the stressors of your life. My emotional capacity is limited."

Time Time is always precious, but because of limited emotional, cognitive, and physical bandwidth in grief, this is a boundary that can get easily crossed. That might include people dropping by to offer support and staying longer than you're comfortable with. You might need to set a time boundary if a family gathering runs long. Clearly and kindly communicating a time boundary might sound like "I'm happy to come to X, but these days I can only be social for one hour at a time. I will plan to leave at X time."

Workplace Many of us return to work far earlier than we're cognitively, emotionally, or even physically prepared for. I couldn't afford to lose my job as a newly single parent, so I returned to work two weeks after Eric died. However, setting boundaries is possible. This might look like letting colleagues know your preference on bringing up the subject of loss. Establishing your need for frequent walking breaks or having the camera off for video meetings may be helpful. Setting a workplace boundary could happen via email. It might sound like "Thanks, colleagues, for your concern over my loss. I've agreed to work on X or Y project, so please don't cc me on any other projects for the next three months."

*You can't always get what you want. But if you know and speak
it clearly, well, you just might find you get what you need.
—Adapted ever so slightly from the Rolling Stones classic
"You Can't Always Get What You Want"*

WHEN YOUR NEEDS CONFLICT WITH OTHERS' WANTS

A *need* is something necessary to survive. A *want* is something that
might improve the quality of life—in other words, a nice thing to have.
We often find ourselves in conflict between needs and wants. This can
happen internally. We often have this battle between our wants and
needs when our Amazon shopping cart is packed, or when we went to
Target for that one thing and came home with ten items.

Of course, it happens in interpersonal relationships too. Like when
children want to run in the road but the parents need to keep them
safe. It happens in romantic relationships when one partner wants the
couple to attend a late-night gathering but the other needs to sleep
after working a double shift.

Even when you figure out what you need and find the courage to
clearly and kindly communicate that to someone or set a boundary, it
doesn't always turn out how you hoped. There's going to come a time,
maybe lots of times, when your need to care for yourself in your grief
causes conflict when the other people won't respect your boundary or
are unwilling to set down their wants. Since I don't know the partic-
ulars of the battle between your needs versus others' wants, I'll offer
you five important reminders:

1. Your needs in grief are valid.
2. Expressing your needs isn't an act of aggression or a sign of
   weakness.
3. You're the best person to determine what inactions, actions, and
   boundaries feel necessary and healing to you.
4. You'll likely become resentful and act out when you prioritize
   others' wants over your needs.

5. You can't pour from an empty cup, so prioritizing your needs is necessary, not selfish.

Be careful to not let the assumptions, judgments, or impatience of others discourage you from traveling your grief journey in your own way. Remember, their expectations don't change what you need.

⚘ AN INVITATION FOR YOU ⚘

check on your needs daily

Our needs and priorities change as we grow. True of life before grief, and most certainly true in the wake of loss. In some seasons of our lives, like early grief, our needs change rapidly, at times day to day. Even in non-grief times, many of us aren't skilled at tuning inward to discover what we need. Practicing this skill, like anything we want to be good at or make a habit of, is required.

I invite you to cultivate a daily practice of checking inward. Knowing what you need on any given day will help you navigate grief with a little more ease and a lot more grace. Remember, the answers might include a variety of actions, inactions, saying yes or no to something, changing your self-talk, or asking for help. My own answers for today are:

1. Take a midday walk.
2. Connect via text (or video if possible) with my best friend.
3. Not check my work emails.

---

what do I need to feel more at ease today?

I encourage you to do this exercise when your feet first hit the floor in the morning, before you stand up. Start with a nice inhalation through your nose and let out an audible exhale. *Whoosh.* Next, place one or both hands over your heart. It's a small gesture of care but it really helps you tune into your inner voice. You can ask this question out loud or silently. And then you wait. Listen without judgment.

Before you stand up, think about how you can put your answers into action.

oh, the places you go and the people you see (and why it's exhausting)

GOING PLACES AND SEEING PEOPLE IS DRAINING

If you live (or have ever lived) somewhere cold, you know that it takes an incredible amount of planning, time, and energy just to leave the house in the winter. You need to put on long johns, extra socks, boots, sweater, jacket, scarf, gloves, and hat. Then there's shoveling the front step and driveway and scraping the ice off your car windshield.

Once you crack open the car door, you've got to turn on the heat and defrost the windows so that when you eventually leave home, you can see where you're going. The car is finally warmed up and the windows are clear and now you're dripping in sweat (yet somehow freezing), and you haven't even left the driveway.

Going places in grief can feel like that. Especially in the beginning. Remember, grief takes a toll on every part of you, so if you're wondering, "When did it get so exhausting—or is it just me?" The answer is no, it's not just you.

Going places requires making decisions and planning and sometimes operating machinery—all things that grief brain makes challenging. You'd have to get dressed (and maybe shower, depending on how many days it's been), and that requires energy your body likely doesn't have due to ongoing stress and lack of sleep. Plus it seems that you've felt more feelings in the past twenty-four hours than you have in the past year. Your emotions are dysregulated, and, like a toddler after having a tantrum, all you want to do is flop down on the floor.

And then there's the prospect of seeing people. Ugh. People.

There's a chance you'll see people you know, who know about your "situation." Maybe you're mildly hopeful their presence will make you feel better, but you're mostly terrified that you'll burst into tears and leave the encounter feeling worse than before. There's also a strong likelihood that you'll see people you don't know and who don't know what happened. And because they don't know, they'll treat you with the casual annoyance of everyday strangers and you feel so fragile that you fear any hint of incivility will shatter you to pieces. You're going to have to negotiate conversations either way, and that takes work too.

So no, it's not just you. Going places is exhausting.

NEW PEOPLE—TO TELL OR NOT TO TELL?

When we do see someone from the "they don't know about it" category, there's a moment in each encounter where we consider whether we'll simply name our loss. (For me, that would sound like "I'm a widow and my husband died recently of an undiagnosed brain tumor.") Or we might avoid the topic altogether. Crickets.

We might feel anxious that a stranger will ask an uncomfortable question: "Oh, are you married?" Oddly, sometimes we might worry that acquaintances won't bring up the loss at all—that they'll miss a huge part of who we are now. Either way, we imagine how people will respond, and we assess their worthiness to witness our pain. That's a lot of cognitive and emotional labor before we've even opened our mouth.

Along the way, we'll tell some people, and sometimes we'll feel better for it. We'll feel seen, an important quality in building a connection with someone new. Sometimes they'll be a grief thief, making it about them or trying to relate in a way that we find insulting. I once mentioned at a dinner gathering that my husband died of a brain tumor and the new guy at the table said, "Oh, that's just like my friend's wife who had a brain tumor and a bunch of surgeries. But she's fine now." Yeah. He said that. Those are the times that we'll be sorry we said anything at all.

I wish I could tell you that there's a warning system that could alert you, but there isn't. So only share if you're hopeful it will make you feel better or create an important connection. Remember that you don't owe anyone your story. In fact, not everyone deserves to hear it. Next time you spend time with someone new and you're wondering what to share, ask yourself, "Has this person earned the right to hear my story?"

In the beginning, I dreaded all situations and avoided saying much at all, so the topic of Eric and my loss didn't come up. Then for a while I became insistent on bringing up my widow status to everyone I met. I was terrified that I was becoming known to people as just Lisa. Not as the Lisa who was married and deeply in love with her husband Eric—and that felt wrong.

In more recent years, I have settled into a "take it as it comes" approach. I've let go of most of the shoulds I carried about these encounters, including the notion that I shouldn't say something because it might make the other person uncomfortable. Maybe you're in the "never bring it up" phase or the "talk nonstop about it" phase. Either way, it's OK. My only suggestion is to try reflecting after each encounter and adjust as needed for the next one. Do whatever serves you best and remember that what's best will change over time.

THEIR OPINION OF YOU IS NONE OF YOUR BUSINESS

"What other people think of you is none of your business." Have you heard some version of this? On an intellectual level, I wholeheartedly believe it's true.

At the same time, we're social beings who are deeply influenced by cultural norms, sometimes including the opinions of others. So the notion that we're always capable of not caring about others' opinions of us is unrealistic. This is especially difficult to do when we're spending time with people who knew us in the "before"—before the loss happened. It feels impossible not to wonder if they're comparing us against our old selves or judging our behavior based on their grief beliefs.

Early in my grief, I admit that I absolutely made it my business to care about the opinions of others. When I showed up in spaces with the other couples who knew me as part of an "us," I wondered what they were thinking. If I somehow found myself happily engaged in a book discussion or laughing at a friend's story, without warning, my mind would start spinning. I'd find myself wondering, "What are they thinking about my behavior? Did his best friend look over and judge me for smiling again? Did my friends falsely conclude this meant I must be 'over it'?"

It would be easy for me to say that the opinions of your friends and family (and even strangers) are none of your business. I could remind you that they've never walked in your shoes, never experienced your loss in the way that you have, and so they don't have the right to judge. In fact, I am doing that. And what I'm telling you is true. And I know it feels impossible not to fall into that trap from time to time.

YOU DON'T NEED TO PERFORM

There's a lot of pressure to act happy when you go places and see people. I've mentioned how our culture's general obsession with mantras such as "happiness is a choice" discourages grievers from bringing their authentic selves into most rooms. It's not just coming from vague sources like culture either. You might hear things such as, "It would be nice if you smiled. It's your sister's wedding after all," or, "When we get there, can you tell everyone you're doing better?"

The reverse is true, too. You don't need to act sad either. As much as we feel pressure to move on and appear happy and grateful, we get the opposite message too sometimes. The expression "you can't win for losing" comes to mind here. We hear the comments and the judgment and the examples in media that loved ones "clearly didn't care" or "must be over it already" because they seemed in good spirits, content, and even joyful at times. I say screw other people's ignorance. You don't need to hide signs of the good days you're having. Take them as they come. Savor them.

HAVING ANSWERS FOR INNOCENT QUESTIONS

When we go out, people ask us questions. How dare they!

No, but really, collectively our conversation skills aren't particularly grief-aware, which means that when we go places and see people, we're going to get questions that seem innocuous to others but feel like a gut punch to us. Questions such as, "Do you have children?" or "How many children do you have?" sound innocent enough, but if you're someone who's lost a child, you feel that blow in your core. One of the strategies I encourage my clients to consider is to come up with some standard answers they feel comfortable with so that they can feel more in control of the conversation. There is no right answer. I have a friend whose first child died, but she now has two more. She generally chooses to say, "I have three, one of which is in heaven." Another client says about his marital status, "I was married to the love of my life," and leaves it at that.

CONTAGIOUS

When we go places and see people, it can feel as if others think our pain and grief are contagious. From awkward and distant body language to changing the subject to cutting the conversation off altogether, it can feel as if you're in quarantine even when you're in the company of others.

Though it's likely no solace to you, others' aversion to your pain has everything to do with them and nothing to do with you. Many of us haven't learned how to be with our own suffering so we freak out and shut down when we witness pain in others. When talking to someone you'd like support from, I encourage you to name what you need. It might sound something like "Hey, I'm sure you're not doing this on purpose, but you treat me like I'm contagious. That makes me feel isolated. I could really use your closeness and support."

This treatment is especially true when the loss is abrupt, violent, or unexpected—such as the death of a child. My friend Rachel Carnahan-Metzger has spent a decade working as a pediatric palliative and now hospice social worker. In her first appearance on my podcast, she shared how she witnessed this treatment regularly with families she worked with. "When you know someone and when your worst nightmare has happened to them, it's hard to show up for that. And the bereaved families can feel that. They know it. They can feel how hard it is for others to show up for them knowing they're someone's worst nightmare."

⚵ AN INVITATION FOR YOU ⚶

to feel better prepared

Especially early in grief, and honestly any time we encounter new people, we feel at the mercy of our emotions or the dynamics or power of the people we're encountering. That can make seeing people a daunting prospect and have us leaving interactions with feelings of self-judgment or regret. I want to say this again because it's important: You *do not* need to perform for others in your grief. You don't owe anyone anything other than your authentic self. That doesn't mean you must bare all that you're feeling. It also doesn't mean you have to hide what you're feeling away to appease anyone's likely discomfort with your pain.

There are some common topics or questions that might make you feel like a deer in the headlights when seeing people in grief—questions such as "How are you doing? Do you have children/how many children do you have? Where do your parents live? Are you married? What does your partner do?"

While the responses you're comfortable with will likely change over time and with circumstances, I invite you to take time to think about some standard replies or answers that will feel good for you. Make sure to note the specific qualities of the person or interaction that make this the right response for the situation.

---

responses that work for me

When someone asks:

A response I'd like to use is:

Qualities of person or interaction:

people say stupid shit

I'M SORRY PEOPLE SAID THAT TO YOU

Have people said stupid shit to you in your grief? And when I say stupid, I mean ignorant, hurtful, dismissive, and sometimes offensive. Do you know the ones I mean? Comments such as:

"Everything happens for a reason."
"At least they aren't suffering anymore."
"They're in a better place now."
"You'll find love again."
"You still have/can have children."
"You just need to move on."

The night my forty-four-year-old husband was taken off life support, I heard the first of what would become way too many of these stupid expressions. Friends and family had been invited to come to the hospital to say their goodbyes. One person approached me and said (I will assume with good intentions), "Don't worry, Lisa, at least he'll be in a better place soon."

I was in shock over the entire experience. Though I was speechless, I know for certain I was thinking, "Fuck off." I also wanted to punch him right in the face. Don't worry, I didn't. I don't condone violence. Between you and me, though, I did enjoy imagining it from time to time in the weeks after that encounter.

As if grief isn't hard enough, having people say hurtful, discounting, or downright rude things to us feels like salt in the already deep and painful wounds of grief. Do you have a small or large list of occasions that this has happened to you? In the wake of your loss, has someone addressed your grief by starting a sentence with, "At least . . ."? Has it been rare? Occasional? Does it feel like it happens all the dang time? Regardless of the frequency, I'm sorry this has happened to you too.

As if grief isn't hard enough, having people say hurtful, discounting, or downright rude things to us feels like salt in the already deep and painful wounds of grief.

OOPS, MAYBE YOU'VE SAID STUPID SHIT TOO

You can't see me, but my hand is raised. I cringe when I look back and consider some of the things I've said to grievers in the past. How about you? Have any regrets? It seems impossible to have avoided it since we live in a grief-illiterate culture. Our models of grief support advice include the historically crappy sympathy (a.k.a. pity) cards that offer these trite and harmful expressions.

Many of us didn't even recognize these expressions as harmful until we went through our own hell and found ourselves on the receiving end. Knowing that we've all likely said stupid things might help you have some compassion for others when they say these things to you. And it might not. Maybe not yet. That's OK. Still, it's important for all of us to acknowledge the consequences of our words regardless of our intentions.

DISCOMFORT WITH PAIN IS A PROBLEM FOR EVERYONE

Others' discomfort with your pain is their problem, not yours. Collectively, we suck at holding emotional pain, both our pain and that of others. Especially when that pain looks like anger or rage. Our inability to hold pain has major consequences for our growth, healing, relationships, and grief journey. We put the comfort of others over our own emotional needs, even in the face of our own great loss and suffering.

We stuff painful feelings down so as not to make waves, create awkwardness, or open the door for others to tell us what is wrong with us, how we're feeling, or how we can fix it—as if our pain is unjustified or that it's something anyone can even fix. This obsession with niceness, of avoiding discomfort at all costs by not bringing up our pain, is toxic for everyone.

EDUCATE, TELL OFF, OR IGNORE

They said the thing. Now what? Whether the words came from a stranger, someone grieving the same loss as you, or a friend/colleague who is "grief adjacent" (a term I heard from the wise and witty Nora McInerny), the choice to respond or not is yours. As far as I can tell, there are only three choices: Educate, tell them off, or ignore it.

Educating people requires that you clearly state how their words made you feel. Be prepared to offer an explanation so that they can learn why what they said wasn't OK. This option is beneficial because it gives them a chance to recognize the harm and hopefully change their behavior with you and others in the future.

As I said, telling them off is another option. This might involve swear words or something more subtle such as eye rolls or shaking your head. This option can certainly feel satisfying in the moment, but it doesn't always feel good in the long term, depending on the target.

The third choice is to simply ignore it and change the topic or leave the setting. This option may benefit your peace of mind or conserve your energy for more important things.

Honestly, any of these options are acceptable. I've used them all. Your use of each will likely depend on:

1. How much you value the relationship
2. What you know about their capacity to hold themselves accountable
3. The severity of the harm or impact of their words
4. Whether this was an isolated or frequent occurrence

5. The setting and delivery (in public/private, in person, phone, email, text)
6. The amount of energy you have (a.k.a. how many fucks you have to give)

Note: If you want to make amends for the stupid shit you said but the person has chosen to ignore you, I suggest you approach the person later and say something such as, "I realize (too late, I'm afraid) that my words were hurtful when I said to you, (fill in the blank). I want you to know that I'm sorry. I'm also working on being more thoughtful in my grief support in the future."

LOST IN TRANSLATION

There's a weird category of problematic things people say to grievers. These are the phrases that are said as if they're a compliment or an observation, but generally leave the griever feeling more misunderstood and isolated than before. Honestly, sometimes I think grievers and non-grievers are speaking two different languages and meaning is lost in translation.

When people said to me, "You're so brave," I heard, "Your life scares me." When a colleague said, "You're so strong," what I heard was, "You should hold it together at all times." What I heard when someone said, "I don't know how you do it" was "I can't relate to you."

Well-meaning comments such as the ones above can make us feel even more like the "other." It affirms to us that we're no longer relatable, we're unrecognizable, and in a way, we're lost. So just in case you're wondering why some of these phrases irritate you, now you know. Also, your reaction to these phrases might change on a daily, hourly, or minute-to-minute basis, especially in the beginning. Totally normal.

That's why fellow grievers are often a comfort, as we explore next in "Who's Got Your Back?" I loved when Christina Applegate's character in the TV show *Dead to Me* said, "Thank you—and just for not saying and doing the same stupid shit that everybody says and does and just makes you feel more alone than you already are, you know? And for not being repulsed by my version of grief."

⚒ AN INVITATION FOR YOU ⚒
say what you need to hear

We've been exploring the harmful expressions and the hurt we often feel when people use clichés and other Hallmark greeting card-like sayings to us in our grief. It's important to acknowledge the hurt, and if you feel able, interested, and safe, communicate that to others.

I encourage you to spend some time thinking about what you really want and need to hear from others. It might be what you'd find helpful when you're intensely feeling the weight of grief. It could be what you'd appreciate in times when grief feels lighter, but you still want others to check in. Maybe you're not sure when, but you have a hunch it would feel helpful.

I invite you to take out your journal and write down at least five things you would like to hear from others in your grief. Once you do, you might even offer these things to yourself by reading them out loud.

If an example is helpful, here are five things I would put on my list:

1. "I was thinking of Eric's smile the other day. Boy, did he light up a room."
2. "I know this month is the anniversary of his death. How can I best support you?"
3. "What is something you want to make sure people know and remember about him?"
4. "I hate that you're going through this. It's fucking bullshit and it sucks so much."
5. "It's OK to feel whatever you're feeling in this moment."

who's got your back?

ISN'T IT IRONIC?

Deep loneliness is one of the most universally experienced feelings in grief. We feel lonely when our need for rewarding social contact isn't met. Loneliness comes from feeling as if no one has our back. One of the most ironic things for many of the significant losses we endure is that the very person we would instinctively go to for emotional support and social connection is the one who's gone. It makes no sense. And yet I can't tell you how many times I've cried and said out loud, "Eric, I wish you were here to help me with this."

Maybe you've done something similar.

There's more irony at play here. In the report "Our Epidemic of Loneliness and Isolation," U.S. Surgeon General Vivek Murthy indicated that across many studies and measures, Americans appear to be less socially connected. Even as we move further into a globalized world, our sense of connection is decreasing. That statistic is not uniquely American either. So wherever you're reading this book, this type of social disconnection and loneliness likely applies to you too. I'm not trying to be a bummer with this news. Instead, I'm normalizing why you might be feeling impossibly lonely and why it's so important to discover who's got your back and how to let them support you.

DISCONNECTION IN THREE PARTS

One way we experience loneliness is by feeling disconnected. In the wake of loss, this happens in three parts.

Person First is the disconnection we feel from our dead or distant loved ones. The severing of that sense of "we/us" is devastating and heartbreaking. It's also the disconnection that's most recognized and acknowledged.

World Less noticeable to non-grievers is the disconnection we feel from the world around us. This disconnection might feel like "no one understands me." For others, we notice this disconnection only with certain people. Oddly, it often happens with people we had anticipated feeling more connected to in the wake of loss.

Ourselves The disconnection we feel from ourselves is the third and perhaps most disconcerting one of all. When Eric died, I felt lost and disconnected from myself. I didn't recognize who I was, as my identity felt shattered. Grief researcher Mary-Frances O'Connor beautifully explains why this happens. O'Connor reminds us that our titles—wife, mother, friend—are inherently about the relationships we have with others.

So when that person dies or disappears, our sense of self is broken. Our brain struggles to make sense of our new title. Think about it. The label *Mom* implies two people—mother and child. *Sibling* implies two people. *Friend, grandparent, partner, aunt, uncle, niece, nephew—* they all include an identity intrinsically tied to another person, and now that other person is gone.

JUST SHOW THE HELL UP

So many times in the early days of grief, I felt like screaming, "Show up. Show up. Show the hell up!" I don't think I'm alone. Have you done (or felt like doing) this?

I probably screamed these words when alone dozens of times. I still do it from time to time as the years have passed. Particularly around those land-mine days (anniversary of death, birthdays, Hallmark holidays, etc.). This isn't to say that people didn't show up for me. They did, and I'm eternally grateful. Several of them still do, which is remarkable because as time passes, people tend to stop showing up.

Have you heard the expression "Be careful what you wish for because it might come true"? What happens when supporters do show up? Yes, a lot of the time it's amazing and exactly what we needed, even if we didn't know what that was beforehand. Irony shows up here too. Because even though most of us have felt like screaming "Show up!" out of deep hurt, loneliness, fear, and maybe even anger, sometimes something weird happens when supporters do show up. It feels awkward, weird, and uncomfortable. Sometimes their presence or their words somehow make you sadder. Occasionally, you may feel angry and resentful, wishing they would just go away. WTF? Has this ever happened to you? It's happened to me.

WHEN THEY DO SHOW UP

When people show up to offer support, have you wondered why you feel better after these encounters? Even if one friend brings you the same boring frozen casserole and another shows up with chocolate ice cream and wine? It's because some people know how to hold space and bear witness. What does that look like or feel like? They know how to make your time together about you and your needs in a way that makes you feel comforted and cared for, not pitied or judged.

I've practiced a sustained meditation on holding space and bearing witness for decades. It was the subject of my master's degree thesis. Some key elements required of the person showing up to hold space and bear witness include:

- Setting their energy prior to arrival
- Arriving with no expectation that you need to fix
- Creating safety
- De-prioritizing themselves
- Sustaining attention on you
- Accepting you
- Not judging you
- Showing compassion for you

THEY FIND YOU BROKEN BUT NOT IN NEED OF REPAIR

Even though you feel broken, you don't need fixing. I know it may not feel that way. What you need is to mend. Mending isn't instantaneous.

It takes time, patience, self-compassion—all the things we're talking about in this book. Even if you wanted supporters to fix you, they can't. All they can do is be there to hold the weight for a while or offer you some salve (love, acceptance, compassion, kindness). They can pick you up when the heaviness of grief brings you down. Better yet, they might get down on the ground to keep you company while you rest.

Besides the friend you specifically called to help fix the leaky pipe or the broken lawnmower, you likely weren't asking for friends to come fix things. You especially didn't expect them to show up to try to fix you. Yet so many people do.

WHY HAVING YOUR BACK IS HARDER THAN YOU THINK

Showing up in a meaningful way doesn't seem as if it should be so hard. So why do we generally suck at it? Well, it's challenging for many of us because it's often the exact opposite of advice we're given about what it means to help. Isn't it our job to show up and fix everything with our opinions, our suggestions, our platitudes? Aren't big gestures and tough love the best options? Nope. They're not. That's what makes it hard. The healing support we need from others in our grief is the opposite. It's often quiet, still, inactive, nonjudgmental, requires short but ongoing check-ins, and rarely results in some aha moment or fix.

When I summon the courage to tell you that I feel broken, please don't try to convince me that I'm whole.

ASKING SOMEONE TO "JUST SEE ME AS I AM"

It's hard for the people who love us to see us in our brokenness. That's why they often try to convince us (and themselves) that we're more whole than we are.

It takes tremendous courage and vulnerability to be seen in our full, messy, and broken humanity, but that's what helps us feel less alone and more connected. When we struggle to recognize ourselves because of the pain of our loss, one of the most healing gestures is for someone to see us and love us just as we are.

It probably feels unfair that you have the burden of educating people on how to help well. I get that. Unfortunately, people tend to need a little coaching in this area. If you feel up to it, and have a person in your life whose idea of help is to try to fix you, say something like this:

> "I know you want to help me, so I want to share this with you. I need you to acknowledge and affirm what I say. There will come a time when reflecting to me a list of all my strengths, heart, and wisdom will be welcomed. But for now, in this moment, when I tell you that I feel broken, please just honor and affirm my experience. Trust that I will do the work of mending and healing, but first, I just need you to see me as I am."

If you both like simplicity and swearing, you can tell them this instead:

> "Sometimes, the most helpful thing you can say to me is, 'This is fucking bullshit and it sucks so much.'"

SHARING IN GRIEF FEELS GOOD (SOMETIMES)

It feels good to be around other grievers, doesn't it? I think so. Well, except when it doesn't. It's complicated. I really wasn't around other grievers in the early years after Eric died. A few close friends had experienced the loss of parents, so that was comforting. I did go to a partner loss support group for a little while because my daughter was attending a group in the same center. It was generally helpful. I think. I don't know. I don't remember much from that time.

When doesn't it feel so good? When a fellow griever is in denial or is clinging to the "move on" theory of grief and trying to get you to go along for that ride. When else? Honestly, sometimes early on in my grief, when I was with someone else who was also grieving Eric, it didn't feel good. I hate to admit it, but it happened sometimes. I found it hard to explain (even to myself) why sometimes it felt good for other people to share their grief over Eric with me and other times it made me angry. Has that ever happened to you?

But yes, being with other grievers often does feel good. Amazing actually. Over the years I've met and befriended a lot more grievers, in part because of the work I now do. I notice it's easier to feel a deep and instantaneous connection with them—more so than with non-grievers. Why? Generally, they're less likely to say the stupid things or act awkwardly around me when they find out I'm a widow. They tend to show up on those hard milestone days when others don't. They're less likely to try to fix me or talk me out of my feelings. Their very existence makes me feel less like an alien. There's rarely any "lost in translation" moments in conversation. In other words, they're more skilled at having my back and I feel good because I know how to have theirs too.

Rabbi Julia Watts Belser, yet another guide in my grief, describes this experience so perfectly:

One day, I'll hear you say to me: I can't. It's just too hard. And I will feel the truth down to my bones, recall another day, a different hour, how once I said those words to you. You did not tell me lies. You did not feed me platitudes like saccharine pearls. You said: I know. You offered me a hand, that silent signature of flesh and breath. You offered me a pause. And then we both kept on.

—*Rabbi Julia Watts Belser*

I WISH YOU HAD A FRIEND LIKE JOE

One of the most important people in my early grief journey was my friend Joe. He didn't live in my town. He didn't have children or much family at all. But he had long been an honorary member of our extended family. He knew Eric and I'm sure he was grieving for him too. Still, somehow, he managed to be there in a way no one else was. He checked in regularly, but never with an "I'm worried you're going crazy—are you OK?" kind of vibe. He stayed up talking (or not talking) to me on the phone countless nights in those early months when I just couldn't sleep. He wasn't afraid to crack jokes or swear or just sit in silence with me on the other end of the line. He sent me stupid videos and favorite playlists. He never made me feel bad for having happy moments or questioned me when those moments inevitably ended in big, ugly, heaving sobs.

The amazing thing is that Joe did all this while his body was slowly giving way to the ravages of muscular dystrophy, a disease he'd had for as long as I knew him. Eventually, it was my turn to show up for him. To take care of him without judgment or pity. To keep checking in. And in the end, I was there by his side when he took his last breath, just a few years after Eric did the same.

I hope you find a friend like Joe in your grief. Someone who can show up and:

- doesn't need anything from you.
- is steady and present and frequently checks in.
- is available for middle-of-the-night panic texts or phone calls, during which all you need is reassurance that someone's there.
- doesn't get offended when you cancel plans at the last minute.
- drops off/sends coffee or a gallon of ice cream or a bottle of wine—all unannounced.
- sends cards in the mail full of swear words to validate you that this whole situation sucks so fucking much.
- doesn't try to fix you, cheer you up, or ask you to look on the bright side.
- knows how to show up, shut up, and listen—and who keeps showing up.

⚶ AN INVITATION FOR YOU ⚶

identify what helps you

I know it can feel impossible to know what you need, especially in your early grief. Identifying your needs can also feel like a moving target, changing from day to day and sometimes hour to hour. That's normal. Yet that makes it hard to figure out who could be supportive or what having your back even looks like.

So I invite you to spend some time thinking about what good grief support feels like to you. Today. I'm offering two prompts. The first prompt: Who is currently doing a good job making you feel supported and how are they doing that? Get as detailed as you can. Maybe instead of saying, "Derrick brings me food each week," you could write down, "Derrick checks in with me weekly, then brings me pre-prepared but healthy meals. I like it when he offers to unload them into my refrigerator for me."

Sometimes we don't currently have enough supportive people, or we can't figure out exactly what they do. In that case, try completing the second prompt: I feel supported in my grief when people (fill in the blank). Again, write as much detail as you can: "I feel supported when people make eye contact and offer to give me a hug."

P.S. Different people may have your back in different ways. No judgment.

---

people who make me feel supported:

(their name and how they do it)

i feel supported when people:

(include details, even small ones)

# of course
it's complicated

IT'S COMPLICATED

Merriam-Webster's dictionary offers two definitions for the word *complicated.* They differ significantly both in tone and effect. A similar thing happens when we use that word to describe grief.

"Consisting of parts intricately combined"

This definition sounds like an accurate description of what happens when we grieve, doesn't it? We are deeply interconnected with the ones we love, which explains the pain and confusion grievers endure as we feel torn apart. When we experience our response to loss across all our parts—cognitive, emotional, physical, spiritual—we're reminded of our complex nature. The unique form of each of our grief experiences results from an intricately connected set of factors, including the circumstances of the loss, our relationship with that person, our resources for support, the expectations the world has of us, and so much more.

"Difficult to analyze, understand, or explain"

This one has a very different tone and yet it also accurately describes grief. For starters, it feels impossible to use our intellect or analytical skills to solve the enormous puzzle the loss creates in our brain. We struggle to comprehend the incomprehensible, finding it difficult to truly understand that our person is gone forever. Also, it's often challenging to communicate our inner experience of grief or to explain why we feel the way we do on any given day in our grieving journey.

Given both definitions, I think it makes absolute sense that *complicated* is often used in reference to the grieving experience.

CIRCUMSTANCES AND SCENARIOS THAT CAN MAKE THINGS COMPLICATED

At the time you experienced your profound loss, you weren't an empty vessel, devoid of history. That means the experiences and circumstances of your life (past and current) combined with the scenario surrounding the loss might add additional complexity to your grieving experience.

What follows isn't an exhaustive list, just some of the common contributors to complexity in grief. If you recognize yourself in some of these categories, remember that it's just information. Consider it an invitation to discover if there's more for you to learn or any additional support you might need. Most of all, if any of it resonates with you, my hope is that you will feel more seen and held in your complexity. You may even feel relieved because it's not just you. Like many people, you're just having a complex response to a complex set of experiences—and that's normal.

Cause or Timing of Death

There are some causes of death that generally make the grieving process much more complex. Those include things such as death by suicide, medical malpractice, accidental death, homicide, or any type of violent death. When a child or young person dies, often referred to as an "out of order death," the grief is complex for the parents or loved ones who never expected to outlive their person. Another way timing can complicate grief is when the discovery of death is delayed. I've worked with clients who didn't discover their loved one's death until months or even years later because the person had gone missing from their lives for one reason or another.

Non-Death Losses

Non-death losses are often ambiguous and can include things such as catastrophic injuries and chronic or terminal illnesses. There's complexity when loved ones are still present, but not in the ways or forms you knew them. This might include loved ones with Alzheimer's disease or who struggle with addiction. Sometimes there's ambiguity and complexity because we only have their presence in our minds and hearts, not physically. In these cases, when someone has disappeared from our life for whatever reason, it's a complex process to accept the loss while finding meaning with the life that still exists.

Trauma

We explore the relationship between trauma and grief in "Too Much Too Soon." What I'll add here is that trauma is the most common source of complexity in grief that I've seen in my work. It's something that has impacted my family as well. I've seen the way unresolved trauma, either related to the loss or from the past (including trauma related to attachment issues as an infant) can complicate a person's ability to move through the grieving process. If trauma is something you've experienced and you feel as if your grieving process is complex, please make sure to find someone who specializes in trauma for additional support.

Difficult, Abusive, and Absent Relationships

"Don't speak ill of the dead." We've all heard that chestnut before, haven't we? But sometimes the dead weren't so great to us in life. Sometimes they treated us badly or were abusive or neglectful. Sometimes they disappeared long before their death occurred. Sometimes we hadn't had the chance to form a relationship in the first place, as is often the case in adoption, or they disappeared after we connected, as when a parent leaves the family.

Sometimes these people aren't missed. Maybe because the emotional, psychological, and sometimes physical labor involved in being in a relationship with them was too much. For some of us, what we feel in their absence is relief. The source of complexity is due to the conflict we feel between the social pressure to grieve the loss and the way we really feel. We may also just miss parts or aspects of them, our history with them, and not them. In fact, what we're often grieving isn't them but the idealized relationship we never got to have with them. Other times the complexity arises because what we're grieving is the missed opportunity to repair relationships.

Feeling conflicted about the people we lost is more common than you might think. There is so much pressure to idolize the deceased that we're not afforded permission to have anything less than eulogy-worthy thoughts, feelings, and memories. In case you feel conflicted, let me be the one to remind you that however you feel is OK! It's acceptable and perfectly reasonable for you to feel sadness and anger. It's understandable if you feel relief and yearning for their return. It's even OK if you're not exactly sure how you feel about them yet.

Denied the Right to Claim It

Being denied the right to name and claim your grief or express your grief in the style that serves you best also leads to significant complexity in the grieving process. This issue is more pervasive than you may think, and we explore this in more detail in "Access Denied."

Feeling conflicted about people we lost is more common than you might think. There is so much pressure to idolize the deceased that we're not afforded permission to have anything less than eulogy-worthy thoughts, feelings, and memories. In case you feel conflicted, let me be the one to remind you that however you feel is OK!

COMPLICATED EMOTIONS AND THINKING PATTERNS

We discussed in "Emotions and Feelings and Moods, Oh My!" that it's more helpful to look at the presence of our emotions as information rather than having an inherent good/bad value. When people have a complicated relationship with grief, a cluster of emotions and thought patterns come up more intensely and frequently and tend to hang around longer. This isn't surprising given some of the circumstances listed above.

Some common emotions and ways of thinking that show up with intensity and longevity, indicating a more complex grieving experience, include numbness, ambivalence, terror, guilt, regret, remorse, resentment, rumination, shame, and survivor's guilt.

We've all likely experienced these emotions and thought patterns from time to time. Having one or more of the ones listed above isn't inherently bad or a sign of being stuck. Experiencing them more regularly and in ways that interrupt your ability to feel other emotions may be a sign that the complexity of your grief is slowing your healing.

LAYERS UPON LAYERS

Grieving is an inherently layered process for everyone who experiences it. To move forward, we're invited to examine all the parts that have come unraveled and disconnected. We're called to sort through the layers of our emotions, memories, and experiences and to determine how best to fit them together again. We're invited to consider which pieces to weave back in and which ones to let go of as we make room for new pieces to incorporate into our emerging story.

For some of us who have had a complicated relationship, it may feel more confusing to sort through. Is it the grief about the person or is it about what we didn't have—a loving parent or a close relationship with a sibling? We may feel both, which can add another layer of complication. For others, we might have to confront letting go of the hope for reconciliation or repair that will never come. Grappling with all these layers can make grief feel more complicated too.

USING "AND" CAN MAKE IT FEEL LESS COMPLICATED

Much of why the complications of grief can feel overwhelming is that we're faced with false choices. When your grief is complicated because of the circumstances mentioned earlier, the pressure to choose from false binaries is even more challenging and harmful.

False choices show up as either/or ultimatums, such as, "Either you

154/relating to yourself and others (or not)

loved him, or you're relieved he's dead, not both," or, "If you really loved your other children, you would stop being so sad about the one who died." Even though it's hard to hold the complexity of opposing ideas or emotions, we can do it. In fact, we need to do it because trying to force ourselves to choose one and ignore the other is often the reason we get stuck.

When clients experience complex feelings around grief, my goal is to get them to a place where they can hold both seemingly contradictory thoughts or emotions at once. More important, my aim is to help them set down the guilt they may have for holding these thoughts or emotions in the first place.

This might start with asking, "What would it feel like to say, 'I still miss them,' and 'I'm also relieved that they're gone and can no longer hurt me'?" If they're willing to say it out loud, it's a good first step in figuring out what old belief or narrative is getting in the way. The goal is for them to be able to say both statements and find more ease or peace when they do.

NOT EVERYONE FINDS GRIEF COMPLICATED

Part of what can make your complicated feelings more challenging is that other people in the person's life may not feel the same. Sometimes in families, one person had a fully loving and healthy relationship, while another didn't. That means the story of the loss is a very different one, often leading the person with the complex experience to feel minimized or dismissed. This might be self-inflicted judgment (nothing anyone else is doing or saying, just the result of comparing yourself—a.k.a. being your own grief thief). Just as often the critique comes from another person and can lead to conflict within families. (See "Access Denied.")

GRIEVING THE ROLE, NOT THE PERSON

Earlier I touched on the fact that in cases where we had a difficult or even traumatic relationship with someone, we find grief complicated because while we don't feel we're grieving the person, we feel some sort of grief anyhow. What we often miss is that the death or disconnection is prompting us to grieve the role or experience we never had.

For example, when an abusive parent dies, the children may not miss the parent, but instead grieve for the child version of themselves that never got a chance to experience a loving and caring parent.

This isn't the only time that not honoring the need to grieve the role makes things more complicated. Many of us are grieving someone we loved and with whom we had a good or even great relationship. For many of us, we've attended to the grief we feel over the person, really being with all the emotions of not having that person in our lives anymore. And yet something's still gnawing at us. Often the thing that we've missed is our grief over the role or title we no longer hold.

One of my clients, who lost both her parents within a month of each other, kept saying that there was something else *there* to the loss of her aged parents. It wasn't just their deaths or even their absence from her life. Something else was causing her distress. As she shared stories of them, I heard and reflected to her that it sounded as if she found a lot of pride, satisfaction, and joy in being their daughter. I suggested that she might need to give specific care and attention to grieving the loss of that role. Her confusion and distress signaled her need to honor that aspect of her grief that had been previously hidden.

That invitation to see loss from another perspective is what allowed her to recognize and say out loud, "I think that's what I might be grieving most of all. Now I'm no one's daughter." In case you've felt some version of this and didn't think you had permission to grieve your title, I want to tell you that it's OK. Grieve.

WHEN COMPLICATED BECOMES DISORDERED

Here's a puzzle for you. Yes, all grief makes life complicated. Most grief has complicating factors. But not all grief is complicated grief. Huh? Maybe you've heard the terms "complicated grief" or "prolonged grief disorder" (PGD) tossed around in recent years. In fact, PGD was added in 2022 to the American Psychiatric Association's *Diagnostic Statistical Manual* (DSM-5).

The general description reads, "Prolonged Grief Disorder (PGD), or complicated grief, can happen after a person close to you has died within at least 6 months (12 months for children and teens). You may feel a deep longing for the person who died and become fixated on thoughts of them. This can make it hard to function at home, work, and other important settings." Please note that this is just the description. It doesn't include all the criteria needed to qualify it as a disorder.

THINK OF IT LIKE AN INFECTION

You know I love a metaphor, and PGD psychiatrist and researcher Katherine Shear shared one that I've found helpful. She explains that while grief is like a normal inflammatory response to the injury of loss, complicated grief is what happens when an infection takes hold. This results in a delay in the healing process and an increase in suffering, which "occurs because aspects of a person's response to the circumstances or consequences of the death derail the mourning process, interfering with learning, and preventing the natural healing process from progressing."

This metaphor offers a more accessible way of thinking about the difference between when grief is a normal (and naturally uncomplicated) response to loss and when it has become unnecessarily complicated and harmful.

Many psychiatrists, other mental health providers, and grievers themselves see this diagnosis as a valuable way to reduce the unnecessary suffering experienced by the small percentage of grievers (estimated around 10 percent) who meet the criteria needed to qualify for PGD. In my experience working with clients, I've certainly encountered people who get stuck in their suffering for years and struggle to find any relief or take any steps toward healing. Typically, this has been a result of a wide variety of reasons, including untreated trauma, underlying attachment issues, abuse and neglect, and ongoing and compounding losses. In fact, you may be one of those people. If so, or if you suspect this to be true, I think finding a provider who can run diagnostics and deliver skilled grief support is vital.

YES, IT'S COMPLICATED, AND . . .

Still, I have a lot of complicated feelings about that description as a disorder. How about you? I'm not here to dismiss the research, the validity of the diagnostic criteria, or your lived experience if this makes you feel seen. I am here to add a "yes, and."

Yes, there is cause for having prolonged grief disorder as a diagnosable condition *and* I have concerns. I fear this will push back the progress we've made culturally, among the helping professions and as individuals, to recognize grief as a normal response to loss. I fear this adds to the everyday pathological vocabulary we use to talk about grief in general. As a griever and grief activist, I'm concerned that it reinforces the myths that "normal" grieving is a short, linear, neat, and completable task.

I worry that this diagnosis will reinforce a right/wrong grief belief that is currently a significant contributor to the unnecessary suffering of so many grievers. This was one of the harmful myths I held early on that negatively affected my grief. Maybe that's true for you too. My concern is that once again, it locates the "problem" in the individual while ignoring the responsibilities of policies, systems, and a culture that contribute to the complexity grievers experience.

⚵ AN INVITATION FOR YOU ⚶

find a container for your complexity

The bottom line is that when it comes to complication in grief, we all struggle to one degree or another. And while we won't ever know all the information or have all the answers, sometimes a part of how we find our way to coexist with the ambiguity and uncertainty more peacefully is to give voice to the complexity of our thoughts and emotions.

The place to begin is to find a way to articulate the thoughts and emotions that don't have a name—the ones that are contributing to the complexity you're feeling. There are so many forms of expressive exercises to help you discover your voice, including letter writing to the deceased/disappeared and sometimes to yourself.

For now, I invite you to start closer in. Get out your journal and start by responding without editing or judgment to the following prompts. Whatever thoughts or feelings come up, write them down. They're not facts. They're not the whole story or explanation for your grief. They're just information.

Be kind and compassionate with whatever arises. Nothing you write makes you a good or bad person, a better or worse griever. It's about validating what your body already knows deep down and creating a container for it to be held—a container that isn't your mind. Writing it down gives you distance and a chance to gain some perspective and perhaps begin to loosen the block that these inhibited thoughts or feelings are having on your healing. This can be something you bring to a support group or use with your mental health provider.

---

*feelings that keep coming up that are hard to admit
to others are:*

*when people ask me about my loss, what I really wish
I could say is:*

*what I wish people really understood about how
complicated it feels is:*

access denied

DENIED THE RIGHT TO GRIEVE

Being denied the right to grieve is such an offensive idea, isn't it? Inherently, grief is an individual experience, so how can there be gatekeepers to grief? Just the notion makes me want to shout, "It's my grief, and I don't need your fucking permission to grieve!" And while I'd technically be correct, it's more complicated than that.

Regardless of how independent you are, we humans depend on social interaction for our health and well-being as we live in a world in relationship with others. We are a part of and dependent upon a complex set of systems (e.g., workplace, medical, legal, religious institutions). We live in collectives, known as societies, that dictate spoken and unspoken rules on just about everything. I mean everything.

Those rules are sometimes formalized, including things such as laws and policies, but can also be informal, including cultural norms. Even though these rules are not always communicated explicitly, cultural norms are extremely powerful, and we see their influence in our lives through our collective willingness to follow them. This includes things that we're expected to wear to work versus how we dress around friends or what's considered appropriate behavior in restaurants versus how we act in a sports stadium.

We see it in the gender norms that normalize girls wearing skirts or having long hair while boys are bullied and harassed for such expression. We collectively understand and enforce the cultural norm that masculinity means men don't display emotions such as sadness. We have and follow cultural norms around tipping servers in the US that don't necessarily exist in other countries. We have cultural norms for how to be in the world.

Not surprisingly, those rules don't disappear when it comes to grief and grieving. Certain laws and policies influence our right and ability to grieve. We see this in the existence of weak, irregular, and in some cases no paid bereavement leave for most people, in most workplaces, over most types of losses. That's just one gate. Perhaps more consequential in denying grief are the cultural beliefs and norms we hold about it.

As in other arenas of our lives, these cultural norms are applied differently and disproportionately affect some groups of people or some types of losses more than others. The result is what Kenneth Doka calls "disenfranchised grief." Coining the term in the '80s, he described this experience as "a loss that is not or cannot be openly acknowledged, socially sanctioned, or publicly mourned." In other words, there really are gatekeepers to our grief.

WHO SERVE AS GATEKEEPERS?

Various levels of society create the conditions where grief isn't acknowledged and displays of mourning are dismissed. Institutional (policies, procedures, rules, and laws), cultural (TV, movies, social media) and interpersonal (what we learn from our family, friends, teachers, coworkers) levels of society often work in tandem without even knowing it. Though there's rarely malicious intent, the result is still the disenfranchisement of people's grief. These gatekeepers are the holders and disseminators of harmful grief beliefs, and they use them to stand guard. They include:

Culture and Media

This is essentially the meta gatekeeper, and in some ways the instigator of them all. Across time and space, the institutions that create what we call culture include all forms of media and arts, religious institutions, politicians, theologians, and leaders in all fields from medical to governmental. The values inherent in upholding these systems are often littered with damaging grief beliefs that are absorbed by everyone involved—which is really all of us.

Institutions

The formal gatekeeping happens at the governmental level, where we see improving but still weak, limited, and rarely equitable paid bereavement-leave policies. Laws also prohibit some prisoners from attending funerals or memorials. It's not only our legal system that serves as a gatekeeper. The policies set by employers (if you're lucky enough to work for a company that has such policies) often ignore the inclusion of many losses that are significant to the griever (e.g., aunts, uncles, friends, unmarried partners, miscarriage). They rarely consider the need for time off to be extended beyond the five to fourteen consecutive days given.

When leaders in any industry prioritize productivity over human suffering and disregard exhausted employees, they're gatekeeping grief too. When religious or cultural leaders disavow gay/same-gender/queer relationships, they deny the grief that this population faces. The failure of many medical providers to acknowledge or educate patients on the physical and cognitive effects of grief is another example of how groups disenfranchise grief. Whether these rules and policies are formal or not, the values beneath them strongly impact grievers' ability to feel seen in their grief and even sometimes safe enough to express it.

Interpersonal (One or More Individuals)

The most influential gatekeeper to some aspect of your grief might just be someone you know. Sometimes people in your life deny your right to grieve, saying things such as, "You hardly knew them," or, "They were just your pet." They sometimes shut down aspects of your grief. This can even happen when you have a "culturally acceptable" form of grief. Yet some people in your inner circle serve as gatekeepers. This can be subtle or bold through offhand remarks or directives letting you know that your sadness has gone on long enough or that you shouldn't talk about it anymore. (See "People Say Stupid Shit.")

You

Sorry to bring you bad news, but as I share in "Watch Out for the Grief Thief," sometimes it's you. We often disenfranchise our own grief. This includes downplaying or altogether dismissing our right to grieve a particular loss, grieve after a certain amount of time, or grieve in our own style. And if it makes you feel better, sometimes I'm the annoying gatekeeper in my own grief too. We've all served in that role from time to time.

The Levels Work in Concert with One Another to Create Cultural Norms

Remember, cultural norms also play a strong role. The media, arts, thought leaders, and often religious institutions are standing guard here. These can often be subtle, informal, yet extremely powerful actions, including how grief is portrayed on TV and in movies (widow's grief ends when a man comes to sweep her off her feet). The messages of toxic positivity, pull yourself up by your bootstraps, and good-vibes-only from politicians, thought leaders, artists, and social media influencers are clear indications that your grief is not acceptable for public consumption.

NOT ALL GATES LOOK THE SAME

As I mentioned, all gatekeepers have their own tricks, making it sometimes challenging to detect or determine the best way to get around them. These gates make grieving more complicated and contribute so much to the unnecessary suffering we experience. Not all gates look the same. As a rule, there are two kinds:

Formal, Obvious, and Permanently Locked

You can see these a mile away. They include the bereavement policy that doesn't include your loss or the religious institution that won't allow you to have a service because it doesn't acknowledge your relationship with the deceased. They are the laws and policies that systems uphold that can literally, emotionally, and psychologically deny your right to grieve.

Informal and Subtle, with the Door Ajar or Unlocked

This form of gatekeeping is run by grief thieves, and they are sneaky. These gatekeepers may or may not be denying your right to grieve at all. They may limit how much grief you're allowed to feel or express—or even the duration. Sometimes it's hard to even notice these gatekeepers are closing the gate. They may express a cliché ("They wouldn't want you to feel bad.") or compare or minimize your pain with sentences that start, "At least . . ." (See "Watch Out for the Grief Thief.")

Sometimes the gatekeeping is even sneakier because it involves nonaction, such as when people don't show up, don't talk about the person, or don't address the loss at all. It's a subtle form of gatekeeping when they don't ask how you're doing or accommodate the situation based on your loss. I've known many people whose parents put away all the pictures of their dead loved one and never talked about them again. That's a quiet inaction that sends a loud message: You don't have the right to grieve.

WHEN THE GATES GET CLOSED

Grief can either be validated and supported or disenfranchised in the wake of any type of loss, but some of the most common scenarios in which your grief might be disenfranchised include:

The Relationship Isn't Valued or Honored

Culturally, some relationships aren't considered as important or meaningful as others. As a result, some losses aren't considered grief-worthy. That can include the death of ex-spouses, extended family members, in-laws, unmarried partners, friends (close, distant, or online-only), and coworkers. Podcast guest Autumn Campbell pointed out one insidious but all too common form: disenfranchisement over the grief of miscarriages and stillbirths.

Pet loss is another commonly disenfranchised loss because the relationship isn't valued. Even people grieving the death of an elder can be disenfranchised when people dismiss the need to be sad because the person lived a long life.

Sometimes it's less about not being valued, and more about a stigmatized relationship. The grief over these losses is frequently denied with more force. This can often include LGBTQ relationships or people involved in affairs. As an anonymous guest on my podcast shared, many people like her felt denied permission to express grief over their abortion because of the stigma surrounding it.

Cause of Death Carries a Stigma

Sometimes grief is denied because of how someone died. When there's social stigma around the cause of death, grief over these losses is often ignored, seen as taboo. This includes death by suicide, accidental alcohol or drug overdose, HIV/AIDS, drunk driving, and while committing a crime or being imprisoned.

Non-Death Losses

In many ways, non-death loss is one of the biggest categories of disenfranchised grief, as too many people still hold a deeply rooted false belief that grief is only valid in cases of death. It's common for people to be denied the right to grieve in cases such as Alzheimer's disease, addiction, traumatic brain injury, mental illness, catastrophic injury, chronic illness, infertility, or adoption. When people are estranged from loved ones because of abuse or neglect, the grief they feel over that absence is ignored. People whose loved ones have been given a terminal diagnosis rightly experience anticipatory grief but are often told that they're wrong for feeling that way.

Losses People Choose

While I believe (and hopefully you do too) that we even have the right to grieve the losses we choose—maturational losses such as leaving home, relationships we chose to end—not everyone feels this way. In our cultural propensity for all-or-nothing thinking, these types of losses are often denied or dismissed with messages such as, "You don't get to complain because you did this to yourself," or, "You shouldn't grieve that. You're better off without them."

Certain Grief Expressions and Behaviors

Sometimes it's not the loss itself that's denied, it's the grievers' right to express their grief in a style that serves them best. As we explore in

"Everyone Is Stylish in Their Own Way," we each have our own style of grieving, and it can cause conflict that can escalate to the level of denying someone agency over their own grief experience.

INDICATORS THAT THE GATES ARE CLOSED

Are the gates closed? Well, for many of us, the disenfranchisement is obvious. The gatekeepers have employed both formal and informal tactics to communicate to us that our grief isn't valid or worthy of attention. We know when the gates are closed because of the lack of social and often systemic validation of the loss itself or the grief we're expressing. That lack of acknowledgment makes us feel unsafe to talk about grief, so we don't. We keep it to ourselves. Lacking support, we feel more isolated and alone, as if we're wrong or abnormal for feeling the way we do.

GATE CODE ALWAYS CHANGES

It feels as if the code to the gate is always changing, even when you're trying to access acknowledgment for the same loss. Depending on the person or institution you're approaching, the timing since the loss, or the behavior you're demonstrating, sometimes the code doesn't work. You may notice this when a friend who previously indicated support through validation and empathy suddenly stops showing up. It might have happened to you when you notice the family changing the subject every time you bring up your deceased pet.

In these times you might be tempted to pick up the mantle of gate-keeper and tell yourself, "I'm too much. My grief is too much." I encourage you to notice when this happens and consider an alternative. Maybe you directly address the friends or family member and ask for their continued acknowledgment. It might mean you find new outlets for support.

IMPACT AND LEGACY

The consequences of gatekeeping grief start with the unnecessary suffering of the individual griever, but it goes well beyond that. The effect and legacy of disenfranchised grief include:

Interrupted Healing

Even when we know it's time to start grieving, it's not that easy. When the world is explicitly and implicitly telling us that we're wrong for feeling certain ways, we can't help but take that in. As a result, we may begin to hide our grief altogether, or just in certain places. Our fear of judgment or of being alienated means that we're less likely to seek the support we need. That's a perfect storm for grief to go unaddressed and result in all types of emotional, psychological, and even relational consequences.

Doors That Lead to More Doors

The pervasiveness of gatekeeping and gatekeepers going unchecked creates a situation where the doors are duplicated. When our boss, our parent, or our friend denies our grief, we suffer. But if we believe the lie that we don't deserve to grieve, we're not the only one who suffers. When we deny our own grief, we often end up closing the gate to others too. "If I can't honor or experience my own pain, you're not allowed to claim yours either."

This happens within families, across friendships, and even plants the seeds for the institutional responses to loss. When we don't see others around us expressing their grief or being supported in grief that's like ours, we begin to believe that our grief isn't valid either and end up gatekeeping ourselves. If we don't attend to or even transform our pain, as priest Richard Rohr explains, "We will most assuredly transmit it—usually to those closest to us: our family, our neighbors, our co-workers, and invariably, the most vulnerable, our children."

Across Generations

The gates that are duplicated don't just stay within our family, friend group, or era that we're experiencing our loss. Disenfranchised grief, if not addressed, has consequences across generations as both the beliefs and the harmful consequences they cause are passed down.

At the cultural level in the US, there are both social and family norms around grief that are often passed down generationally. Sometimes these norms manifest in ceremonies and traditions, but most often they are in the spoken or unspoken expectations and limitations around grief and mourning.

My friend's family has been taught not to cry at funerals. Her grand-mother never cried and once elbowed her mother during a funeral as a signal to stop crying. Her mother quickly learned that crying at a funeral was unacceptable and told her own daughters not to cry before attending their first funeral. Maybe you can think of one or more examples such as these about the norms your family taught you about grief.

There's also growing knowledge around intergenerational grief and trauma, including the way it changes us culturally and genetically (called epigenetics). This subject is profound and important and too extensive to include here. However, if you're an eager learner like me, check out Rachel Yehuda and Resmaa Menakem. They are two of my favorite thinkers and guides.

Disproportionate Application

Anyone can be disenfranchised but as we touched on earlier, there are groups of people and types of losses that are locked out more than others. As a result, they suffer unnecessarily, and the consequences can outlast the suffering of that individual griever or groups of individuals.

The most egregious example of a group of people being denied access to grief in the US is people of color. Their grief over horrific and ongoing losses caused by racism have been consistently and systematically denied. Gaslighting, a tool of grief thieving, and disenfranchisement have been the predominant strategies used.

Historically, people who identify as women have been disproportionately affected. This disenfranchisement continues today. While the losses themselves differ, infertility, abortion, miscarriage, and still-birth are some of the most systematically and culturally disenfranchised losses. Think about it. If you're the next woman to experience one of these losses and you haven't seen or heard from others about their experience or even know what support for grief looks like, you're going to suffer too. Even the 2022 repeal of *Roe v. Wade*, removing a woman's right to bodily autonomy, is a profound loss that many refuse to acknowledge.

In different ways, people who identify as male have also been denied their right to grieve. Sometimes this takes the form of denying the legitimate need to grieve certain losses (e.g., friends, miscarriage, stillbirth). More often it's the enforcement of cultural norms that do damage, including discouraging these men from expressing grief and seeking support. Toxic masculinity in our US culture tells men, "Man up. Don't cry; that's weak." These problematic cultural norms make it more difficult for men to process and express their grief in healthy and helpful ways.

BREAKING DOWN THE GATES

So how do we become a rule breaker for ourselves or someone we care about whose grief is disenfranchised? How do we begin to break down the gates? Whether you do it to feel validated and find support for your grief or on behalf of a friend or family member, there are a few strategies to consider:

Listen To and Believe Them

Brené Brown recently wrote, "We need to dispel the myth that empathy is 'walking in someone else's shoes.' Rather than walking in your shoes, I need to learn how to listen to the story you tell about what it's like in your shoes and believe you even when it doesn't match my experiences."

You don't have to have experienced it too to be able to relate or understand. When grievers tell you their thoughts, feelings, or experiences of grief, listen to believe. Listen without judgment. This is probably the single best action you could take to break the practice of gatekeeping that leads grievers to feel disenfranchised.

Interrupt the Gatekeepers

Throughout this book, we explore a lot of the practices and language used by gatekeepers to disenfranchise grief. One way to support others whose grief is being denied is by interrupting the people guarding the gates. When you hear something or notice actions that deny the right of grievers to express their grief in their own way, interrupt it.

This might sound like, "Mom, I just heard you tell my sister that she shouldn't talk about her miscarriage so much because it makes others uncomfortable. When you do that, you're telling her that she doesn't have a right to grieve the loss the way she needs to, and that's harmful." As we will explore, interruption is a skill we need to develop to combat the times we're disenfranchising our *own* grief.

Lead By Example

We all carry cultural and family norms of grief, and we teach them to others in subtle and direct ways throughout our lives. Through our actions and words, we are modeling grief, so that means we have a choice to uphold or change the norms we inhabit.

One of the most powerful things you can do to dismantle the practice of disenfranchisement is to lead by example. This can include the interruption strategies we just discussed or showing up and listening to believe the friends, family members, and coworkers who trust you to hear their story.

This can also include talking about and inhabiting your own grief differently with others. You might notice that you diminish or shy away from accepting support or from talking about the difficulty you're experiencing as a way of gatekeeping your own grief. Interrupting your own gatekeeping practices by accepting help or confiding in friends about the realities and complexities of your grief gives them permission to do the same with their grief. By claiming and acknowledging your own right to grief and grief expression with others, you're leading by example, helping create a more grief-literate world where no one is excluded.

⚜ AN INVITATION FOR YOU ⚜

discover the gates in your grief

Whether our grief is denied outright or in smaller, more subtle ways, we all experience disenfranchisement. The tricky thing is that we often don't see how, when, or why we're trapped behind the gates. I invite you to discover the gates in your grief so that you can consider how to take them down. Take some time to identify at least one example of gatekeeping in your own grief and one way you might interrupt or dismiss others' attempts at disenfranchisement.

An interpersonal gatekeeper might sound like, "I notice that every time my brother sees me crying or talking emotionally about my girlfriend who died, he tells me, 'Man up, dude, and move on. There's plenty of girls out there.'" An interruption strategy might sound like, "What I need when I'm upset is for you to acknowledge how much this sucks, not try to talk me out of feeling this way or offer me solutions to get over her." This exercise to examine how you might gatekeep yourself is perfect for what we explore next, in "Watch Out for the Grief Thief."

One way I notice that [culture and media, myself, institutions, or someone in my personal life] are gatekeeping my grief is:

One strategy I can use to try to interrupt this is:

pitfalls and hazards

identifying the grief thief and other speed bumps when navigating loss

watch out
for the grief thief

WHO WANTS TO STEAL GRIEF?

Who would even want to steal grief? Um, no thanks. Don't want it. You can keep it.

What the "grief thief" is really stealing is your grief support. Grief thieves are those who stealthily (and sometimes clumsily) shift the focus, conversation, and sense of support from you to them in an instant. Some are bold, daylight bank robbers and others are everyday pickpockets. Are they doing it on purpose? Maybe. But most often, they're not. Are they doing it because they didn't get enough support for their loss? Possibly.

SIGNS THAT YOU'RE BEING ROBBED

How do you know when you've been robbed? Sometimes the signs are obvious: You see it happen in front of your own eyes. Other times you are pickpocketed and don't even notice. Only later do you realize you feel emptier from the encounter.

Below are some telltale signs that a grief thief is on the prowl. In response to you sharing something about your grief (or sometimes before you've even finished a sentence), you hear:

"The same thing happened to me."

"I know exactly how you feel."

"That reminds me of my friend/neighbor/co-worker/cousin . . ."

"Oh my god, that's just like the time . . ."
"They wouldn't want you to be/feel/say . . ."
Any sentence that starts with "At least . . ."

Regardless of the thief's intention, the consequence is the same. You leave the encounter with less instead of more. You no longer feel seen and held in your grief. You lose a bit of trust and confidence in this person's ability to support you. Your emotional energy is drained instead of recharged. And now you (and maybe others present) are attending to the thief's grief instead of yours.

Another way to discover if your grief has been stolen is to assess how you feel after the interaction. Ask yourself, "Do I feel emptier or enriched from that conversation? Did I feel heard and understood or ignored? Did I get a chance to speak about what was on my mind and in my heart or was the conversation shifted away?" If you walked away feeling emptier, ignored, or denied the chance to speak, you've likely been robbed.

BEWARE OF OTHER CONS AND SHAMS

Sometimes the harm of grief thievery isn't so obvious as the examples listed above. Whether robbed by others or ourselves, there are cons and shams to watch for. These subtler crimes still might leave you feeling emptier and less able to hold your grief the way you need to.

Running the Gratitude Con

Are you thinking, "Isn't gratitude a good thing?" Yes, gratitude is a good thing. It's actually a great thing. That's true not just because it sounds morally appealing. There's a lot of research that backs up its value.

A 2021 article on the Harvard Health Publishing website reported that "in positive psychology research, gratitude is strongly and consistently associated with greater happiness. Gratitude helps people feel more positive emotions, relish good experiences, improve their health, deal with adversity, and build strong relationships."

I can practically hear an audible sigh of relief coming from you. Yes, an attitude of gratitude can be extremely powerful and healing. I incorporated a daily gratitude practice years ago and it's one of my most useful tools for my well-being. Gratitude is necessary, yes. And it's not sufficient on its own, especially in the early phase of grief. The approach of "all you need is an attitude of gratitude and you'll be fine" excludes the reality that you can be both grateful for some things and deeply sorrowful, disconnected, or even angry about them too.

The gratitude con can steal your belief that your feelings are valid or have you deny that you have those feelings in the first place. Forced gratitude can stifle your willingness to reach out for help. It can interfere with the learning you need in order to live into your emerging story. So yes, gratitude is great, *and* be careful that it doesn't steal your need to own and claim your grief in a way that serves you.

Yet there are valid reasons that you're having a hard time accessing positivity. Remember, our brains are wired to be on the lookout for danger, and what you've just experienced was exactly that: emotionally dangerous. So if in your grief you see a "Good Vibes Only" sign and want to tear it down and stomp on it, that's totally normal.

The Toxic Positivity Sham

Having a positive mindset has proven to be helpful to our emotional and mental well-being. It's used a lot in the literature of workplace success and achievement too. Yet there are valid reasons that you're having a hard time accessing positivity. Remember, our brains are wired to be on the lookout for danger, and what you've just experienced was exactly that: emotionally dangerous. So if in your grief you see a "Good Vibes Only" sign and want to tear it down and stomp on it, that's totally normal.

Like the gratitude con, the toxic positivity sham is deeply rooted in our cultural narratives. Toxic positivity is a shallow response to someone's display of pain, offering false reassurance instead of responding with empathy and compassion. The reason people run this sham is because of their own discomfort with sitting with negative or difficult emotions.

Again, like the gratitude con, the toxic positivity sham offers a false choice. In this instance, toxic positivity says, "Be positive and happy or be stuck in your grief. Pick one." Heartache and pain aren't choices. They aren't signs of moral failure. They're normal responses to loss. Just like all emotions, they aren't limited nor are they mutually exclusive. There are times when we can hold both. Forcing positivity at the expense of feeling and honoring other thoughts and feelings is unnecessary and harmful. Hold on to positivity when it serves you, but don't let it con you out of your other possessions.

The Gaslighting Sham

Gaslighting isn't just a tool of narcissists; anyone can run this scam under the guise of grief support. According to *Merriam-Webster's* dictionary, gaslighting is a "psychological manipulation of a person usually over an extended period of time that causes the victim to question the validity of their own thoughts, perception of reality, or memories and typically leads to confusion, loss of confidence and self-esteem, uncertainty of one's emotional or mental stability, and a dependency on the perpetrator."

Gaslighting is such a stealthy crime, a strategy of psychological manipulation that makes you question your own value, way of thinking, and ability to care for yourself.

Gaslighting can include a range of tactics. Especially in grief, this includes distracting, denying, minimizing, and even sometimes blaming. Some telltale signs that someone is gaslighting you as you grieve include phrases such as:

"You're making a big deal over nothing."

"You're too sensitive."

"You're overreacting."

To determine if someone is gaslighting you, pay more attention to what they do and how they make you feel than to the words they say.

Some ways to get out of the scam include seeking perspective from others by sharing what was said and how it made you feel. You can also practice strategies to gain self-love, such as a loving-kindness meditation. If you sense that the person is not saying these things purposefully, try shining a spotlight on the crime. "Hey, when you said this, I felt gaslit and left feeling worse about myself instead of better." However, if there's anything other than full accountability and a change in behavior going forward, cut off or at least minimize communication with this person. This is a great place to practice setting a boundary.

THE PROBLEM WITH THE LINEUP

In grief, comparison can be criminal behavior too. Yet it happens all the time. We often put grievers in a metaphorical lineup. Picture those lineups you see on television and in movies: "Turn to the right. Turn to the left. Where were you? What happened the night of . . . ?" And then we compare and evaluate their stories. We judge to see who's guilty or, in this metaphor, who gets to claim the title of "Most Grief Worthy." Everyone else is dismissed and any attention is considered stolen from the grieving one.

The lineup scenario doesn't just happen in grief. We hold an all-or-nothing and be-the-best mentality in virtually every arena of our lives. We live in a time and place where we have awards for everything: Most This or That, Top 10 Yada Yada Yada, Best Blah Blah Blah. We're obsessed with superlatives. We think they're the absolute best. See what I did there? But seriously, this "winner takes all" thinking is the perfect environment to create a grief thief. You and I live in this land of comparisons too, so the danger of being robbed isn't just from others.

WATCH OUT FOR THE THIEF IN THE MIRROR

On a regular basis I find myself telling clients, "Don't worry, there's enough grief for everyone." In my role as a grief activist, I feel as if I need to be Oprah Winfrey sometimes, shouting, "You get a grief! And you get a grief! And you get a grief!" Though grief is not as fun as the cars Oprah gave away, sometimes I feel it's necessary to remind people that our cultural grief avoidance makes us think that there is a limited supply of grief. As a result, we end up hoarding it or stealing it from others.

In a recent session, a client explored the grief he was experiencing over his divorce. He said a few phrases that might sound familiar to you: "Well, it's not like what my friend whose husband died had to deal with. I'm the one who left, so my wife deserves the support from our friends, not me." He went on to diminish his grief by adding, "I can't ask my neighbors for help. They have problems of their own." He was his own grief thief.

Do these descriptions sound familiar? If you look in the mirror, do you find a grief thief there sometimes? I do. Honestly, even though I'm the one writing this book, I'm still my own grief thief from time to time. It's insidious.

I'M GOOD, IT'S FINE, AND OTHER LIES THAT COME AT A COST

When we feel as if we're drowning in grief but say, "I'm good," we think we're protecting ourselves from feeling the pain or experiencing the resulting awkwardness. We answer, "It's fine," believing that we're saving others from the burden of holding the truth that we, in fact, are not fine.

The little lies we tell ourselves and others aren't a shield that keeps us safe. They rob us. We miss out on the relief that expressing an emotion can offer us. We damage our connection to our authentic self. We lose out on the chance to be witnessed. We give up the chance to receive support. We rob other people of the chance to feel helpful too. While there are obviously situations where it's appropriate and efficient to not "tell the truth, the whole truth, and nothing but the truth," be careful that it doesn't become such a habit that you miss out on the richness of the grief support you deserve.

SHARING THE GOODS

In case you're worried that I'm the most cynical person on earth, I'm here to say that there are lots of occasions when bringing up similarities, sharing stories, comparing, and offering words of perspective are valuable. Sharing the goods can feel good. Some of the most helpful and supportive conversations I have are with fellow grievers. (See "Who's Got Your Back?")

That's been true even with people who've experienced very different types of losses than me. My best friend's son died nearly a decade before I met her. She experienced a full-term stillbirth. I laid with my forty-four-year-old husband when he died. Very different experiences and timing, to say the least. Yet our conversations about grief are the most meaningful and helpful I have had with anyone. It's affirming to hear other grievers admit to feeling certain ways or having similar thoughts. It's nice to feel less alone when they say things such as "OMG, the same thing happened to me when I went back to work." I also learn tips, tricks, and strategies for navigating grief from fellow grievers (and am more open to learning from them than from others).

DETERMINING WHEN IT'S NOT A CRIME

So when is the right time to share and compare? When is it not taking but giving? How can you decide when it's not a crime, when you won't end up being a grief thief? Keep the following five things in mind when deciding if the time is right.

Comfort In, Dump Out

Ring Theory by Susan Silk and Barry Goldman is a helpful tool to keep in mind when you're grieving over the same loss. In your mind, draw a series of concentric rings. Place yourself and this other person in the layers based on the proximity to the center of the loss. If you're farther out, be careful of sharing or complaining about your pain to this person.

The best approach? Offer comfort in, toward people closer to the center of the circle, and dump your own feelings out, to people on the outer layers. Don't make the primary griever support you. If you're the significant other of the primary griever (maybe a parent died), offer comfort in, to your partner. Then because you likely have your own grief or intense feelings watching your partner grieve, make sure you process that with someone further out, such as a colleague or friend.

Assess Timing and Perspective

One important consideration is the difference in length of time since the loss. As you're likely experiencing, perspectives and needs change as time passes. It might be that a large gap between the recency of your respective losses makes sharing and comparing feel unhelpful or even harmful. Like everything, there are no absolutes, of course. Sometimes it can be helpful in early grief to hear from someone further down the road. I've certainly experienced that. Just make sure you consider the length of time since the loss before you proceed.

If you're in conversation with someone whose spouse died two months ago and you lost your partner ten years ago, be cautious of doing too much relating or interjecting at first. After the person shares, you might say something such as, "I hate that you're going through this too. I know everything is all so new and probably feels so confusing. It's been ten years for me. Let me know how I can help, even if that's giving you some perspective from down the road."

Start With Acknowledging and Affirming

Starting a conversation by ignoring someone's experience is the best way to ensure that you've become a grief thief. So always start with acknowledging and affirming what the person just shared. And don't do it in a perfunctory way so that you can hurry up to share. Offer it up and pause. This may be the first time someone affirmed the person, and it might open a willingness and need to share more. You might say something such as, "I'm sorry to hear that you're struggling with sleep. I can imagine that's normal in grief, but that sure doesn't make it easy."

Check In

I might seem like Captain Obvious here, but I recommend you check in and ask before you share. You might ask the person if it's OK for you to share a similar experience you had or ask if it would be helpful to hear what you learned from it. As always, start with acknowledging first. This might sound like, "I'm sorry that happened to you. I had something similar happen and I wonder if it's OK or would be helpful to share."

Share, Don't Judge

Just because you felt a certain way or tried a strategy that worked (or didn't), that doesn't mean the same will be true for the other person.

Be on the lookout for direct or indirect messages of judgment. When you're sharing your experience, be mindful, ensuring that the other person understands that it's OK to feel differently. I prefer language such as, "I don't know if you've found this . . ." or "This might not be the case for you, but I liked when . . ."

THE BEST DETERRENT

So much of the unnecessary suffering we experience in grief is caused when grief supporters enlist the thief tactics mentioned earlier. Holding space and bearing witness ensures that you won't be a grief thief. I've held a sustained meditation on this topic for decades. (See "Who's Got Your Back?") Recently, soul sister Autumn Campbell shared her definition of holding space and bearing witness, and it was so beautiful that I wanted to offer it to you. She says:

"Instead, what our grief, pain, rage, and trauma needs is a practice called Holding Space. Holding Space helps us provide close, quiet, active empathy. When someone shares their story with us, we can act as Witness: we listen deeply, we do not share our own feelings or stories, we simply create an environment that nurtures and protects the uninterrupted time that our friend, family member, colleague, etc. needs to share their story and feel seen, valued, and understood."
—Autumn Campbell

I offer some dos and don'ts for supporting a griever in appendix B. Feel free to share it with the grief supporters in your life. Oh, and one other note on this topic: This chapter includes examples of suffering that happen because of grief thieves, when someone's loss is otherwise recognized as valid. A more insidious version of this is disenfranchised grief, something we explore in "Access Denied."

⚰ AN INVITATION FOR YOU ⚱

look out for the grief thief in the mirror

Unfortunately, some of the most harmful effects of this crime are self-inflicted. It can be hard to recognize when we're stealing from ourselves versus when we're trying to practice gratitude, have perspective, and work toward making meaning. The truth is, it's not always clear. So like the invitation in "*Should* Is a Dirty Word (and Not the Swearing Kind)," spend some time investigating your language—both how you talk to yourself about your grief and how you talk to others about your grief—and see if you sound like a grief thief.

Remember to practice noticing and not judging. Many of us are prone to negating our own hardships, so like so many things in life, it will take practice to replace the grief thief habit. Get specific and write down recent examples in your journal. Make sure to capture the ways you validate yourself too. Your answers can be useful for reflection with a therapist or grief guide or to revisit down the road to see where you were and where you are now.

---

self-talk about my grief

Negating ("At least . . ."; "I shouldn't complain because . . .")

Comparing ("But they have it worse because . . .")

Affirming ("It makes sense that I feel this way")

Reflective ("I'm grateful for . . ."; "I've learned that . . .")

talking to others about my grief

Negating ("At least . . ."; "I shouldn't complain because . . .")

Comparing ("But they have it worse because . . .")

Affirming ("It makes sense that I feel this way")

Reflective ("I'm grateful for . . ."; "I've learned that . . .")

there is no grief GPS

I'D PAY GOOD MONEY FOR A GRIEF GPS, WOULDN'T YOU?
I've looked everywhere. I've read the books, the blogs, and the articles. Listened to the podcasts (and even created one of my own). I've scoured Google. I've done the research. And what I discovered is that a grief GPS, like the legend of Bigfoot, is a myth. That's too bad for so many reasons, not the least of which is that I would follow Morgan Freeman's voice anywhere (because . . . you know . . . Morgan Freeman's voice). Like you, I would've paid good money for a GPS system to help me navigate this dizzying, scary rollercoaster ride of grief.

I know from firsthand experience that the myth of the perfect GPS-guided route is likely making your real-life experiences of off-roading through the challenging terrain of grief feel as if you're making one terrible mistake after another. You might find yourself thinking, "Why am I so lost? Didn't I already pass this spot?" Or, "I thought I had it figured out but now I don't know." You may have even said, "X person seems to know what to do and where to go. Why am I the only one who's lost?" Gentle reminder: You don't know what's really going on for X person. More importantly, there is no one right route. Period.

Gentle reminder: You don't know what's really going on for X person. More importantly, there is no one right route.

Still, I know you may be hanging on to some doubt because the myth is so pervasive that it feels as if it could possibly be true. That sliver of doubt is likely causing you a lot of insecurity and self-judgment. One way to ditch this myth is to remember that grief came long before GPS was invented, and our species navigated the journey just fine (if not messily) without it. What has always been there? Other people.

NO GPS? NO PROBLEM. GUIDES CAN BE HELPFUL TOO (OR NOT)

Have you ever bumped into someone in your grief who, without first listening, launches into saying something such as, "The thing that I did that you should do is (fill in the blank)"?

Oh, I bet you have. I'm not sure I've met a grieving person who hasn't. First, bless them for trying (said in a thick and sweet Southern accent). Second, please fuck off.

Before you write everyone off, though, let me clarify something. Sometimes listening to and learning from fellow grievers can be exactly the guidance you need in that moment. Sometimes asking for directions from fellow travelers, ones who may be a bit farther down the road, can be helpful. They can point out when the shoulds of grief are getting in the way. (See "*Should* Is a Dirty Word [and Not the Swearing Kind].") And if some of those fellow travelers are British, they can help you tell those shoulds to "bugger off" (because everything is better with a British accent).

You can learn from their missteps, wrong turns, and dead ends too. You can take advantage of the hard-won wisdom they've gained from the places they've already been, the gear they brought with them, and the people they met along the way. They're what I call our grief guides.

I've learned a lot from the guides in my life, many of whom have experienced very different losses than my own but still found a way to accompany me, gently guiding me back on course and encouraging me along the way. Some guides are close friends; many were once strangers, guests on my podcast. And some are the artists, writers, philosophers, and poets who I will likely never meet. I share some of their wisdom throughout this book.

So even if someone can't be your guide or can't really offer advice or specific directions (only useless tidbits such as, "Turn left once you go down the road a bit, right after you see the big old oak tree."), it doesn't mean that the person can't support you in a meaningful way. To be accompanied on this road—to know that someone is there to witness you, to watch you, to maybe even help carry the weight of your pack sometimes—is truly one of the most valuable gifts you can receive. Do you want to know something surprising (that you may not believe yet)? Letting others help you is a gift for them too. Truly. (See "Your Turn to Buddy-Breathe.")

FEELING LOST AND HOMESICK

Homesickness is a quality of grief that is too often ignored. For many of us, the losses we experienced were the people who made us feel at home, no matter where we were. They may have been members of our family of origin or those in our chosen family. Or maybe our treasured pet, our physical home, or even our homeland. We may feel homesick when our person is still physically present but gone in some way, as in the case of ambiguous losses such as dementia or addiction. We can even feel homesick for a place or relationship we never had, as in the case of adoption.

Regardless, navigating the world without their presence may cause you to feel as if you're in a perpetual state of homesickness, a longing to return to a real or imagined sense of home. I know what an unsettling sensation that is, but I think it's made more difficult when we don't name it. How do you know if that's what you're feeling? Well, it may show up as feeling anxious. Maybe you're experiencing feelings of restlessness and you find yourself pacing and perhaps wandering into rooms only to discover that's not where you wanted or were meant to be. It might feel like yearning and longing or a feeling in your environment or in your body.

In the "Now What?" section of this book, part of what I share is that some day in the not-too-distant future, you will stumble upon moments of feeling at home. That might be a relief, and it might quickly be followed by confusion or even guilt. Then somewhere further down the road, you'll feel more at home than lost most days. Although it may be hard to believe right now, some day you may even feel mostly at home wherever you are.

Don't worry, this isn't the "everything happens for a reason" BS. It's just the nature of our lives as we continue rewriting and living into our emerging story. As a result of new experiences, new connections, hard work, healing, resting, and feeling all the feels, we find ourselves somewhere that feels like home.

Regardless, navigating the world without their presence may cause you to feel as if you're in a perpetual state of homesickness, a longing to return to a real or imagined sense of home.

But at the risk of repeating myself, every grief journey is unique, even the various ones you will take over the course of your lifetime. This means that the vehicles you travel in, the directions you take, the gear you need, and the stops you make along the way to the place that resembles home might look a little bit (or a lot a bit) different for you. Ugh. No GPS. So what we're left with is being open to the questions.

FOCUS ON THE QUESTIONS, NOT THE ANSWERS
Focusing on the questions instead of insisting on the answers is hard. Really freaking hard. Finding some level of grace and peace when we feel lost is so difficult for us—both at a physiological and nervous system level and at the cultural level. At the nervous system level, we're wired neurobiologically to find answers to keep us safe. (See "Your Body Knows.") In Western culture, we're inundated with expert culture and the emphasis that there is a single answer if only we try harder or work smarter.

Those two things mean we don't have a lot of practice being open to questions, so of course we suck at it. For one thing, it takes vulnerability, something that very few of us are comfortable experiencing, let alone expressing. We strive to have answers while being resistant to ask questions. But how else will we learn?

I consider the poet Rainer Maria Rilke one of my grief guides. Early on in my grief, I stumbled upon these words in his book *Letters to a Young Poet*. He wrote, "And the point is, to live everything. Live the questions now. Perhaps you will then gradually, without noticing it, live along some distant day into the answer."

And the point is, to live everything. Live the questions now. Perhaps you will then gradually, without noticing it, live along some distant day into the answer.
—Rainer Maria Rilke, Letters to a Young Poet

To be completely honest, at first Rilke's words made me angry. I found myself thinking things such as, "Easy for you to say, dude." Soon after, I found myself repeatedly returning to these words. Like the wisdom of starting close in from David Whyte, this invitation to live into the questions and let the answers emerge took some pressure off me to hurry up and "get better" or "do better at grief," which is something that consumed me for some time, especially as a mental health "expert." I wonder if you feel that way too sometimes.

We all have different questions, depending on our loss, our circumstances, our history. To offer you an example, a question that came up for me, one that haunted me at first, was "How am I going to raise our daughter on my own?" I wonder what questions are beneath the surface for you.

⚓ AN INVITATION FOR YOU ⚓

live into the questions

I invite you to take a moment to read and then reread the words of Rilke and see what they offer you. It's OK if, like me, you want to cuss at first. If that's all you can or want to do now, that's OK. Maybe sticky note, highlight, or dog-ear this page to return to later. If you're ready for something else, you might also try one or both of the exercises below.

share the question with someone you trust

After you've done the above and found maybe a bit of peace or ease while sitting with the question, find someone you trust to share the question with. Make sure to explain that you don't need answers, that you need someone else to hold the question with you for a while. This is important because all of us, especially the people who love us the most, desperately want to fix us.

Try saying the question out loud. Allow yourself to be, to feel, and to say what comes up. Remind yourself (and this person) that you're not looking for answers at the end, you're simply making space for ideas, feelings, and experiences to unfold. The person's job is to witness you and to help you feel safe and loved.

be with the first question that comes to you

In your journal, write down the first question that comes to you. Then sit with the question. Notice what you feel in your body. Notice where your mind goes. Likely your mind will begin immediately searching for the answer. That's normal. Instead of judging yourself for searching for an answer, practice noticing that your mind is traveling toward the answers and make a U-turn. Return to the question. Maybe even say it out loud to yourself.

See if you can take some deep breaths, inhaling deeply, exhaling slowly. Explore what it would feel like to make peace with the question and with the fact that for now, you might not have an answer.

ambiguity s-u-c-k-s

UNCLEAR IS MORE THAN JUST UNKIND

Ambiguity is defined as the potential to have more than one meaning or explanation. Synonyms for the adjective form, *ambiguous*, include *inexact, uncertain, indefinite, unclear,* and *confusing*—all words that make me queasy to my core. How about you? And like the word *complicated, ambiguous* is a spot-on way to describe what grieving feels like.

When we face the unknown, the unexplored terrain that is life after loss, we desperately seek certainty. Ambiguity feels like our enemy. We crave anything to help us scaffold back together a story of our lives that makes sense. We reach for checklists, top 10 lists—anything to bring order to the chaos of our lives.

There are a lot of psychological, physiological, and evolutionary reasons why we're not fans of ambiguity. In a nutshell, it's because humans are storytelling creatures and need coherent stories to feel safe, which can make uncertainty and lack of clarity feel scary (and even dangerous).

That's why you're not alone in thinking that ambiguity sucks. Say it with me: "Ambiguity sucks." It really helps if you elongate *s-u-c-k-s* while yelling as loud as you can. If you want to throw an expletive in the middle there, you know I support that too. Go ahead, yell it out. I'll wait.

Am I right? It's kind of cathartic.

TYPES OF AMBIGUOUS LOSS

There's the ambiguity all grievers experience and then there's something called "ambiguous loss." Starting in the '90s, Pauline Boss, the principal theorist behind ambiguous loss, was seeking to understand and clarify a unique set of losses that create a unique set of challenges for grievers. Ambiguous loss happens, Boss explains, when "there is no verification of death or no certainty their person will come back or return to the way they used to be."

As covered in "Of Course It's Complicated," ambiguous losses, which are primarily not deaths, make the grieving process more complex. This type of loss stifles and sometimes freezes our ability to move through grief. The ambiguous nature of the loss also increases the chance for it to go unrecognized by others (and sometimes by ourselves). Boss describes two main types: a loss that happens when the person is physically absent but psychologically present or when the person is psychologically absent but physically present.

Physically Absent, Psychologically Present

You might have experienced this type of loss and not acknowledged that it was a loss you could grieve. This often includes divorce, adoption, physical estrangement due to a poor relationship, distance due to immigration, or military deployment.

More catastrophic forms of this type of loss include disappeared and missing people due to kidnapping, war, terrorism, or natural disasters. Depending on the circumstances, the physical absence may also be a result of a struggle with addiction or mental illness (e.g., depression, PTSD) where the person's presence may fluctuate, creating even more ambiguity.

Physically Present, Psychologically Absent

The second type of ambiguous loss is one many of us have experienced—or will—in which a person is alive, maybe in our day-to-day physical presence, but psychologically, cognitively, or emotionally absent. That includes having loved ones with the symptoms of dementia or Alzheimer's disease.

Other examples include the losses we experience when someone in our lives is struggling with addiction, traumatic brain injury, or significant and untreated mental illness. Though I didn't name it as ambiguous loss at the time, I experienced this the year prior to Eric's death when he became physically, psychologically, emotionally, and behaviorally unrecognizable.

OTHER AMBIGUOUS LOSSES

There are other ambiguous losses that haven't traditionally been included as examples in the above definitions but that pose similar challenges. These include experiences that cause losses to our sense of certainty, control, safety, freedom to act, and even to our understanding of ourselves and the world around us. They're often disenfranchised too. (See "Access Denied.") We experience these losses as ambiguous both when they happen to us—to our bodies—and when they happen to those we love.

Chronic and Life-Threatening Illnesses

Chronic and life-threatening illnesses such as cancer, lupus, amyotrophic lateral sclerosis (ALS), multiple sclerosis (MS), muscular dystrophies (MD), Lyme disease, and Parkinson's disease can profoundly impact an individual's quality of life. In these instances, loss of abilities, agency, freedom from pain, and freedom of movement can cause the person to lose the sense of self and often causes disruption or loss of employment and relationships. Given the uncertainty around the course of the illness, presence and intensity of symptoms, and the possibility of recovery, the ambiguity is profoundly impactful.

Catastrophic and Life-Limiting Accidents

Catastrophic and life-limiting accidents include sports-ending injuries, paraplegia, quadriplegia, blindness, loss of hearing, and other impairments. Though unique, each condition creates significant uncertainty and ambiguity about the body's future capacity, ability, mobility, freedom, and sense of agency.

Traumatic Events

For people who've experienced trauma as the result of events such as human trafficking, abuse and neglect, sexual assault, war, terrorism, and all manner of violent crimes, the losses are profound. They can include losing a sense of self; emotional, physical, and psychological safety; trust in others; an ability to self-regulate; and more. The ambiguity of these losses comes from the uncertainty around if or when these abilities can and will be regained. It can also result in a cascading series of other losses, such as relationships and jobs. (See "Secondary Losses: The Sneakiest Bitches of Them All.")

Death Without Answers

For those whose loved ones died without any clear cause, the ambiguity is profound. Even though there's certainty around the death, there remains confusion, uncertainty, and lack of understanding of the reason. These can include death by suicide, infant death, violent death, and other accidental or unexplained deaths.

STRUGGLING WITH MASTERY

In the context of grief, the notion of mastery isn't about control as we might think of the word. It's about gaining skills, competency, literacy, and understanding—essentially what we're doing as we grieve and move toward building a coherent new narrative of our lives in the wake of loss.

There's no competition in grief. Remember, as I mention in "Watch Out for the Grief Thief," there's plenty of grief for everyone. Yet Boss observed, "The greater the ambiguity surrounding one's loss, the more difficult it is to master it and the greater one's depression, anxiety, and family conflict."

If you're experiencing ambiguous loss—perhaps the disappearance of a loved one—you'll likely recognize some of the reasons, as Boss explains, why mastery is challenging:

1. We're uncertain if the current situation is temporary or final, so we struggle to problem-solve or to know when or where to start.

2. We struggle to know how, where, or when to adjust our roles and responsibilities because of the uncertainty surrounding the permanence of the situation.

3. There's rarely any ritual or support like those traditionally offered in the wake of death losses.

4. For many would-be supporters, these types of losses are reminders that life isn't always fair or predictable, and people tend to withdraw support (as if it's contagious).

Ambiguous losses add an additional layer of difficulty because we struggle to identify some basic facts, find certainty, or understand how the little information we do have will influence the future of our story. For many of us who experience this type of loss, we find ourselves having writer's block, even somewhat frozen in grief.

THE MYTH OF CLOSURE

Closure, defined as finality, is useful when you're finishing a baseball game or completing a medical procedure. It's less helpful, and in many ways a harmful expectation, when it comes to any type of loss. The expectation of closure is exceptionally harmful when it comes to ambiguous losses.

Grieving these types of losses requires learning in a different way. It's about bearing the grief, and to do that, Boss offers six nonsequential guidelines:

1. Make meaning out of loss.
2. Relinquish one's desire to control an uncontrollable situation.
3. Recreate identity after loss.
4. Become accustomed to ambivalent feelings.
5. Redefine one's relationship with whatever or whomever has been lost.
6. Find new hope.

In "There Is No Grief GPS," I invite you to practice "being with the questions." In the case of ambiguous loss, Boss similarly focuses on this, suggesting that our focus is best placed on the question of how to live with the loss.

SIMILARITY TO TRAUMA

For many with ambiguous losses, the experience can be traumatizing due to the ongoing nature of the loss. Though not the same as PTSD, some of the physical and psychological responses can be similar, including depression, anxiety, guilt, psychic numbing, flashbacks, and distressing dreams.

Support for ambiguous loss is relational because the rupture, or loss, is a broken attachment. This differs from traditional trauma support, where the goal is to return the individual to health. By the way, this isn't meant to be diagnostic. If you're feeling overwhelmed and distressed—ignored by yourself or others because your loss isn't a death loss—know that I see you. You've endured a difficult ambiguous loss and your body and mind are doing their best to respond to an extraordinary situation.

Having a grief guide, or more than one, is beneficial regardless of the type of loss you've faced. I've had many guides along the way. Given the uniqueness and challenges of ambiguous loss, I encourage you to consider seeking support from a provider who has experience working with individuals and families facing these types of losses. They can be particularly helpful in guiding you through the steps required for your healing.

⤙ AN INVITATION FOR YOU ⤚

*reconnect with the certainty of love**

Experiencing ambiguous loss, or any level of ambiguity that grief brings, means that we're steeped in uncertainty. In this place, it can be challenging to feel connected to anything, to any idea, even to ourselves. What poets, philosophers, artists, and thinkers all agree on is that we are hardwired to love. We are love, even when we can't see it or feel it. So amid ambiguity, I invite you to reconnect with the certainty of love.

If you'd prefer to be guided, I've got you covered. Scan the QR code with your phone and you'll be taken to a guided meditation for Certainty of Love that I recorded just for you.

If you'd like to guide yourself for the next few minutes through a meditation, I offer the mantras on the next page from my Certainty of Love meditation along with a few simple instructions.

I invite you to get into a position that is most comfortable for your body, where you feel held and supported. Since you'll be reading, this will be an eye-open meditation. Spend a few moments taking some easy breaths in and slow breaths out. If possible, place one hand on your heart. You may read these words out loud or to yourself. I encourage you to inhale deeply and exhale slowly in between each line to seal these words in your heart. When you're done, you can spend a few moments with your hand over your heart. Be with yourself with love and compassion.

*A note for trauma survivors or those with trauma symptoms. While mindfulness meditation can be beneficial, for some the intensity and request to focus or close the eyes can exacerbate symptoms. Some adjustments to consider are keeping your eyes open, taking breaks when you need to, and maybe even having a visual anchor in the room to ground you in the present.

certainty of love meditation

When despair clouds my vision,
may I see love, feel love, radiate love, receive love.

When fear immobilizes my body,
may I see love, feel love, radiate love, receive love.

When loneliness seeps into my joints,
may I see love, feel love, radiate love, receive love.

When anger constricts my heart,
may I see love, feel love, radiate love, receive love.

When joy brightens my day,
may I see love, feel love, radiate love, receive love.

When delight dazzles my senses,
may I see love, feel love, radiate love, receive love.

When hope swells my heart,
may I see love, feel love, radiate love, receive love.

When amazement leaves me breathless,
may I see love, feel love, radiate love, receive love.

May I see love, may I feel love,
may I radiate love, may I receive love.

should is a dirty word (and not the swearing kind)

DIRTY WORDS (AND NOT THE SWEARING KIND)

By now, you know how much I love a good expletive from time to time—well, frequently. Who am I kidding?

I stand with my earlier argument that using curse words is not only fun but can also be therapeutically valuable. So it may come as a surprise to learn that there are two dirty words I absolutely detest. I work diligently to remove them from my vocabulary and encourage everyone I know to drop them from theirs, especially when referring to their grieving process.

The word *should* indicates obligation, duty, or correctness, typically when criticizing someone's actions. Of course, this word is useful in various life circumstances. It can help keep us safe, as in, "I shouldn't touch the hot stove," and it helps us act on agreed-upon moral responsibilities, "I should check on my elderly neighbor who I saw fall down."

Given that this definition features the words *obligation, duty, correctness*, and *criticism*, we can see how using the words *should* and *shouldn't* in reference to grieving is the opposite of therapeutic. These words are toxic and detrimental to our healing.

When we use these words, we are incorrectly supporting the myth that there is a single right way to grieve. Each time we use them we're reinforcing the belief that we have a moral obligation to think, feel, or behave a certain way for others. The consequence of these incorrect assumptions is contagious and dangerous, as it's also grounds for us to judge and criticize others for their performance of grief.

Given that this definition features the words obligation, duty, correctness, and criticism, we can see how using the words should and shouldn't in reference to grieving is the opposite of therapeutic. These words are toxic and detrimental to our healing.

OUR GRIEF BELIEFS IN ACTION

Using *should* and *shouldn't* signals that we believe some thought, feeling, or action has a generally agreed upon value (good or bad). Every time we say these words, we're also asking ourselves to change or adapt our feelings and behavior connected to this belief for the sake of others or as a sign that we are worthy of belonging.

MOST COMMON AND HARMFUL TOOL OF THE GRIEF THIEF

In "Watch Out for the Grief Thief," I expose all the tactics and strategies of the grief thief, including the should words and where we learned to run these cons. I think the shoulds are the most common and harmful tool of the grief thief, which is why I dedicated an entire chapter to our use of the words. It's the explicit and implicit way shoulds operate that make them so common and so very dangerous to our well-being in grief.

The Explicit and Obvious S

Just like the other tactics of the grief thief, the use of the shoulds can be explicit. This includes the words being spoken out loud to you about the appropriateness or inappropriateness of your thoughts, feelings, or behaviors in grief.

They don't need to be spoken to be plainly heard. Oftentimes, the behavioral responses of others to your grief expressions serve as a clue that they're applying *should* rules to you. The benefit of shoulds and shouldn'ts spoken out loud by others is that they're easier to spot and apprehend. We can call people on their false beliefs, ask for them to speak differently, and set a boundary if they can't stop the behavior.

The Implicit and Subtle S

The implicit and subtle shoulds are the sneakiest and most damaging variety because they go undetected. Even when we can somehow catch a momentary glimpse, they somehow slip away. These shoulds often appear only in our self-talk or in the actions and inactions we take without much conscious intention. Their quiet presence makes them difficult to catch and remove. Their frequency makes them costly to our well-being.

ORIGINS OF OUR SHOULDS

As I explore throughout this book, the grief beliefs that inform our shoulds have been learned and reinforced in so many areas of our lives: family, friends, religions, culture, media, systems. One of the most obvious but missed sources of our shoulds is right under our nose.

In the late '60s, Swiss American psychiatrist Elisabeth Kübler-Ross offered the Five Stages of Grief theory in her seminal work *On Death and Dying*. Finally, the world released a collective sigh of relief: "There is structure and order and an outline for how 'to do' grief right!" (Note the sarcasm in my writer's voice.)

In our eagerness to find clarity and instructions, we ignored the fact that Kübler-Ross was describing the stages of people coming to terms with their own death, not the loss of their loved ones. Even so, she wasn't saying that grief was neat and linear. Our collective consumption of the five-stage theory has added to the already enormous arsenal of shoulds and shouldn'ts that get in the way of the messy, heartbreaking, and sometimes beautiful work of navigating our grief journey.

YOUR INNER KNOWING

As a result of grief, and for many other reasons such as past trauma, many of us live our lives disconnected from our inner wisdom. That's why the S words have so much power over us. We've been taught, encouraged, and rewarded for quieting and ignoring that voice, instead prioritizing the rules, regulations, and expectations of the systems and culture we inhabit. We say "Yes" when deep down we want to say "No." We take on more work when our energy is already depleted.

One of the biggest reasons we've lost touch with our inner wisdom is that culturally and medically we've learned to see our physical, mental, and emotional health as separate. That's obvious in the ways we've learned to ignore the signs and signals our bodies send us when they're desperate for our minds to listen. When we ignore our inner knowing, it takes up more space, it gnaws at us through our body, our thoughts, our emotions. It can come out sideways or in ways we don't expect. It really needs you to listen.

But how?

PAUSE TO RECONNECT

Our disconnection from ourselves causes us to make choices and believe things that keep us stuck, or worse, cause us to become more depleted. So how do we begin to reconnect?

Pause.

I mean it. Practice pausing. I know it seems too simple, but I've found that pausing is the best first action I can take to recognize when the shoulds are in charge. As I share in "Start Close In," we don't have to figure it all out, just determine the next best step. For me, that step almost always includes pausing.

Pausing gives me a chance to take some slow, deep breaths, which help regulate my nervous system, making it less likely for me to act out from the shoulds. Pausing offers me a chance to respond, not react. The pause, whether it's one minute or one day, gives me a chance to connect with my inner knowing by being curious about:

- my instinct to say "Yes" to requests of my time and behavior.
- my instinct to say "No" to offers of help and support.
- what my body feels like, and what it's trying to tell me.
- my self-critical language (that often include the shoulds and shouldn'ts).

Pausing is useful in so many circumstances in grief, even beyond your critical inner narrator using the S words. Pausing is useful in grief (and life) every time you're asked to do or decide something or are given an opinion about your grief process. And after you get in the habit of pausing, your next best step is to listen inward for the clues. Are your feelings or actions responding to the shoulds or to your actual needs?

THE S WORDS LEAVE CLUES

The S words are such a ubiquitous part of our everyday vocabulary that we rarely notice them. Even when we do notice them, we often dismiss them. We treat them as just an expression and not as causing any real harm.

This is why we need practice in identifying clues that we're ignoring our inner wisdom. Once you start practicing, some clues become obvious while others remain stealthy. Some of the most obvious clues I've heard, both by listening inward and to the clients I've served over the years, include:

Shoulds

"I should keep myself busy."

"I should get rid of his clothes now."

"I should focus on and be grateful that she's not in pain anymore."

"I should get back to work."

"I should feel better by now."

"I should be able to handle this better."

Shouldn'ts

"I shouldn't keep looking at old photo albums."

"I shouldn't be so sad because we weren't that close."

"I shouldn't cry in front of my children."

"I shouldn't be mad at him"

"I shouldn't have moments of happiness."

"I shouldn't be so lazy."

LISTENING WITH THE THREE Cs

After you pause, check inward for the shoulds that are overriding your intuition and adding to your suffering. When we listen inward to these familiar stories, the ones that sound convincingly true, it's helpful to listen in a specific way. This listening requires what researcher Susan David calls the Three Cs: curiosity, compassion, and courage.

The familiarity of these shoulds make us believe in their absolute truth. That's why we need to approach them with a curious mind, letting go of the assumption that they are facts. Since these beliefs often come from parts of us that think we need protection, it's critical to offer ourselves compassion. We all have stories. That's part of the human condition. Judgment will only further empower the hold they have over us. Courage is required because we're asking ourselves to step into the unknown. Courage is acting in the face of fear. As we listen in with curiosity and compassion to these should stories, we need to be brave because we're asking ourselves to let go of the known and step into the unknown—into our inner wisdom.

LIBERATING YOURSELF

Developing the practice of pausing and listening with the three Cs gets us ready for the next best step—liberating ourselves from the shoulds. As the wise author, poet, and activist Sonya Renee Taylor explains, "When we liberate ourselves from the expectation that we must have all things figured out, we enter a sanctuary of empathy." The first time I read these words my body had a visceral reaction, as if I was being wrapped in a loving embrace. How about you?

What would it mean to your emotional, physical, mental, and spiritual well-being if you could liberate yourself from the shoulds of grief?

What would it mean to your emotional, physical, mental, and spiritual well-being if you could liberate yourself from the shoulds of grief? What would it feel like to express your emotions without inhibition? How might you experience your body differently? Would it shift your access to resting and digesting? How might you move through your day differently? How might this liberation shift anxiety and the feeling of being overwhelmed? How might it change how you relate to others in their grief?

You might notice that these are leading questions and suspect that I have some answers for you. Bottom line? You will feel better.

By now you likely know that I'm a "should detective." Ask any of my grief support clients, my friends, my students, my daughter, really anyone I spend meaningful time with, and they'll agree. I'm on the lookout for shoulds everywhere I go. That's because when the shoulds go unchecked, we suffer unnecessarily, especially in our grief. That's why every single client of mine will tell you that a significant part of our work together is to develop a practice of pausing, listening, and liberating ourselves from the shoulds. I tell them, "Swear all you want in these sessions. It's therapeutic. And know that I'm going to push back when you use the two dirtiest and most harmful words—*should* and *shouldn't.*"

⚜ AN INVITATION FOR YOU ⚜
be a should *detective*

Our grief beliefs can operate in stealthy, sneaky ways. Every time we use *should* or *shouldn't*, it's a clue that the S words are on the prowl. Shining a floodlight on them is the best way to stop them in their tracks. To learn how to do this, we need to brush up on our detective skills.

For one day or, if you're feeling ambitious, for one week, I invite you to practice your should detective skills. Take some time, with intention, to notice every time you hear "should" or "shouldn't" as it relates to your grief. The words might show up when talking to others about some aspect of your grief. The S words are often sneaky, appearing just as thoughts in your head. Also be on the lookout for when the S words are spoken by others to you or about you.

In your journal, reflect on and record your answers to the prompts below. Sometime afterward, be on the lookout for common recurring themes or circumstances. This will help you be savvier in your ability to catch shoulds in the future. When you do discover them, you might take a page from the TV series soccer coach Ted Lasso and tell yourself, "I'm gonna just file that under stinkin' thinkin'."

Be curious about recurring themes. Knowing that they're your most deeply ingrained grief beliefs will help you stay alert for their reappearance. This will help you continue your work as a should detective.

---

practice being a should *detective*

1. What was the expression or language?

2. Who was the messenger?

3. What was the context?

4. How did hearing it make me feel?

5. Is this a belief I want to keep or ditch?

6. How can I reframe this to be healing, not harmful?

holidays, anniversaries, and other grief hazards

HOLIDAYS AREN'T THE ONLY DAYS

Unlike work, we don't get to take a day off or a weeklong vacation to escape grief. That means we're actively grieving, especially early on, three hundred sixty-five days a year. The level and intensity of these grief experiences will diminish over time. Yes, you may go days, weeks, and maybe even months without grief's noticeable presence. But it doesn't disappear completely. It's not surprising that holidays and anniversaries are times when grief reappears or grows more intense. We refer to these times as STUGs (sudden temporary upsurge in grief). (See "Wait. Am I Still Grieving?")

What is most surprising? All the other days that trip us up. For me, these days have included Eric's birthday, my birthday, our daughter's birthday, the anniversary of the day he proposed, our wedding anniversary, the anniversary of his death, the sixteenth of every month, Tuesdays, Valentine's Day, Father's Day, the days I have to check the "widow" box and leave the second parent line blank, when I visit a place we've lived or traveled to, when I do something he always wanted to try but never got the chance. Do you have a list like this too? I'm guessing you do.

Like all things in grief, the intensity and presence of the STUGs have diminished, but not all of them have disappeared. That's why it's important for you, and everyone who supports you, to remember that holidays aren't the only days of intense grief.

In the first year after losing someone, you're discovering what days or circumstances will be the booby traps that activate your grief. Some you'll see coming. Others will trip you up along your path. The challenging and surprising thing to know is that you may or may not experience the pitfalls in the same way or with the same intensity every time. Like much of grief, these days are sneaky too.

PREPARATION, NOT PREVENTION

While you won't necessarily be able to list all the pitfalls, nor will you be able to rank the likelihood of triggering a STUG perfectly, it can be helpful to inventory your grief hazards. Why? Because there are some strategies you can implement that will help you prepare for the days and seasons of grief.

I'm not suggesting you're going to prevent yourself from feeling grief, nor do I think that's the goal. I do know that much of why we find these days so difficult is because we haven't practiced much of the skills we've talked about elsewhere in this book. Below are ten skills to consider practicing before and during your next grief-inducing days.

1. Name What's Hard

It feels as if everything about these grief days, such as holidays, is hard. I understand that feeling. And getting specific about what aspects will be most difficult matters. Clarity can reduce feeling overwhelmed and helpless, giving you the opportunity to prepare.

Take some time to write down what is hard. Is it certain days, being with certain people, specific locations? Is it expectations you have of yourself? Is it the expectations you believe specific people have about you? Knowing the details will help you prepare. Equally important is to write down what feels good, or at least what helps things sucks less. Maybe it's doing things in shorter time bursts, attending smaller versus larger gatherings, or spending time in nature.

2. Be a Should Detective

As we explore in "*Should* Is a Dirty Word (and Not the Swearing Kind),"
shoulds can be a pitfall in our grief. They seem to creep up more often
during the most hazardous days, especially holidays, because the expectations for joy, gratitude, happiness, and celebration (pretty much
all the things we don't feel much of in grief) are in our face. Being a
should detective will help you reduce the pressure of being, feeling, or
doing anything other than what rightly calls to you. So I invite you to
practice being a should detective during these times.

Every time you hear yourself say out loud (or in your mind), "I
should or I shouldn't XYZ," pause. Take a breath. Ask yourself why?
Where does that belief come from? Does it make sense to hold on to
in this moment, given the depth of your grief? Maybe keep track of it
in a journal or talk about it with a trusted friend or partner. See if you
can liberate yourself from the should.

3. Adjust Your Expectations

It seems the only worthy goal for holidays or anniversaries is joy. Anything less is a sign that you're a Scrooge. Bah humbug. To be honest,
holidays and anniversaries are not that different than the rest of the
year, as we live in a culture of toxic positivity, only covered in an extra
layer of decorations and lights. I'm here to remind you that joy doesn't
have to be your goal in these seasons.

Adjust your aim to meet yourself where you're at. If having a joyful
holiday season, birthday, or anniversary doesn't feel right for you, ask
yourself what does? Maybe this year your goal isn't a joyful celebration.
Maybe it's having a few joyful moments or hours or days. Maybe joy
isn't in your vocabulary at all. Maybe seeking ease or peacefulness feels
more reasonable. Honestly, maybe it's just about surviving and getting
through. That's OK too. Once you've adjusted your expectations, share it
with the people closest to you so that they can support you in achieving
your goal.

4. Plan For Your Needs Versus Others' Wants

During holidays, we feel extra pressure to meet other people's wants.
This might include the wants of our children, parents, friends, and

even colleagues. We often sacrifice what we need. In grief, we're especially concerned with being labeled as "a bummer," so we say "Yes"
when we really feel like saying "No."

Yet all we owe others is to be our authentic selves. And if that's a sad
version of you, a non-cooking version, or a version that says "No" more
often, then so be it. As we explore in "Knowing and Honoring Your
Needs," when you prioritize other people's wants over your needs, you
end up feeling resentful, right? How often do you show up with your
less-than-best self? What are you teaching those around you about
standing up for what they need in their times of struggle?

As you anticipate one of these land-mine days, keep an inventory of
what you need to help you achieve whatever aim you set. That might
mean saying "No" to traditional and long-standing gatherings. That
might mean not cooking. That might mean having people visit you
instead of you traveling to them.

5. Inventory Your Calendar

Take inventory. What have you already said "Yes" to? How many of
these activities or gatherings are likely to be hard? Given what you've
already discovered from the previous tips, how many events or gatherings like these can you handle right now? Equally important, what's
on your calendar that feels good or nourishing? (See "Make Space.")

If your calendar doesn't align with your goals, make adjustments.
Maybe you've recognized you're at your max for large gatherings.
Great. This will make it easier for you to say, "Thanks for the invitation,
but my calendar is already full." Perhaps it will require you to send a
note: "Thanks again for the invitation, but I realize I'm overcommit-
ted and won't be able to join you." You may also realize there's not
enough restoration built into your calendar, so schedule blocks of time
for things that nourish you—such as time in nature, exercise, creative
endeavors, or maybe even play.

6. Find Your Exit Buddy

As Crush, the wise one-hundred-year-old turtle in the film *Finding
Nemo*, asked, "Do you have your exit buddy?" While you're the only

one experiencing this loss, that doesn't mean you need to navigate your grief alone. One of the things about knowing ahead of time that these grief-inducing days are going to be hard is that it gives us time to plan and build in support.

Even if we've named what's hard, ditched the shoulds, adjusted our expectations, prioritized our calendar, and focused on our needs, we still might find ourselves needing to leave a holiday gathering early, escape an awkward conversation, or get help holding the weight of our grief for a while. That's where our exit buddy comes in.

So I invite you to think about who your exit buddy is (a.k.a. support people or resources) that might help you navigate this day or season. Good news: You can have more than one.

You might talk to a friend and ask if you can call on a specific day when you anticipate attending a difficult gathering. Or it might be talking with a trusted friend or family member ahead of an event to come up with a signal or plan a mid-event walk. You might get extra appointments on the books with your therapist or let family members know that you might leave early, so not to worry.

---

who are my exit buddies?

---

7. Expect the Unexpected

While there are obvious days of grief, some days are less so, and how we will feel each time they come around is an even bigger mystery. Plus these days are often full of extra tasks, deadlines, and expectations. It feels as if there is absolutely no wiggle room. But the truth is, grief doesn't care about any of that. Grief is messy, nonlinear, and, well, a sneaky bitch. One of the best things we can do for ourselves is to expect that things won't go according to plan, including how, when, or where our grief might show up.

I invite you to develop a mantra or two to offer yourself some grace when grief does what grief does. Maybe you'll say to yourself knowingly, "Wow, it's just like Lisa says, grief is such a sneaky bitch." Or maybe you'll offer yourself compassion by saying, "It's OK to feel how-ever I'm feeling in this moment. That's the nature of grief."

I invite you to develop a mantra or two to offer yourself some grace when grief does what grief does. Maybe you'll say to yourself know-ingly, "Wow, it's just like Lisa says, grief is such a sneaky bitch." Or maybe you'll offer yourself compassion by saying, "It's OK to feel however I'm feeling in this moment. That's the nature of grief."

---

8. Help Someone Else
Yes, it's important to prioritize your needs over others' wants. And one of the tried and true (and scientifically backed truths) is that helping someone else who is also suffering can help us feel better. Helping oth-ers can put things into perspective, interrupt the ruminating common in grief, or simply fill what seems like a sparse social calendar.

If you find yourself weighed down by grief and in need of a shift in perspective, consider helping someone else. This might look like par-ticipating in a volunteer program around the holidays, such as visiting senior citizens or serving meals to the homeless. Remember, it doesn't have to be big or formal. It could be something as simple as texting or calling another person who's grieving or surprising a neighbor with your favorite holiday cookies. Any random act of kindness will do.

9. Old, New, and Emerging Rituals
Traditions can be beautiful. They help us feel connected with others across time and space. Traditions can also feel hard when we're deep in our grief. Traditions can trigger grief during many of the pitfall days such as holidays, birthdays, and anniversaries. It's hard to know when it's appropriate to carry traditions forward or let them go. The truth is, there may not be a clear sign, nor is there a right answer.

So the next hazardous day that is embedded with traditions make space for old, new, and emerging rituals. Take some time to think about which traditions feel important for you to carry forward. You might discover that some feel hard, but with a little adjusting, they might feel good (or at least less hard). Don't forget, you can also give yourself and your family permission to try something new.

One of the most important things we can do in our grief is to find a way to carry our person with us as we live into the emerging story of our lives. So be creative and explore ways to incorporate the love, life, and memories of your loved one into your traditions and rituals.

At the same time, no pressure if nothing comes to you. There's always next year. Adding something new or not participating in a long-standing tradition one year doesn't mean it's a permanent thing. Give yourself grace. It's truly the best gift you can give yourself.

10. Pause, Breathe, Repeat

We live in a productivity-obsessed culture that prioritizes outcome over process and glorifies busyness. Grief is stressful, and it impacts us cognitively, physically, and emotionally. We're busy learning and adapting to a new reality, one that makes no sense and has no instructions. The added stressors of grief-inducing holidays compound our stress.

That's why I invite you to consider focusing on a different P word for these land-mine seasons: Pause. Pause when your feet hit the ground in the morning. Spend a few moments focusing on your breath. Inhale deeply and exhale with a big "woosh" sound.

Before you stand up and get on with your day, take a moment to consider what actions (or inactions) will help you feel better, even just a little bit. Pause before you respond to the invitation to another event and ask yourself, "Does this fit with what I need?" No surprise: I invite you to pause when you hear the shoulds pop up (which they tend to do more on these days). Pause and ask yourself, "When's the last time I ate? Drank water? Took a deep breath?"

⚜ AN INVITATION FOR YOU ⚜

inventory your days

A lot of the skills required to reduce the unnecessary suffering we often experience during holidays, anniversaries, and other grief hazards need to be implemented before the days come. That's why making a list of the grief-inducing days, based on a combination of past experiences and intuition, can help you feel more ease and comfort. It can make these unbearable days a little more bearable.

Get out your journal and spend some time writing down the days that have been hard in the past. If you want, you can also write down one or two things that made these days especially difficult and one or two things that might make them more bearable next time they come around.

> ### *inventory your grief days*
>
> *Name the day or season*
>
> *One or two things or skills that made it more difficult*
>
> *One or two things or skills that can make it more bearable*

secondary losses: the sneakiest bitches of them all

AFTERSHOCKS

The initial loss we face is massive and destabilizing. Like an earthquake, it shakes our very foundation. The rebuilding we must undertake is daunting to say the least. More like unbearable. Somehow, we pick ourselves up, and we perform the rituals of mourning. We take care of the responsibilities of cleaning up the debris. Then at some point, we're faced with the task of figuring out how to rebuild.

Amid all that, or maybe even some time later, the aftershocks happen, and more pieces of your life are falling apart. These are the secondary losses we experience in grief. From lost friendships to financial insecurity and more, they don't get the headlines or recognition that the earthquake did, but they cause just as much damage. Rarely acknowledged, supported, or mourned, secondary losses are truly the sneakiest bitches of them all.

Rarely acknowledged, supported, or mourned, secondary losses are truly the sneakiest bitches of them all.

COMPOUNDING DAMAGE

Whether it's the death of a loved one, the dissolution of a relationship, or some other type of loss, the original loss triggers secondary losses that can compound the pain. It's important to be on the lookout for these losses and identify when you're experiencing aftershocks. Naming these losses can help make sense of why you might be feeling overwhelmed. Getting specific about what you've lost in addition to your primary loss can help you identify what's missing in your life and what kind of support you need.

SPIRITUAL OR CONCEPTUAL

Some secondary losses are spiritual or conceptual. Profound losses often lead grievers to lose a sense of themselves, experiencing some form of identity crisis. Many of us lose confidence in ourselves and in our ability to navigate a world that has become unrecognizable. As we explore in "This Is Your Brain on Grief," many of us face a temporary but frightening loss in our cognitive functioning. Profound losses, particularly out-of-order deaths such as the death of a child or any abrupt or violent death, often cause a spiritual or existential crisis, leading to a loss of faith on some level.

SECURITY AND SAFETY

The profound losses we experience, such as the destruction caused by earthquakes, don't just damage what existed. Our sense of safety and security is also shaken, which is a loss that often goes unrecognized. Sometimes that loss of security has tangible consequences: loss of income and financial security, loss of a job, even loss of a home. Often, we no longer feel psychologically or emotionally safe, sometimes even physically safe in the world. Depending on the loss, particularly if it involved trauma, what we're grieving in addition to the primary loss is our sense of safety.

RELATIONSHIPS

We often experience secondary losses in the form of strained or broken relationships with people who couldn't or wouldn't show up.

Sometimes when a couple loses a child there can be tension and disconnection in the relationship if each person has different grief styles. As I share elsewhere in this book, many of us lose our relational identity. When we look in the mirror (metaphorically), it's hard to tell what we're looking at. It's not really us. It's a blur of grief and the person we lost. It's hard to see ourselves. This is a secondary loss. For me, not being married, not being a wife any longer, was another loss I didn't see coming.

TANGIBLE OR DELAYED

Sometimes the aftershocks of loss are delayed, and we don't know if or when they're coming. For many of us, the loss of memories over time is a delayed cost we didn't realize would hurt so much. Some losses are delayed, and they are ones you don't see coming, such as discovering something damaging or harmful about the person you didn't know before the loss. For example, learning about infidelity after the death of the partner can be its own form of loss. And there is loss when we face the inevitable act of selling or donating items belonging to the one we lost. Truth be told, we don't always feel the loss the moment we part with these items. Sometimes it's down the road that the loss is realized.

As we touch on in "Ambiguity S-U-C-K-S," missed opportunities that result from our primary loss represent secondary losses that we rarely recognize or validate. One example is not having a coparent when a partner dies.

DAMAGE GOES UNCLAIMED

The damage of secondary losses isn't just that we must experience them. The compounding damage occurs when these losses so often go unclaimed. They are disenfranchised losses. (See "Access Denied.")

If someone breaks into your home or car and your insurance claim is denied, it makes repairs, rebuilding, or replacing items incredibly difficult. This is one of the ways secondary losses are so sneaky. When a young child dies, parents often lose access to the sense of community and connection they had as part of a playgroup. Such a profound absence of fellowship and friendship is often dismissed.

ASSESSING THE LOSSES

Naming and labeling the secondary losses you've experienced is a helpful first step. Self-acknowledgment is important for many reasons. It offers you insight into the complexity or gravity of grief you're experiencing but can't quite explain.

It also offers you a chance to figure out what you can or want to repair or have returned. That might be a lost friendship or a path to financial security. Getting specific about what you hope to repair is helpful when you begin the rebuilding process. With this knowledge, you'll be better prepared when you seek the support of fellow grievers or mental health professionals. Some of us will be content just naming the loss for ourselves. However, many of us need to feel seen, at least by another person. We want others to affirm that they understand: Our grief is not just about the person who died, but also about living with the other losses.

TEMPORARY OR PERMANENT?

Some secondary losses can be permanent. For example, the financial insecurity that these losses cause might require you to sell your house. You'll never get it back. Other losses are temporary, such as our ability to participate in school or work. For many of the secondary losses we endure, it's unclear in the beginning whether they're temporary.

One of the most common secondary losses happens when our relationships are compromised. This is most often the case when the secondary losses we face are relational. You may discover early on in your grief that some people you expected to be there for you aren't. This is a secondary loss. And you have every right to feel disappointed or angry. You may decide or acknowledge that the connection is broken. (We explore the reasons people often suck at showing up in "Who's Got Your Back?") Therefore, all I'll offer here is the reminder that some of these people may come back around. They might learn how to be a better friend or partner or family member. So before you conclude that this loss is permanent, consider not writing them off just yet.

WHEN IT'S PILING UP

Sometimes we confuse secondary losses with cumulative losses, when primary losses are so close together that we haven't had time to begin processing the first one when the second or third ones come at us. This might be the death of loved ones a few days, weeks, or months apart. We can experience this reaction even when there is significant time between the two losses if we haven't processed the previous loss. And the truth is, we may be experiencing both cumulative *and* secondary losses.

⚷ AN INVITATION FOR YOU ⚸

assess your losses

Since we often miss naming or acknowledging the secondary losses we face, I invite you to get out your journal and explore them. Think about the various categories of secondary losses and reflect on if or how they might be contributing to what you're experiencing in grief. Remember, we can't move forward with repairs until we first assess our losses.

spiritual or conceptual

security and safety

relationships

tangible or delayed

missed opportunities

skills
and tools
that
help grief
suck less

discovering ways to soften
the hard edges of grief

notice mindfully

BRING INTENTION TO YOUR ATTENTION

Noticing something seems so passive and can feel insignificant. Yet *noticing* is an action word that has a big impact on our well-being. We're always noticing or paying attention to something; our awareness is always somewhere. The challenge for many of us is that most of the attention we give is rarely intentional or in the present moment and frequently carries a significant amount of judgment.

In grief, our attention is anywhere but the present. So often we're engrossed in replaying moments from the past or running "what if" scenarios about actions that we imagine would've resulted in different outcomes. Our thoughts also race into the future, where worry is often in charge. When our mind does pause in the present, we're often frightened by the emotional intensity we find there, so we instinctively set our minds elsewhere, from tackling tasks and responsibilities to seeking ways to numb. Regardless of where our attention has wandered, we rarely go there with intention, but we frequently bring judgment along.

Mindfulness is the practice of deliberate and nonjudgmental awareness of the present moment. What does it look like when we bring these qualities together?

Deliberate We make an intentional decision to cultivate our awareness. This is not a one-and-done action. Mindfulness practice means that we'll have to focus on awareness over and over and over. The need for repetition when our intentions fall away is not a failure.

Present Once we've set an intention to bring our awareness somewhere, we want to arrive in the present moment. We're observing our thoughts, feelings, and sensations as they come into view.

Nonjudgmental The third quality (and perhaps most challenging for many of us) is to bring a curious and kind gaze to whatever we discovered when we brought our deliberate awareness to the present moment. We're invited to observe without judgment.

While being deliberate in what you're noticing in grief, you might ask yourself one question: "What sensations am I noticing in my body in this moment?" Cold? Tight? Relaxed? Tingly? Pain in my knees?

But why should you care about this mindfulness stuff? As we explore elsewhere, there's no getting around the emotions of grief or the reality that it will affect you physically and cognitively. The good news is that mindfulness has been proven to reduce the intensity of the effects.

We often feel at the mercy of our thoughts and emotions. The truth is that these thoughts and emotions are sneaky and unpredictable, and developing the ability to approach our experiences with deliberate, nonjudgmental awareness gives us a much-needed sense of agency amid the chaos of grief. Mindfulness is new for many of us, so it will take practice. That's why we need to be aware of the obstacles we encounter and develop strategies to remove them so that we can start noticing things mindfully.

THE MOST VALUABLE AND ACCESSIBLE FREE RESOURCE

Mindfulness is the most valuable resource we have in grief. How? Mindfulness practices have been scientifically proven to reduce stress levels, increase emotional resilience, promote better sleep, cultivate self-compassion, and have a positive relationship with self-care. It also helps us discover new meaning in the wake of loss or another tragedy. (See "Meaning-Making [Even Though It Didn't Happen for a Reason].")

That's why the practice of mindfulness is the most valuable investment I've made in reducing the unnecessary suffering I experience. Beyond the scientific data, I speak from experience. My regular mindfulness practice has helped me:

• learn how to be with the grief emotions that threaten to over-whelm me.

• interrupt the mean and bossy inner grief critic who tells me that I'm doing everything wrong.

• clear the fog of my grief brain, allowing me to think with more clarity.

• create a connection with myself so that I can more easily iden-tify and prioritize my needs.

Sounds good, right? What could make it better? This grief resource is free and available 24/7. We can be mindful in any moment. We don't need to be at a yoga retreat or in a meditation class. I use mindfulness throughout my day, and I mean every day, beginning with a mini-mind-fulness moment: noticing the sensation of my feet on the floor, placing my hands over my heart, and offering myself a mantra for the day.

I even use it throughout the day when I feel overwhelmed or fran-tic, shifting my attention to the present moment, taking a few rounds of deep breaths, and offering a kind word to myself. I frequently use mindfulness to detect the shoulds that sneak in and make me feel bad. I also practice mindfulness through longer, daily meditations, anywhere between five and twenty minutes. Sometimes these med-itations are self-guided, but I often use free software apps and other online resources.

The profound value of mindfulness for our everyday well-being is also why I use it in every client session, class, workshop, and even talks I give on stages big and small. In case you're thinking, "I can't do all that," I hear you. I'll also remind you that comparison is unhelpful in life and in grief. I have been incorporating mindfulness practices for nearly a decade, so like grief, don't judge your practice against mine. Just start somewhere, and when you do, be kind to yourself and remember that you're not alone.

SURFING THE WAVES OF GRIEF

You may have heard that grief comes in waves. We know that the in-tensity of our memories and emotions related to loss ebbs and flows, sometimes coming in strong like tidal or tsunami waves and other times gently lapping on the shore.

Jon Kabat-Zinn, creator of mindfulness-based stress reduction (MBSR), offered a perfect metaphor about how mindfulness helps us navigate the rough waters of life (and grief): "You can't stop the waves, but you can learn to surf." Kabat-Zinn studied the emotional, cognitive, and physical benefits of mindfulness meditation on people with chronic pain, stress-related disorders, and other illnesses. He discovered that MBSR lessens stress on the brain and improves how we process emotions. The results also showed positive effects on the immune system.

The skills required for "surfing" is another perfect metaphor for the skills we need to ride the waves of grief with more ease and grace. As a scuba diver, I love the ocean. But I've never surfed. Honestly, I love the deep sea but the power on the surface scares me.

So I lean on the wisdom of J'aime Morrison. She fell in love with surfing late in life, and it turned out to be a profoundly important passion that has helped her navigate the waters of deep grief after the death of her husband. The sheer power and force of ocean water require surfers to build tremendous body strength. Waiting in the water, riding long waves, and then getting back on the board after being repeatedly knocked down requires surfers to be adaptable, agile, and durable. The most important technique for surfing the ocean (and the waves of grief) is being present—a skill that takes tremendous practice.

MINDFUL SELF-COMPASSION

"Would you talk to your best friend with that mouth?" That's a question I pose to my clients, my daughter, and myself so often in grief. I find that just asking the question is enough to interrupt the judgment we level at ourselves.

"Would you talk to your best friend with that mouth?"

The question invites us to have self-compassion, a practice that allows us to talk to ourselves with kindness in the same way we would speak to a friend. I know self-compassion is a buzzword that sounds nice in theory, but hard to attain or experience, especially in the depths of grief. To understand what it takes, world-renowned self-compassion researcher Kristin Neff shares three elements:

Self-Kindness versus Self-Judgment This involves warm and caring thoughts of your suffering and pain, approaching your experience with tenderness and a gentle embrace. This replaces the inner critic voice that lays harsh judgment of your suffering on your shoulders.

Common Humanity versus Isolation This element, Neff explains, requires you to acknowledge that suffering, pain, and imperfection are part of the human experience. To grieve and to make mistakes is to be part of the human community. This replaces the common but irrational isolationist thoughts we have that sound like, "I'm the only one who . . ."

Mindfulness versus Over-Identification Remember that mindfulness is the practice of noticing your thoughts and feelings in a balanced way? It asks that you neither ignore your heavy or negative emotions nor amplify them.

Self-compassion has benefits for your physiology and ability to be flexible and adaptable, skills we know are crucial in navigating grief. As Neff explained in our podcast conversation, "Self-compassion reduces sympathetic activity, for instance, that lowers cortisol, reduces inflammation, and increases things such as heart rate variability, which allows us to be more flexible. Self-compassion literally helps us calm down and be more flexible as we respond moment to moment."

In case you're concerned about any downsides, research has shown self-compassion is not self-pity or self-indulgence and it doesn't make you lazy or have an over-inflated sense of self. It's simply the recognition that you, like all humans, deserve compassion.

MINDFULNESS HELPS YOU SEE WHAT'S HIDDEN

One of the challenges we face in grief is that what we pay attention to creates a myopic and sometimes harmful perception of reality. The unprecedented intensity of many of the emotions we experience in grief are like a magnet for our attention. As a result, we miss the other emotions and experiences available to us because we struggle to shift our gaze.

We can also miss out on the emotions that need to be recognized because the judgment we bring to their presence in our mind keeps them concealed. One of the benefits of mindfulness is that it serves as a tool to help you discover what's hidden. Sometimes what's hidden the most is the love, connection, and even support that are already available to us.

"Remembering Blue Skies" is one of my favorite mindfulness techniques for uncovering what's hidden from us when the clouds of grief interfere with our view. I'm not certain of its origins, but this mindfulness practice invites you to picture a clear blue sky. Then you're asked to connect with the feeling it elicits. For many of us, that's ease, relaxation, and maybe even joy. Next, we might imagine a few fluffy clouds, representing everyday struggles. We might notice that they don't distract us from our view of the blue skies.

Then you're asked to picture dark storm clouds rolling in. The stormy cloud cover, like the intense emotions and moments in our grief, can convince us that darkness is permanent. We can begin to believe that we've always felt this way and we always will. But if you've ever been on an airplane on a cloudy day, you know the blue sky is always there. You just have to get through the cloud cover to see it. This practice can help us remember that clouds always pass and that no matter what we're feeling, the blue sky is always there.

⚜ AN INVITATION FOR YOU ⚜

breathe mindfully

Since we know that slowing ourselves down to bring a deliberate non-judgmental approach to the present moment doesn't come naturally for many of us, we all need practice. Not to get "good at it" or to be an expert. We practice because it helps in the moment. The more we practice, the more moments of ease or reduced suffering we experience. The more moments of ease we have in a short period of time, the more we'll want, so we keep practicing.

Below is a simple mindful breathing practice. I invite you to try this practice daily for a week and take a few notes after each practice about your experience.

ready, set

Start by picking a time of day that works best for you. Personally, that's the moment I wake up. It sets the tone for the day. But you might like to try it during your lunch break or even at bedtime.

Set a timer so that you don't have to keep checking the clock. Five to ten minutes is plenty. Start with three if that feels right.

Next, make sure you're in a comfortable position, whatever that means for you.

practice

Bring your awareness to the present and the sensation of your breathing. Your breath will be your anchor.

Next, follow the path of your breath, paying attention to the sensation of your chest and belly expanding on each inhale and softening on each exhale.

When your mind wanders, and it will, observe it without judgment.

Hmm, my mind has wandered. Then bring your attention back to the present moment. Make sure to do it with gentle kindness, like you would treat a puppy who had wandered off.

Return to tracing the sensation of your belly expanding and contracting with each breath.

improv skills help

IMPROV CLASSES, ANYONE?

Have you ever taken an improv class? I did once. (We're not going to talk about that now; I'm profusely sweating just thinking about the experience.) Don't worry, I'm not going to suggest that you take a class—although that could be freaking awesome.

Why are improvisation skills important and why should you care about them? Fair question. *Improv* means to invent or make up words or movements at a time it's needed without having planned it ahead of time. I'm guessing you see how inventing or making something up on the spot can be useful in grief.

Honestly, improv is useful in all seasons of our lives, but perhaps never more than when we're struggling or suffering. None of us have insight into who, where, when, and how we'll experience a loss, which makes it unpredictable. There's no way to fully plan for grief, and there's no amount of preparation we can do that ensures we'll arrive knowing exactly how to cope with the cognitive, emotional, social, spiritual, and relational consequences of our loss.

This is true even if we know the loss is coming (anticipatory grief). While grief might give us a warning sign, we're still not fully prepared. For those of us who've experienced more than one loss, we know this too. Though we had some sense of what to expect, we experienced each loss so differently, requiring us to make up our new story again as we go.

Now that I've (hopefully) convinced you that improv skills will help you navigate the unpredictability and messiness of your grieving journey, you might be wondering what exactly those skills are.

The following ground rules of improv explain how each tenet can make your grieving process a little bit easier (or at least suck a little less).

TAKE A CURIOUS AND NONJUDGMENTAL APPROACH

The first ground rule of improv is to arrive at the encounter with curiosity and without judgment. In grief, that encounter is most often the one we have with ourselves. Oh my, is that approach challenging for our analytically driven brain. Our drive to assess situations isn't just cultural, it's primal. It goes back to our survival instincts. We are wired to have a critical eye. That's why being with your own experiences, thoughts, and emotions in grief is hard. Doing it without judgment is even harder. It's why approaching your experiences in grief with curiosity and nonjudgment takes practice. A lot of practice.

What does taking a curious and nonjudgmental approach to yourself in grief look like? It includes a lot of the skills we explore throughout this book. Being a should detective helps us notice when judgment is holding us to unrealistic expectations. Interrupting the narrator helps us stop the judgment stories we're telling ourselves. Mindfulness, as we explore in "Notice Mindfully," is all about approaching our grief with curiosity and compassion, which requires nonjudgment.

RESPOND WITH "YES, AND"

"Yes, and" is perhaps the most notable improv tool. The premise is to take the idea of others as they are, then add to them. Seems simple enough. It's a sure way to keep a conversation going and build a unique narrative. An actor might start with, "I'm standing in the rain without an umbrella." The actor's scene partner might respond, "Yes, you're standing in the rain without an umbrella. And I notice that there's an umbrella flipped upside down just a few feet behind you." More than keeping a conversation interesting, "yes, and" demonstrates that more than one thing can be true, or that situations can hold complexity or ambiguity, in essence replacing either/or thinking with both/and.

Did you notice that I use "and" a lot in this book? It's my favorite word. In fact, the ampersand (the character "&" that sometimes stands in for "and") is part of a large and intricate tattoo that covers my wrist and forearm. I have a black band around my wrist, representing the importance of honoring my losses. That band flows into the & character, which represents that my energy isn't only focused on the loss, but a reminder that I can be with the both/and of loss and life. The top of the & grows into a series of wildflowers spreading and wrapping around my arm. Some of the flowers are in full bloom, representing the joy of being alive. Other flowers are only drawn in outline, representing both the life that was interrupted by the loss and the life yet to be lived. (Special shoutout to the incredible Vickie Chiang for making this vision come to life in the most exquisite way.)

First improv classes, and now tattoos.

Don't worry. I'm not encouraging you to get a tattoo either. I promise. What I'm sharing is how I incorporate one of the most well-known tenets of improv—"yes, and"—into my grieving process and into my life.

LISTEN TO AND ACCEPT THE GIFTS GIVEN TO YOU

"Giving gifts" is a warm-up game in improv where one person gives an imaginary gift, and the recipient must accept it with an enthusiastic "Yes!" along with an explanation of why they love the gift. The giver then must explain why they gave the gift. While the gift and reasons given are made up, the connection that's formed between the actors is real.

What does this have to do with lessons for grieving? I promise this isn't a nudge to say thank you when people say stupid shit to you in grief or for you to express enthusiasm over yet another frozen casserole. The relevant lesson here is that in the exchange of asking for and receiving gifts of support, we're able to feel more connected to the world. This is especially valuable as the very nature of grief leaves us feeling untethered and isolated. Listening, asking for, and then accepting the gifts of grief support reminds us that we belong.

BE PRESENT IN THE MOMENT

In improv, paying attention to what's happening in the present moment is necessary, since the goal is to invent a response to the new information coming at you. If your attention is somewhere in the past or future, your reaction to what your scene partner said will be disproportionate, inappropriate, and likely not helpful for continuing the game.

Grief is no game, but the lesson applies just the same. Yes, remembering and reliving past events and worrying about the future is normal in grief (and life). However, the more time we spend there, the less likely we are to listen to the cues our body and mind are giving us about what we need to care for ourselves. We can also miss the gifts of support being offered to us.

Once again, our neurobiology and culture make it more difficult to spend time in the present. We're encouraged to reflect on and learn lessons from the past and be on the lookout for future danger. This means that focusing our awareness on the present moment takes intention and practice. A lot of practice. To avoid feeling overwhelmed, focus on what's the next best step to ease your suffering. To know what's next, you first need to know where your feet are planted.

This means that focusing our awareness on the present moment takes intention and practice. A lot of practice. To avoid feeling overwhelmed, focus on what's the next best step to ease your suffering. To know what's next, you first need to know where your feet are planted.

You may be thinking, "Yeah, but I'm not good at it, and every time I try being present, my mind races off." Remember, even the minds of veteran mindfulness practitioners wander into the past and future. Your mind will wander too. As we explore in "Notice Mindfully," your goal is to notice when your mind wanders, kindly and without judgment acknowledge that it happened, and invite your attention back to the present moment. Each time you return to the present, you'll be better able to discover your needs and then find a way to meet them.

BE FLEXIBLE AND ADAPTABLE

Just when you think you know where the scene is going, your improv partner throws you a curveball (sorry for the mixed metaphor). You thought the conversation was going to stay on favorite music concerts but then—BAM! Now your partner is talking about space travel. What do you do now? How do you respond? The answer is to be flexible and adaptable. It seems these are skills we're forced to practice constantly, especially in the early phase of grief.

These can include our need to adapt to new living environments, tasks, and responsibilities, requiring us to be flexible when it comes to our schedules and in response to invitations. While we may have practiced, many of us don't enjoy having to use these skills. We just want things to be certain and known and predictable.

BE SPECIFIC AND PROVIDE DETAILS

Another ground rule for improv is for participants to be specific and provide details. Why? Details allow your scene partner to know what's important and help move the scene forward. You tell your scene partner that you're new to the city. You add that you're feeling sad, lonely, and scared because you don't know anyone, plus the subway system is confusing. Being specific about your emotions and the reasons for feeling them helps your scene partner know what's important and how to move the scene forward.

In grief, being specific with the emotions you're having or providing details of what you're experiencing in your body is so valuable. Whether you share the information with yourself, your friend, a doctor, or a therapist, being specific provides information about what's important to you. As is the case with being present, details help everyone better understand the next best step to take.

THERE ARE NO MISTAKES, ONLY LEARNING OPPORTUNITIES

There are no mistakes, just learning opportunities. I love this tenet of improv. It's my AFGO (another fucking growth opportunity) approach to life in an improv performance. Let's say you assumed your character was from South Carolina, so you laid on a thick Southern accent, but your scene partner mentions that you are from England. That's OK, it's not a mistake, it's information. You learned something, and now you decide how to incorporate it so you can move forward. You respond to your partner with, "Yeah, I was born in England, but my mom hated the cold weather and the food, so we moved to Charleston when I was two."

Even though you've never experienced this loss before, like me, you likely hold the belief that you should have it all figured out. You don't. You can't. None of us can. All we can do is try. And when our efforts don't give us the results we were hoping for, the best thing we can do is learn. Maybe you returned to work because you thought you were ready. You ended up crying all day or were in such a fog that you couldn't focus. No need to label your return a mistake. You made the best decision based on the information you had. Your experience at work provided you with new information. It's simply a learning opportunity. Given what you learned, without judgment, you can ask yourself, "What is the next best decision regarding work?"

⚓ AN INVITATION FOR YOU ⚓

practice "yes, and"

Many of us have learned and practiced skills that include either/or thinking. We've gotten good at using "but" when faced with something that feels complex or appears contradictory. "But" cancels out everything before it, like the apology that includes, "I'm sorry for X, but . . ." We know firsthand that grief is full of complexity and seeming contradictions. That means we must acquire some new skills. Yes, we've got to adapt.

I invite you to practice incorporating "and" into your everyday vocabulary. This includes trying it in conversations about grief and your well-being with others and using it in the conversations you're having with yourself. You might try saying the following five "and" affirmations to yourself at the start of each day. I encourage you to get out your journal and add in the times you found yourself using "but" or having either/or thinking so that you can create your own "and" affirmations.

---

five "and" affirmations to try:

"I can be grateful for what I have and grieve what I lost."

"I can be resilient and still need a break."

"Other people's loss can be significant and my grief is still valid."

"I can be healing and still have hard days."

"I can be happy for others and sad for me."

times I used "but" or "either/or" thinking that discounted my grief:

---

your turn to
buddy-breathe

NOW IS THE TIME TO RECEIVE

As I share in the preface, I learned three important life lessons at the age of twelve. The first time I went scuba diving I was taught to dive in, breathe deeply, and buddy-breathe when necessary. The first two rules I applied right away. (Technically, my dive-in was more of a flip backward off the boat, but I digress.) Life's dive-in moments invite us to live boldly, take chances, and follow our dreams.

The combination of awe and fear when we break the surface and sink into a new and unknown world leads most new divers to hold their breath. That's why rule No. 2, breathe deeply, is so important. In life, this rule is a reminder to be aware of our tendency to hold our breath when we're entering new and unknown seasons. Breathing deeply keeps us from panicking, allowing us to relax and see the path ahead more clearly. There's a certain carpe diem vibe to the first two rules. It's how I try to live my life. Maybe you do too.

Yet we all know there are times we don't dive in of our own accord. We're shoved into the water. When we experience a profound loss, we sink fast into the deep waters of grief without any equipment. That's when we need to remember the third rule: buddy-breathe when necessary.

When a diver runs out of air, dive buddies are there to share their air until any panic subsides. Then both divers rise slowly and safely to the surface. This scenario parallels life in grief. We're shoved into the deep end and it feels as if we don't have the equipment we need to breathe. That's why in the early season of grief we're going to need other people to help us breathe. As we move forward in grief, we'll get to a place where we can carry our own oxygen tank, but early on, we're going to need others to keep us from sinking too deep and running out of air.

A UNIVERSAL RULE THAT'S OFTEN IGNORED

Author, poet, and widow Elizabeth Alexander points out the profound universal truth that to be human means we're all going to be the helpers and the ones who need help. She reminds us of the struggle and our collective need to hold one another in the depths when she writes, "None of us will outrun death. What do we do in the space in between that is our lives? What is the quality and richness of our lives? How do we move through struggle and let community hold us when we have been laid low?"

A quick Google search reveals hundreds of quotes on the virtue and value of helping others. The same search yields little to no references on the importance and necessity of *receiving* help. This is such a powerful example of how implicit messages shape our view of the world: To be a good, virtuous person, you help others. To receive help is nothing to celebrate.

Flight attendants (and every self-help guru) are famous for saying, "Put on your own oxygen mask before assisting others." This a perfect example of the need for self-care. We can't help someone else if we're running on empty. However, that advice is missing a profoundly important footnote. It should say, "At any given moment we might be the 'other' who needs assisting." Just because we can carry the weight of grief on our own for a while, doesn't mean we should. Eventually, we're going to run out of air.

IT TAKES PRACTICE

Most new divers use up their oxygen tank quickly or spend the entire dive staring at their gauges. They either forget the hand signals they learned in dive practice or don't remember to use them to communicate with others. They can get lost, trying to ascend too quickly, and this experience can be overwhelming. That's understandable. You can't really prepare for the experience of being in deep waters in the classroom, just as you can't prepare for grief by reading about it.

Yes, we learn skills in class. We even pass a test. But none of the lessons come naturally. The more we dive, the more we learn how to breathe deeply, stay calm, signal to our dive buddies to communicate our needs, and hone skills needed to remain buoyant in the deep waters of grief.

As a professional "helper," I've learned to be a thoughtful and compassionate supporter for people experiencing deep grief. Over the first decade of my career, I had a lot of training and more importantly a lot of real-world practice. Yet none of that really prepared me for when I was shoved into the deep waters of grief. I didn't have much training or practice at signaling when I was out of air, asking for help, or graciously receiving it when it was offered. That's when I learned that asking for the right help and then allowing myself to receive it takes practice. Lots of practice.

ONGOING COMMUNICATION

As a diver, we would never start our descent into the ocean by swimming away from our dive buddy or ignoring our equipment and conditions around us. Even though we're savoring the indescribable beauty all around us, we're always alert, aware, and communicating with our buddy. Why? So we can ensure that our time underwater is as comfortable as possible, keep our oxygen tank from running out of air too quickly, and avoid injury or unnecessary suffering.

We're aware and alert and communicate proactively when conditions are clear. We use signals to caution one another when visibility is low. Using these skills reduces the chance that we'll need to use our emergency signals, like the one indicating that we're running out of air. Ongoing communication of our needs and awareness of the conditions around us prevent us from getting swept away by a strong current, descending to unsafe depths, or washing into a coral bed.

I've completed hundreds of dives over the past four decades and though I've had a few odd and sometimes scary moments, ongoing communication with my dive buddies is what kept me safe. In grief, ongoing communication can be as minimal as hand gestures or as in-depth as requests and conversations. Whatever form this communication takes, I invite you to use it in all conditions, especially these three:

Proactive Communication

Often overlooked, this type of communication is the most valuable skill to have as you navigate grief. Setting up communication plans with your various grief dive buddies can help you and them stay alert to changing conditions and needs. This might include setting up regular check-in calls, video meetings, or walks with a friend or family member. Scheduling regular check-up visits with your primary physician and any other medical providers helps keep you aware of problems with your equipment. Scheduling check-in sessions with a spiritual leader or mental health provider helps you see things that may not yet be visible to you.

Signaling Caution

From the moment we face loss, we're likely implementing these signals with our grief dive buddies, even when neither we nor they under-stand what we're cautioning. We may just be waving our hands over our head wildly to signal distress without being able to pinpoint the issue. That's OK. Wave away. Having others observe us gives them a chance to swim to us, detect the problem, hold us so that we remain buoyant, and remind us to practice our deep breathing.

Using the Emergency Signal

In grief, we'll all need to use the emergency signal. But how many of us aren't sure if it's appropriate to flash the running-out-of-air signal? And even if we're sure it's OK to do, do we know who will be watching or if they will help? This is why it's so important that we establish on-going communication with more than one buddy as we navigate grief. While we hope we won't need to use them often, knowing that we have people who will listen and watch helps ensure that they'll show up when we need them.

CHOOSING YOUR DIVE BUDDIES

Choosing the right dive buddy (and knowing other divers on a similar adventure) can make the difference between having a smooth and easy experience or a chaotic and frightening one. Sometimes our choices are limited, and we pick the best options at the time. The more we dive into grief, the more we learn what dive buddies work best for us.

In the beginning, we may naturally have the support we need, but over time, supporters fade away or the type of help they offer is no longer useful. For others, it takes us time to even locate a dive buddy, and when we do, we might need to swap them out. Remember, just as most divers will have multiple dive buddies in their scuba lives, we'll also need various sources of grief support along the way.

HOW FELLOW DIVERS HELP

Sometimes what we find most helpful is someone who has been in these waters before. We need a fellow diver who has experienced a similar loss. They can help validate our concerns, and can help us overcome the obstacles we face.

Other divers, even inexperienced ones, can be helpful too. They may not know the conditions we're facing, but they know us. As our friends, colleagues, or family members, they know what we care about, what skills we have, what resources we've relied on during past challenges. They can offer us comfort, companionship, and a reminder that we're not alone.

Fellow divers can be great because they're familiar to us and generally easy to access. Plus, they're often eager to accompany us. I've had some incredible friends and family members act as dive buddies as I navigated the waters of deep grief.

HOW CERTIFIED MASTER DIVERS HELP

The people who love us don't want to see us in any pain or discomfort. They will do anything they can to make it all stop. To make it go away. The intention is thoughtful, caring, and wonderful.

Because our friends, family members, and colleagues love and care about us so much, they often spend a lot of their energy desperately trying to keep us above water, dragging us to the surface before we're ready or in ways that are dangerous to our well-being. Mental health and other wellness professionals, including spiritual leaders, are trained to get on their scuba gear and join us underwater for a while. They have the communication skills to help us breathe into our regulator, keep us buoyant, and even teach us some advanced skills we can use, since we'll be spending a lot of time underwater in the early season of grief. That's why professionals can be a uniquely beneficial source of grief support.

STAYING ALERT TO CHANGING CONDITIONS

Dive trips usually involve a dive plan. We map out the area, the underwater terrain, and the sea life we expect to see. We check for the water and weather conditions and survey the direction of the current. We start our dive swimming in the opposite direction of the current to ensure we won't have to swim against it at the end of our dive when we're tired. Ever heard the expression "the best-laid plans"? All that planning is necessary, and sometimes we still get it wrong. Sometimes the conditions change by the time we reach the dive site or even while we're underwater.

Since we're grieving across a life span, the circumstances of our lives change. That means we need to stay alert to the changing conditions because it will likely affect the type of help we need and the dive buddy best suited to support us. The things that keep us buoyant early on in grief may be unnecessary or even harmful two or three years later. Even the supports that helped us the last time we were grieving may not be helpful this time around because the circumstance of the loss and our lives are different. Remembering to check your plan and conditions regularly will help ensure that you're getting the right support for this phase of your grief.

A GIFT FOR YOUR DIVE BUDDY

In case you're like me, you might be thinking, "My dive buddies probably find me a drag and they'd rather not be paired up with me so often." It might surprise you to know, but that's not true. Think about a time when someone you love was in pain and how desperately you wanted to help. When we bravely communicate our needs and ask for help from those who support us, we're giving them a gift. We're meeting their desire to be helpful. We're giving them a chance to practice their caring skills, which will be useful in all domains of their lives.

You're also giving them a chance to unlearn the harmful rules that we learned in the classroom of life—that needing help is something to hide. Our dive buddies, whether they're friends and family or professionals, all want to help us. Remind yourself of that each time it's your turn to buddy-breathe.

⚞ AN INVITATION FOR YOU ⚟

make a support plan

I recognize that each one of you is reading this book in a different phase of your grief. The conditions you're facing vary widely and your access to various sources of supports does too. Regardless, I hope by now you recognize all grievers need support. The type of support varies (e.g., physical, emotional, psychological, spiritual) as do the people you get it from (e.g., friends, family, fellow grievers, physicians, therapists, spiritual leaders).

Just as you make a dive plan based on current conditions, I invite you to spend some time reflecting on the current conditions of your grief. You can start by recording your current conditions in your journal to see if the current plan is serving you and to see if the conditions require additional support.

---

support plan for current conditions

current conditions
(e.g., number of children you're caring for, physical and mental health issues, financial resources, employment demands, upcoming grief anniversaries)

support currently in place
(e.g., adequate day care, weekly therapy appointments, under care of physician, receiving social security death benefits)

other supports needed
(e.g., locating a trauma-informed therapist, negotiating a flexible work schedule, finding someone to watch the children when you're at therapy)

seek a creative
resource

CREATIVITY AS A RESOURCE

Artists, performers, writers, poets, and all manner of creators are some of the guides I've found most helpful in my grief. My long-standing interest in the power of storytelling and metaphor along with my training in narrative therapy primed me to find their guidance valuable.

I'm not the only one to find these tools helpful. In my grief work with individuals, as a college professor of loss and grief, and in my podcast conversations, I've met many grievers who have found the creative response to loss to be one of their most powerful tools. What follows is a collection of wisdom and insight from some of my favorite creators whose work and words dropped me a lifeline when I needed it most.

IN CASE YOU NEED SCIENCE ON YOUR SIDE

In case you're skeptical of the benefits of creativity in grief and need more data, I've got you covered.

Many grievers (frankly, most adults) believe there's no room for creativity in their lives. They may not think it's practical, for one thing, and in grief, creativity may feel impossible. Plus, many of us are out of practice. As we age and experience the pressures of "adulting" and darker seasons of life, our connection to the powerful magic of creativity tends to fade.

Our priorities shift from the curiosity and wonder creativity requires to the need for efficiency and expertise. When we find ourselves in dark moments or seasons of our lives, including intense grief, our gaze retreats even closer in—to survival. That's understandable and even necessary. Thank goodness the wisdom of our body-mind (a.k.a. nervous system) protects us.

And yet as we talk about in "Your Body Knows," our survival mode is meant to be only a temporary state. During stressful times, the need for survival often gets stuck in the on position. Switching it off allows us the space to recharge and rest.

Creativity, whether our own expression or the work of others, is one of the best ways to turn on the rest switch. It's here where we rediscover that we're safe and connected and belong. It's from this place that we more easily connect to our memories, sit more comfortably with the emotions of grief, and take steps to write the emerging story of our lives.

CREATIVITY AS SUSTENANCE IN GRIEF

Actor Ethan Hawke offers one of the most powerful explanations of why creativity is necessary in times of heartache and grief. In his TED Talk, one that I share with my students each semester, Hawke suggests that creativity matters, even though we spend very little time thinking about it. It's not until, he explains, "their father dies; they go to a funeral; you lose a child; someone breaks your heart. And all of a sudden, you're desperate for making sense of this life. 'Has anybody felt this bad before? How did they come out of this cloud?' [. . .] And that's when art's not a luxury—it's actually sustenance. We need it."

We crave feeling understood. We're desperate to know if others have ever felt the way we do and wonder how they got through it. Art—music, film, sculpture, or some other form—offers the nourishment we need to satisfy those cravings. Most often, we're seeking reassurance in the works of others that we're not alone in feeling the way we do. We find solace and comfort in the song, the memoir, the sculpture, the poem. For some, art is nonnegotiable. Many of us use others' art as the muse we need to contribute our own offering, not necessarily as a gift to the grievers who come after us, but to better understand our own grief.

REDISCOVERING YOUR WHOLE SELF

One of the most beautiful examples I've ever seen of a creative response to loss is the work of friend and artist Krissy Teegerstrom. After our podcast conversation a few years ago, Teegerstrom realized that she'd experienced a secondary and profound loss beyond the death of her father when she was a teen. Her mother's neglect and emotional abuse in the aftermath of his death was a traumatic loss that she needed to address.

As she moved through her healing process, Teegerstrom needed to find and mend the parts of her that were fragmented. In the exhibit *I Was Already Everything*, Teegerstrom pushed herself beyond her familiar forms of expression to create a series of exquisitely designed capes. Using secondhand tools and materials, and with extraordinary details and embellishments, Teegerstrom designed each cape to represent the various parts of herself (e.g., anger, grief, rage, alienation). Her use of beauty to represent even the darkest aspects was intentional. She looked to nature for the example of how even decay can be beautiful. These are all parts that she needed to reconnect with and love.

In her artist statement, Teegerstrom said, "Some fragments are dark and difficult, and some are not, but each fragment was lost to me until I began therapy in 2020. That painful process of truth-telling gave me back parts of myself that I didn't realize were mine all along. We are born whole. What happens to us, especially when we are powerless, is what creates the fragments." Through this exhibit, Teegerstrom not only rediscovered her wholeness in the wake of loss and trauma, but she also gives us a chance to do the same.

THE PROTECTIVE COVER OF METAPHOR

A friend once called me the "G.O.A.T. of metaphors." At age fifty-three, I really think that's the nicest thing anyone's ever said about me. That's because metaphors have been a lifeline in the darkest times of my life. They've allowed me to find my way back time and again when I thought I was lost for good. Countless times metaphors have been the helping hand I could offer to heartbroken friends and grieving clients.

Why are metaphors so valuable? I think writer Parker Palmer explains it best in his beautiful book *A Hidden Wholeness*. Palmer says we can't always tell or hear the truth of something deep in our soul with straightforward language. We retreat from the directness of it. He argues that we need the "truth told slant" (as originally written by Emily Dickinson), and that's best done through metaphor, whether it be in a poem, a song, a story, or even a work of visual art. Using metaphors, or as he calls them "third things," ensures that "truth can emerge from, and return to, our awareness at whatever pace and depth we are able to handle—sometimes inwardly in silence, sometimes out loud in community—giving the shy soul the protective cover it needs."

That's it really, isn't it? Metaphors give us the protective cover we need to see what we might be frightened to admit, and the language needed to describe what we had no words for.

When I feel unmoored, poets John O'Donohue and Mary Oliver help me feel tethered to the earth and all creatures. Poet laureate Elizabeth Alexander offers me insight into my own complex set of grief emotions. Poet David Whyte reminds me to slow down and start where my feet are. The legendary Maya Angelou assures me that I can handle the pain of grief while providing me the courage to give voice to my stories. There are countless songwriters and storytellers who have done the same. Who might that be for you?

DISCOVERING WHAT YOU KNOW

Much of what we struggle with in grief is not having answers. There's so much unknown. In fact, we often find ourselves questioning everything we thought we knew to be true. This is where poetry, among other narrative forms, can be such a beautiful vehicle to discover what we *do* know. My urge to write things down and my propensity to invite you to do the same is best captured by Joan Didion, author of the exquisite memoir *The Year of Magical Thinking*. She explains, "I write entirely to find out what I'm thinking, what I'm looking at, what I see and what it means. What I want and what I fear."

Writing in any form, from notes in your phone and journal entries to poetry and long-form blogs, is a creative resource waiting for you. That last word in that sentence is the important one: You. This form of creative response to loss isn't about creating content for your blog, social media, or even a future book. It's a resource to help you discover more of you. If it turns into something that can be a gift for others in the future, great. But that's not the goal.

IMAGINATION CAN MOVE YOU

In the wake of loss, we find ourselves deeply entrenched in our pain, with our gaze cast exclusively on the absences and deficits we endure. This is the case whether we're grieving the death of someone we loved or the loss of our health and mobility resulting from a chronic or terminal illness. This tendency is valid and honest and a protective reaction deeply embedded in our neurobiology. It is, however, a dark and dangerous place we find ourselves in. It hides the other lighter realities of our present moment and disguises the possibility of a future that feels different.

I decided to reimagine my survival as a creative act. If the chemo sores in my mouth made it too painful to talk, I would find new ways to communicate. As long as I was stuck in bed, my imagination would become the vessel that allowed me to travel beyond the confines of my room. If my body had grown so depleted that I now had only three functional hours each day, I would clarify my priorities and make the most of how I spent the time I had.
—Suleika Jaouad

I think often of author Suleika Jaouad, who experienced cancer as a young adult. (She is again experiencing cancer as I write this book.) In her beautiful memoir *Between Two Kingdoms*, Jaouad reveals how

248/skills and tools that help grief suck less

she uses the power of imagination to take her awareness somewhere beyond the pain or depletion of the present moment. Jaouad writes, "I decided to reimagine my survival as a creative act. If the chemo sores in my mouth made it too painful to talk, I would find new ways to communicate. As long as I was stuck in bed, my imagination would become the vessel that allowed me to travel beyond the confines of my room. If my body had grown so depleted that I now had only three functional hours each day, I would clarify my priorities and make the most of how I spent the time I had."

I hope that her invitation changes your relationship to your imagination as it did mine. This invitation isn't just a reminder to see creativity as a tool to use when you're unable to see beyond the pain of this moment. She offers us permission to think of our limited energy as a chance to prioritize our time for the people and things that nourish us most.

HUMOR LIGHTENS THE LOAD

In our podcast conversation, voice actor Tawny Platis said that humor, in particular dark humor, is a trait or skill she has always relied on in hard times. In fact, humor was one of the things she and her husband shared, even and especially since he had been battling an illness over the course of their entire relationship.

After witnessing his sudden and shocking death, Platis explained that she knew she would rely on humor to survive. "I'm going to make jokes about this. I'm going to use my art, you know, and I know that's something . . . A lot of people don't find comedy an art form, but I'm going to use this in my work. That's how I'm going to get through this and survive is through comedy." She admits she even cracked a joke with the emergency crew who came to take her husband's body away.

You don't need to be a stand-up comedian or tell jokes to feel how humor can make the unbearable weight of grief just a little bit lighter. Laughter triggers "happy hormones" that are long dormant in grief. Having a good chuckle can also reduce the stress chemicals flooding your body. Though I do like to be a wisecrack from time to time, I found consuming humor was more my speed. Jon Stewart, then host of *The*

Daily Show, brought lightness to the countless dark, sleepless nights I endured that first year.

"MAKING" AS AN ACT OF MEMORY KEEPING

Though not as a professional, Christina Bain was a maker—or as she referred to herself, a garment sewist. A mutual friend shared Christina's blog post "What to Make When You're Dying" with me. At thirty-six years old, Christina had already endured five years of chemotherapy and radiation and undergone multiple surgeries to address the colorectal cancer that was ravaging her body.

On the podcast she explained that, as a quilter, she wanted to complete one that she'd started for her husband, Wesley. She wanted to use her skills to make him an object that would serve as a touchstone of their lives together.

Though she was low on energy and knew the act of making the quilt would be challenging, she believed it was worth it "to show up for him now while I can, to pour my attention and affection into this object that will have to stand in for me over the decades he will have without me." In fact, when I later interviewed Wesley for the podcast (after receiving a moving letter about how profoundly grateful he and Christina were that I featured her story), he arrived wearing a sweater she had knitted for him.

As we explore in "Memories for Safekeeping," our fear of forgetting our person is often what creates stickiness and distress—qualities that don't serve us. Finding forms to set down our own memories for safekeeping allows us to both remain tethered to our love for them and be free to move forward. You don't have to be a seamstress or painter or woodworker to enjoy the benefits of making. Christina's gesture is a reminder that the act of making creates a thread that connects us to who we love, even when they can't be reached.

BEAUTY WALKS

For me, the most profound creative resource of my healing has been taking what I call beauty walks. Early in my grief, I started taking long walks when I felt overwhelmed. It was an intuitive response, nothing I had read about or had a goal or plan for. I found that movement calmed down the anxious energy in my body and the change of scenery shifted my relationship with my thoughts.

Eventually, I incorporated mindfulness practice into these walks, and I still go for beauty walks today. Sometimes I'm on a mission to listen for and celebrate as many sounds as possible that I can identify on my walk. Always (and I mean always), my walks include being on the hunt for a beautiful object or view.

Yes, I'm also a beauty detective in addition to hunting for shoulds and joy. I now live in Southern California, where beauty is everywhere, but natural beauty isn't necessary to benefit from beauty walks. Whether on the walks through my old neighborhood in Austin, Texas, or wherever I travel for work, I seek beauty everywhere—even if that's just on the path from my bedroom to the coffee maker in my kitchen.

Seeing beauty in all forms, whether the creator be Mother Nature or human, offers you a gift you didn't know you needed in your grief. Whether you're perched beneath a giant painting in a museum, strolling by art murals, standing beneath a giant redwood in a forest, hiking a mountain path, or sitting on the bank of a river or beside a sculpture in a park, these objects connect you with something outside yourself, something mysterious. I promise that looking for beauty will offer you a reprieve from your grieving heart—every time.

CREATIVE RESOURCES ARE EVERYWHERE

Whether you're able to find healing in the creative works of others or you engage in these endeavors yourself, creativity brings so much value. Each engagement with a creative source is like watering a garden or enriching the soul. With each action, you come back more and more into your "aliveness," as podcast guest Cecilie Surasky calls it.

The opportunities to connect with creativity in your grief are endless. They can take the form of movement, such as dancing around your living room or watching a dance troupe on social media. Creative resources can be found everywhere, from gardening in the soil to swimming in the ocean, or even in simple, everyday walking.

AN INVITATION FOR YOU

discover your creative resources

I promise that discovering and engaging with your creative resources will be valuable tools as you navigate grief. Remember, they don't have to look a certain way, be used the same every time, or even be good in the eyes of others. And it doesn't have to be just one thing. It's easy, really. Look for things that bring you ease, relief, connection, or aliveness. Many of us disconnected from creativity and play long ago, even before the loss we faced.

For this reason, I invite you to discover, or rediscover, a creative resource. Think about how you feel when the weight of grief is bearing down on you. Then think of a creative activity or outlet. Consider what it would feel like to do that activity. Be curious to learn how it might shift the sensations in your body or change the thoughts in your mind. The activity can be something you've already tried and know feels good or you might contemplate trying something new. Get our your journal and write down a few ideas and see what creative resources you have available to you in your grief. If you're tentative, you might ask one of your dive buddies to join you in this adventure.

my creative resources

When I do/see/watch:

The positive changes I notice in my body are/might be:

The positive changes I notice in my mind are/might be:

make space

TIME TO TAKE INVENTORY

When loved ones die, or disappear in some other way, their absence takes up so much space in our imagination, in our thoughts, and in our heart. As we explore in "The World's Still Spinning," everyday life is still happening too. Our relationships, jobs, school, and creditors also require our attention, energy, and time. We're asked to hold it all, yet we still only have the same twenty-four hours in a day we did before the loss and our ability to focus is diminished.

As a result of the increased demand on our mental, physical, and emotional time, it's inevitable that we're going to feel overwhelmed and drop some commitments while forgetting appointments still on the schedule. This happens for a lot of reasons—because we're exhausted, we're scared, or we simply forgot. If that's happened to you, or should I say because that's happened to you, please hear me when I tell you, "It's OK. You're OK. It happens to all of us. That's the nature of grieving."

And it *is* possible to cut down on the time you spend on things that drain you and increase the time you spend on things that nourish you. Finding a better balance between the two requires you to do a few things:

1. Assess what's draining versus what's nourishing.
2. Be more intentional with your time.

3. Make more space in your life (a.k.a. your calendar) for the people, resources, and activities that will support you in your grief.

Get out your journal and use the prompts below to discern what is draining you and what is nourishing you. Be prepared to discover some surprising answers. Once you have a clearer understanding of the two, you can begin to decide where and on what you want to use your time and energy.

what's draining me these days?

what's nourishing me these days?

A NOTE ABOUT THE WORD *BALANCE*

Contrary to the way the buzzword *balance* is used in our everyday lives—to give us the illusion of something we can achieve and, voilà, we're done—I'm aiming for something different. Making space to incorporate your needs as a griever requires an ongoing, ever-adjusting, and intentional practice. As I've said many times, grief isn't linear and the space it takes up in our lives will expand and shrink. That means the balance we seek in grief is not static or about equal allotment of our time and energy. It's about cultivating a practice of noticing the signs that we're off-kilter and then intentionally accessing resources to bring ourselves back into alignment.

That means the balance we seek in grief is not static or about equal allotment of our time and energy. It's about cultivating a practice of noticing the signs that we're off-kilter and then intentionally accessing resources to bring ourselves back into alignment.

RELATIONSHIPS REQUIRE TIME AND ATTENTION

This new life, the one that requires you to experience all the dimensions of grieving on top of your existing life, is going to require something new of you. It will require new skills, new resources, new ways to spend the same twenty-four hours you had before. Any time we set out into the unknown, to learn something new, it requires that we practice. A lot. I know I sound like a broken record here (which as I'm writing this, I'm realizing is likely an outdated reference).

Recently I've been thinking about how our need to make space for our grief is similar to what we need when we start a new relationship. Let's face it, we're in a relationship with our grief. If we want a relationship to feel balanced and to nourish and serve our growth, the relationship requires care and feeding. If you believe in lists (which I think I've already established I'm not a big fan of), you might think there is one perfect way to have a relationship.

Even though perfection is a myth, let's humor the list-makers of the world and explore how the care and feeding of your relationship with grief might make it a better, kinder, more compassionate one. Below are ten important qualities for a relationship. I'd argue that they apply to our relationship with our grief too.

1. *Acknowledge the relationship*: Acknowledge that we're grieving.
2. *Articulate values and needs*: Articulate what we value and what we need as we grieve.
3. *Respectfully negotiate differences*: Negotiate when our needs conflict with others' wants.
4. *Communicate directly and kindly*: Communicate both our experiences and needs.
5. *Hold compassion for self and partner*: Have compassion for ourselves and others in grief.
6. *Attend to needs and interests of self*: Focus on our own needs in grief.
7. *Listen to learn, not respond*: Listen to our emotions not as facts but with curiosity.

8. *Be willing to seek external support*: Acknowledge that we can't grieve alone.

9. *Make time to practice*: Make time to practice our skills and use our resources.

10. *Assess and adjust Numbers 1 through 9 regularly*: Our relationship with grief changes, so stay alert.

FOCUS ON YOUR CALENDAR

We've covered Numbers 1 through 8 on the list above throughout this book, which brings us to Number 9. Making time to practice the skills and use the resources that will support us in grief is a step that many of us overlook.

We generally know what we need, which resources might help make grief suck less, but we haven't figured out how to make space for it. It seems as if it should be simple: Just put it on our calendar. Yet we struggle for several reasons. As we've established, our culture doesn't value self-care and healing. In fact, it places it in direct competition with our productivity-obsessed and overscheduled world. Perhaps most significantly, in grief we're so often overwhelmed by everything that even simple tasks don't feel simple.

I'm here to make the case for you to use your calendar as a tool to help you implement what you've learned so far about how to feel better, or at least how to make grief suck less. Yes, our calendars represent the nonnegotiable appointments, tasks, and responsibilities of our lives. And I'd argue that what's on our calendars, and what's not on them, is representative of what we value most.

We're living day to day, especially in deep grief, so we rarely spend time looking at our calendar. We do tomorrow what we did today, and we have no way of seeing where we could add things that nourish us or subtract things that drain us. Many of us are saying "Yes" to more things than we want or need to and not entering the little and big actions that would be much more beneficial to us. These include all the skills, practices, and resources we've explored so far.

We feel captive by our calendar instead of in charge of it. Just the thought of spending time looking at a bird's-eye view of our calendar for the next week or month might feel daunting. I suspect that's because we're bringing our all-or-nothing and either/or thinking to the task. That's why I offer some tools and tips for approaching your calendar in a way that will allow you to make space for more of what you need.

START SMALL (THINK CARRY-ON LUGGAGE ONLY)

You don't have to do it all. Not right now or ever. And you don't have to get it *right*. You don't need a full overhaul. Instead, think about implementing helpful practices in small increments.

You can't possibly anticipate everything you will need for the rest of your grief journey and even if you could, there isn't a suitcase big enough for it. You will reassess and adjust down the road. So as you get out your calendar, start small and think about adding resources that require varied amounts of time, energy, and courage. Think carry-on luggage versus packing the massive duffle bag.

> *Small* This is a skill, resource, or request that you consider a low-lift of energy and time. Perhaps it's something that takes less than thirty minutes that you can do anywhere at flexible times (e.g., morning meditations or a walk two afternoons a week).

> *Medium* Add a skill or resource that might take more time or energy or might push you out of your comfort zone. This might be reaching out to a friend, scheduling weekly video call check-ins, or setting up a weekly or biweekly therapy appointment.

> *Large* Consider adding one thing to your calendar that may take a lot of time or energy. It might be something that's a one-off event, but it's a task or skill that will make more space for other things once you've completed it. This might be sorting and donating belongings, filing for death benefits, or talking to your boss about an adjusted work schedule.

> *Unpack* Oh and to keep this metaphor going, part of what you might want to do is look at your carry-on luggage (a.k.a. calendar) and decide what doesn't need to be there. Sometimes,

simply removing unnecessary items (tasks, responsibilities, burdens) is necessary to make space for the things we need.

CREATE A BUFFER

I'm going to be extra real here: I don't practice this one nearly enough. For many of us, even when we schedule time to do something, we pack it in between a work meeting and picking up the groceries. If one task runs late, our self-care or healing activity is the first thing to go. Even if that isn't the case, sometimes the activities we do to nurture ourselves in grief can connect us with big emotions that don't necessarily go away because our thirty-minute time segment is up. This is especially important around the known holidays, anniversaries, or other days that are likely to bring on waves of grief. So be realistic about your activity and add in the buffer time you might need.

REFRAME PRODUCTIVITY

One of the challenges we face when making space for our grief is that the rules of unfettered capitalism and productivity are deeply engrained in us. When we look at our calendar, many of us have unconscious expectations about the amount of work hours, family hours, chore hours, or service hours *should* be on there. You know I'm going to call BS on those beliefs. Remember, you're grieving, and that's another full-time job.

As psychologist Dr. Nicole LePera said, "Art is therapy. Dance is therapy. Sobbing on the kitchen floor is therapy. Play is therapy. Setting a boundary is therapy. Allowing someone else to see you is therapy. Find your therapy, prioritize it, and let it heal you." So if you need a reason to justify adding meditation, a nap, reading (this book even), therapy, walks, check-in calls with friends, support groups, or anything else you feel will nourish you, consider this your permission slip.

START CLOSE IN

Remember what we learned in "Start Close In"? In early grief, many of us get lost in horizon time, a segment of time we're often tempted to focus on in our grief but that is so far down the road that it's difficult to know where to begin. When we think about adding something new to our calendars, we're often drawn toward all-or-nothing thinking. We end up feeling as if we must tackle the year, or even the next few months. This isn't necessary or even recommended in the early days of grief. Your needs will change. So start close in. Consider looking only at your next few weeks. If that feels like too much, then the next few days.

WRITE IT DOWN

I'll keep this short: Write it down. Whatever it is, write it down. Five-minute meditation? Add it to the calendar. Fifteen-minute walk? Add it. Listen to a one-hour podcast? (Mine perhaps?) Add it to your calendar. Remember, what you see in your calendar reflects what you're most likely to do. Show yourself that you're a priority and write it down. Now's the time to begin using these new skills and strategies. Get out your calendar.

⚜ AN INVITATION FOR YOU ⚜

get out your calendar

I forgot to ask: Do you have a calendar that works for you? Whether it's a digital or analog calendar, think about what form would support you best in terms of visibility and reminders of the things that matter most. If your answer to my question is "No, I don't," then maybe set down this book and decide what calendar would serve you best. Personally, I like digital calendars because I can schedule alerts and reminders. I need these. Recently, I added a month-at-a-glance paper calendar for an easy visual overview of big activities or goals that will take up a lot of my time. There's no best calendar, just the one that works for you.

If you have a calendar system that you already like, then I invite you to get it out and look at the next week. Using all you've learned so far in this book, spend some time thinking about one or two small, medium, or large activities you could add to help you better care for yourself in grief. Write them down. Block out enough time. Don't be afraid to remove items that are taking up too much space.

On the next page is a list of practices, skills, strategies, and activities you might consider adding to your calendar this week. Remember, even blocking out time to journal counts.

small

morning meditation
8 a.m.–8:10 a.m.
(every day this week)

sign up for meal-delivery program for next month
9 a.m.–9:20 a.m.
(once)

write in journal
9:30 p.m.–10 p.m.
(every day this week)

medium

listen to podcast while walking
5 p.m.–6 p.m.
(one a week for next four weeks)

schedule / have video call with best friend
7 p.m.–7:30 p.m.
(create regular schedule)

schedule body care
(massage, acupuncture, restorative yoga, etc.)
one-hour session
(once or schedule next one at time of service)

large

sort through closet and take clothes to donation center*
Saturday 9 a.m.–12 p.m.

fill out paperwork needed for
financial resources or to resolve legal matters*
Sunday 1 p.m.–4 p.m.

*have a friend help or be on standby for a call

now what?

*bringing curiosity to
the emerging story of your life*

the beautiful, messy, emerging you

TIME AND THE RIGHT ENVIRONMENT

Of course you know the story of the caterpillar becoming a beautiful butterfly. If you're like me, the whole story is: "A caterpillar becomes a butterfly. The end." It's a nice sound bite that highlights our outcomes-driven culture so beautifully. Yet I invite you to consider some important components of this story that get left out, ones that parallel our own stories of grief.

For starters, the caterpillar already possesses the traits and materials needed for its transformation into a butterfly. Time and the right environment allow it to transform. What about the actual process of transformation? We see the "after" as this beautiful butterfly, but before that happens, the caterpillar literally dissolves into a pile of slimy goo before it transitions into a majestic creature that can take flight. I'm fortunate to have monarch butterflies and other species land on the flowers near my house almost daily. It's rare that I look at them and remember that they came from a caterpillar—that they went through a messy process to become what I see before me.

I hope you're picking up what I'm not so subtly putting down here, my friends. You're a work in progress. We're all a work in progress.

You already have everything you need, or the knowledge to get what you need, for the transformation that happens as you move forward in grief. You're also not expected to do this in a quick, costume-change moment. It's going to be a slow, messy process. Wherever you are in your own transformation is exactly where you need to be. No matter how much you've changed, no matter how distant you feel from the you in the "before," remember to look at yourself and see the caterpillar in you. Remember that you're a beautiful, messy, emerging you.

ON THE NATURE OF BEING AND BECOMING

Over the past decade, I've had an incredible and sometimes insatiable appetite for discovering and learning from poets, spiritual leaders, trauma experts, novelists, thinkers, artists, researchers, and scientists. I marvel at the way each one uses language so differently, and from unique perspectives, to teach us about the essentials of what it means to be human.

As I meditated on what I wanted to share with you in this chapter, I kept coming back to the varied and profound wisdom so many of these teachers have had on this topic—the topic of transformation, of crossing thresholds, of emerging. I've found comfort in them as I continue to grapple with living while grieving. Or is it grieving while living? My hope is that their wisdom brings you comfort too.

HONORING OUR COMPLEXITY

As we explore in "Of Course It's Complicated," experiencing a complex web of thoughts, feelings, and embodied responses isn't a sign there's something wrong or that you're not grieving right. It's simply a sign that you're human. Our emergence into the world of the "after" is full of complexity, which is natural. It is also made more difficult because we're convinced that everything can be made simple.

In her book *Becoming Wise*, journalist and podcast host Krista Tippett explores why she finds comfort in the fact that humans are the most complex creatures that exist. "I'm strangely comforted when I hear from scientists that human beings are the most complex creatures we know of in the universe, still, by far. Black holes are in their way explicable; the simplest living being is not. I lean a bit more confidently into the experience that life is so endlessly perplexing. I love that word. Spiritual life is a way of dwelling with perplexity—taking it seriously, searching for its purpose as well as its perils, its beauty as well as its ravages."

Though we're admittedly full of discomfort, perhaps like Krista we can learn to appreciate our complexity as a thing of beauty too.

RECOGNIZING WE'RE ON A CONTINUUM

There's no "Ta-da! You've arrived!" moment in grief, nor in any form of healing. I know how frustrating that news can be. We just want to "get there already." We want to be able to declare, "I'm not broken anymore." While I understand the appeal of making declarations, this type of binary thinking is a setup for self-judgment and loathing.

Resmaa Menakem, an expert on trauma and disenfranchised grief, explains the risk so perfectly. "We tend to think of healing as something binary: either we're broken, or we're healed from that brokenness. But that's not how healing operates, and it's almost never how human growth works. More often, healing and growth take place on a continuum, with innumerable points between utter brokenness and total health."

We so desperately want (as do those around us) to wake up one morning and be miraculously healed. I've been there. I've wished for that. And I see this reminder from Menakem as a gift. He's inviting us to be curious about the stories, expectations, and shoulds that might creep into our thoughts or be whispered in our ears about where we should be at this point. Let his words be a reminder to shift the way you measure your progress. Shift your focus from being locked onto departure or arrival dates. Instead, reflect on all the countless points along the way.

CROSSING THRESHOLDS

What does it mean to cross a threshold? No, not the metal strip at the bottom of a door. The other kind. *Threshold* is defined as the place or point where something starts to happen, where a change or new experience occurs. We cross a profound threshold with the sheer force we experience in the wake of loss.

As we move forward in our grief, we experience the heartbreak, pain, and confusion of loss in every minute of our day, in every cell in our being. It's nearly impossible to pause and reflect on the shifts that have happened and continue to happen beneath the surface. Though we can't see or understand its magnitude, transformation and transfiguration are happening deep within us. The late Irish poet and philosopher John O'Donohue's words on crossing thresholds are offerings that I hold on to in times of tumult and transition. "I always think that's the secret of change—that there are huge gestations and fermentations going on in us that we are not even aware of. And then, sometimes, when we come to a threshold, crossing over, which we need to become different, that we'll be able to be different, because secret work has been done in us, of which we've had no inkling."

I always think that that's the secret of change—that there are huge gestations and fermentations going on in us that we are not even aware of. And then, sometimes, when we come to a threshold, crossing over, which we need to become different, that we'll be able to be different, because secret work has been done in us, of which we've had no inkling.
—John O'Donohue

INTIMATE DANCE OF JOY AND SORROW

When I was in high school, I spent every afternoon taking dance classes, moving my body to modern, contemporary, and hip-hop choreography. I was good, not great, but that didn't matter. Dance was a place of refuge and discovery for me. I was able to move through the deep pain of grief and trauma I experienced during those years and find moments of ecstatic joy brought on by the music, the choreography, and the collective celebration that transpired. When my dance teacher shared Alvin Ailey's *Revelations* with the class, it broke my heart open in ways I couldn't really understand until years later. The Alvin Ailey American Dance Theater describes this piece: "Using African-American spirituals, song-sermons, gospel songs and holy blues,

Alvin Ailey's *Revelations* fervently explores the places of deepest grief and holiest joy in the soul." It might possibly be the piece of choreography (or any art form) that best represents the intimate dance of joy and sorrow.

I know how disconcerting it can be to hold the both/and of joy and sorrow. In this messy and ever-emerging place you find yourself in as you navigate grief, remember that joy and sorrow are intimately connected by their very nature. When I find myself struggling to be with this duality, I lean on the words of writer and poet Kahlil Gibran. In *The Prophet*, he writes, "When you are joyous, look deep into your heart and you shall find it is / only that which has given you sorrow that is giving you joy. / When you are sorrowful look again in your heart, and you shall see / that in truth you are weeping for that which has been your delight."

While seeking big joy may feel far off at this moment, consider the wisdom of Cyndie Spiegel, author of *Microjoys: Finding Hope (Especially) When Life Is Not Okay*. In our podcast conversation, she describes microjoys as being immediately attainable, intentional, and deliberate. The most important thing she shared about seeking joy amid grief (in case you're feeling some guilt or resistance) is that "microjoys are just respite from grief. They don't take it away; they are just co-existing with it. It empowers us to move through grief in a way that feels natural to us."

⚘ AN INVITATION FOR YOU ⚘
be a joy detective

The should words aren't the only thing I want you to be on the lookout for in your grief. Developing joy detective skills are equally beneficial to you as you navigate grief. These may feel like a near impossibility early on, so if you're reading this and you're not ready, I get it. Skip ahead.

If joy feels out of reach or not quite descriptive of your experiences, consider these synonyms: delight, glee, elation, gratification, triumph, rejoicing, happiness, jubilance, exhilaration, radiance, pleasure.

If you weren't repulsed by the idea of joy, here's why you might find being a joy detective so valuable. Joy is one of our most valuable resources in our healing and in our capacity to build resilience. I'll add that joy has physical health benefits too. Yet often out of shame, guilt, or just a lack of practice, we overlook or intentionally ignore these moments of delight. Joy can be elusive because should drowns it out, as in the thought, "That was so fun. I feel so happy. Ugh, I shouldn't feel happy. What's wrong with me?"

I invite you to practice your joy detective skills. Take some time and—with intention—notice, describe, and savor every time you feel joy, or one of its synonyms. You might catch yourself declaring a feeling of joy to someone in conversation. You might declare it to yourself out loud. (Yep, I do that sometimes.) Track joy's appearance for one day or, if you're feeling ambitious, feel free to put a tail on it for a whole week. In your journal, reflect on and record your answers to the prompts below.

skills of a joy detective

skill 1: notice, describe, and savor

Notice and describe the expression/language you use.

Notice and describe the context/circumstances surrounding your joy.

Pause and, if you can, look in the mirror at yourself (or take a selfie).

Notice and describe your inner experience of joy (e.g., I feel butterflies in my stomach, I feel a lightness in my body, I see a twinkle in my eyes, I can see the curve of my smile).

Pause and savor this feeling. Perhaps offer some gratitude for the presence of joy in this moment. Consider if there's someone you want to share this with so that they can help you remember that you felt this way.

skill 2: discover themes

Be curious if there are certain recurring themes. Are there certain people, places, activities, or times of day that allow joy to be more present?

memories for safekeeping

HONORING CONNECTION WITH MEMORIES

There's a theory that appears in grief textbooks that you'll want to know about. Up until the end of the last century, the dominant theory on healthy grieving suggested that the function of grief was to let go and detach from the relationship with your deceased loved ones. The idea was that new relationships and a healthy life were impossible without this step.

Thankfully, by the mid-90s, a new model of grief emerged called continuing bonds (CB). As the name implies, the model encourages continuing a connection or relationship with the deceased. CB acknowledges that, rather than representing your denial, the actions you take to honor the love, including keeping and sharing memories, can improve your functioning and well-being in the present. Whew, we knew that intuitively, didn't we? I'm glad the academics caught up, even if some of our friends and family haven't yet.

Memories are critical to our ability to maintain a connection to our loved ones. A critical thing to know about memories is that they are created, adapted, and maintained through the stories we tell of our experiences. Partly true and partly fiction, our memories are malleable, but that doesn't make them any less valuable. Earlier in this book, I share how feelings are data with a story attached. Regardless, the notion that memories are created and adaptable through story is a reminder that we have some agency when it comes to creating and storing our memories for safekeeping.

The notion that memories are created and adaptable through story is a reminder that we have some agency when it comes to creating and storing our memories for safekeeping.

HURRY BACK AND GO AWAY

Sometimes remembering hurts too much. I think writer Haruki Murakami captured the duality of our relationship with memories in grief so beautifully when he wrote, "Memories warm you up from the inside. But they also tear you apart." Our memories are all we have left of the person we lost. That makes the memories sacred, something to savor and hold dear.

It's in the memories that we can feel closest to the ones we've lost. We hear their laugh, see their smile, feel their love. It's also in their memory that the pain of their absence is greatest. Memories will bring you both joy and heartache. This is another reminder to honor the both/and of grief.

Sometimes, our memories pour out of us in unexpected ways at unplanned times. Sometimes they don't take the shape of storytelling. Sometimes they're our tears. As author Ruth Ozeki wrote in her beautiful novel *A Tale for Time Being*, "Sometimes when she told stories about the past, her eyes would get teary from all the memories she had, but they weren't tears. She wasn't crying. They were just the memories, leaking out."

UNEQUAL AND MYOPIC ACCESS

It's not just you. In the beginning, memories are often so tied up in how things ended. This isn't only true of death loss. It can be true with ambiguous losses, the ending of relationships, or even when we recognize a dream cannot be realized. Often the only memories we're able to grasp hold of are related to the details, conversations, and events we experienced in the last moments. Truth be told, in the beginning, sometimes it feels as if we can't remember anything, recent or long ago.

As I mention in "This Is Your Brain on Grief," there is good reason for that, and thankfully it won't last. Though our memories are stored in many places, our prefrontal cortex, the part that goes offline in times of stress or traumatic responses, is the part that helps us locate them. Over time, you will find it easier to recall many experiences. You will be able to rebuild a fuller, richer context for the life you had together. I wish I could give you an exact date, or a formula for how and when this happens. But as I promised you at the beginning of this book, I won't bullshit you.

FEAR OF FORGETTING

It's so odd: We often worry that we'll forget our loved ones and memories of the life we shared. One of the most common worries in grief is the fear of forgetting the moments, details, and experiences that matter most. Closer to the loss, our grief brain makes remembering anything beyond what just happened very difficult. As time passes, thankfully we regain our capacity to remember more. At the same time, that means we're farther away from when the moments happened, so we struggle to retain it all.

Sometimes we're afraid of forgetting our loved ones' physical presence: the way they smelled, the way the corner of their mouth turned up unevenly when they smiled. Sometimes we try to capture Polaroid moments before the loss. Other times we don't know the loss is coming. As I lay with Eric for hours before he died in my arms, I tried to memorize him. Because I knew then, though at the time I didn't realize how much it would matter, that remembering the details about him wasn't going to come so easy someday. That it was going to take so much to remember those details.

Other times we're afraid of forgetting the big and little moments that made up our lives together. That's been a big one for me, because as I shared earlier, Eric was my memory keeper. I used to tease him about his ability to remember random details about TV shows we watched or places we went. Perhaps that's the same for you.

Part of what makes recalling these special moments so bittersweet is that our person is not here to fill in the gaps in our memory. When we see a photo or hear a song or someone asks us a detail about the memory we are sharing, we find ourselves scrambling and wishing our loved ones were here to corroborate. We're left wondering if we're getting the details right at all.

AND THE PRESSURE TO FORGET

While we're busy scrambling to remember as much as we can about the people or pets we lost, other people in our life are pressuring us to forget. Well, maybe they don't want us to forget, but they're certainly suggesting that we keep the memories of our people to ourselves. You might have experienced this when you hear family members change the subject when you recall a relevant story that includes your loved one. You might hear concern that holding on to these memories is somehow a sign that you have a problem.

Perhaps the pressure you feel is more indirect, as when you're entering the dating scene and you sense that your potential romantic partners won't want to hear about your dead wife, husband, or partner. You might get the sense that your ability to hold on to and share memories makes some people uncomfortable.

Sometimes the pressure is internal. This might be because we're hanging on to damaging grief beliefs that we're supposed to "move on," and that would mean forgetting. You know what I have to say about that. However, our motivation to forget some memories might be self-preservation. Whether the memories are a frightening image we captured at the sight of our loved one's death or the possible suffering experienced during the person's illness, there are some memories we'd rather forget.

ACTS FOR SAFEKEEPING

I'm so fortunate to know artist and materialist poet Dario Robleto. His extraordinary work spans genres, time, and space (literally). Through his work, he explores the moral dimension of memory, including art's role in being a memory keeper. He offers some of the most profound reminders about the power of memory. "Memory is a tool, a weapon against decay and against loss being permanent." Therefore, we grievers strive to share our memories, tell our stories, cast them in bronze in a way, to prevent the permanency of loss. Robleto also reminds us that if we work to carry forward the memories of those who've gone before us, then "love survives the death of cells."

Memory is a tool, a weapon against decay and against loss being permanent.
—*Dario Robleto*

The ways in which we can safekeep our memories range from the small, simple, and intimate acts, such as telling someone about our loved one, to large, complex, and public displays such as monuments: the 9/11 Memorial & Museum, the Holocaust Museum, and others. Very few of us will erect a building, but that won't prevent us from safekeeping our memories.

We can tell stories to the people in our lives during everyday conversations over dinners or at remembrance ceremonies. We can capture our memories for safekeeping when we write journal entries, letters, and blogs. If you have more to say, you might someday write a memoir or a biography to capture your memories. Of course, ceremonies such as memorial services and funerals are a place for sharing memories. Periodic graveside visits or annual rituals such as Día de los Muertos help us celebrate life and share memories of those who've died.

Sometimes the opportunities to capture and deepen our memories arrive more spontaneously and form a bridge between the present and the past. I experienced a moment like this with my daughter a few years ago.

Just before dawn, we stood at the top of Haleakalā, a 10,000-foot-tall mountain on the Hawaiian island of Maui. It was freezing cold that night. We were so high up that we felt as if we could catch the shooting stars that sprinkled the sky. As she and I watched the miracle of the sun rising above the clouds, I looked over at her and wept. Eric and I had been in that exact same spot, long before Lily was born. I felt him there. Later, I told her stories of what he experienced in the same spot she stood. In that moment, I realized that we were erecting a bridge that connects him to me to her and now to you. I'm creating a path to carry the memories of his light, his generosity of spirit, and his curiosity into the future.

There are so many incredible resources and examples of acts for safekeeping our memories in anticipation of or in the wake of loss. Francis Weller's *The Wild Edge of Sorrow* is one of my favorite books about rituals. Lorraine Hedtke's TED Talk beautifully explores the rituals of remembering. Some remembering practices include cooking the loved one's favorite meal, creating an altar with items that spark memories, dancing to the person's favorite song, wearing a favorite piece of clothing, or even holding a conversation with the person during the day or in your dreams. What are yours?

⚜ AN INVITATION FOR YOU ⚜

capture memories for safekeeping

Author and poet Elizabeth Alexander explained our desire to capture this chapter of our lives for safekeeping when she wrote, "And so, I write to fix him in place, to pass time in his company, to make sure I remember, even though I know I will never forget." I particularly love the phrase "to pass time in his company." It's a reminder that our loved ones will always be with us.

My invitation for you today is simple: Spend some time capturing a memory for safekeeping. You may want to grab an existing journal or open a document you've already started and add a memory that has recently come up as you read this book. You might consider reaching out to a mutual friend or loved ones and ask if they'd like to spend some time sharing stories. Perhaps you are already working on a scrapbook, a blog, or even a memoir. Do whatever serves you best in this moment.

If you haven't started a memory-keeping practice but want to begin, use your journal to jot down some ideas about activities or rituals you'd like to explore.

meaning-making (even though it didn't happen for a reason)

MAKING MEANING (BUT NOT NEEDING A REASON)

My jaw tightens and my fists clench every time I hear someone say, "Everything happens for a reason." Maybe you have this reaction too. It truly makes me want to use all of comedian George Carlin's *7 Words You Can't Say on TV*, plus more (and by now you know my curse word vocabulary is extensive). It's especially cruel that this phrase is most often said immediately after the loss, at funerals and memorials, when the griever is still in shock, unable to even begin trying to comprehend incomprehensible loss.

As we explore in "People Say Stupid Shit," the good intentions of the people saying this phrase are irrelevant. The consequence is the same: unrealistic and harmful pressure on the griever. This phrase bullies grievers into ignoring the validity of their whole-body response to loss. It communicates that they shouldn't feel as bad as they do. It conveys that sadness, or any other big emotions experienced from loss, is a sign that they're not looking hard enough to find the reason for the loss, as if it's a moral or mental failure on their part.

While I'm keeping my promise not to delve deeply into theoretical models of grief in this book, I do think it's important for you to know that there are currently multiple understandings and opinions of the role of meaning-making in grief. In the fields of psychology and counseling, the models vary somewhat, but they're largely in agreement that grieving requires us to construct and reconstruct the meaning we have of the world, of ourselves (our identity), and of the loss (the attachment we lost).

In the *APA Dictionary of Psychology*, *meaning* is defined as "the cognitive or emotional significance of a word or sequence of words, or of a concept, sign, or symbolic act." Finding meaning in life is about having narratives that provide us with a sense of coherence for all the experiences of life, from heartbreaking moments to joyful ones. Psychologists argue that finding meaning helps our emotional and mental well-being.

As someone trained in narrative therapy with a passion for the power of words, I appreciate the invitation to bring awareness to the stories we create. I've experienced firsthand the shift in my mental and emotional well-being when I pay close attention to caring for the stories I tell of my experiences. The same goes for all the clients I've supported over the years. In fact, it's what I've been inviting you to do throughout this book. And what I think some professional helpers and most well-intentioned grief supporters misinterpret is that to move forward in grief, grievers must find meaning in their own lives, not in their loved one's death.

Writer, podcaster, and professor Kate Bowler says, "The only thing worse than saying 'everything happens for a reason' is pretending that you know the reason. When someone is drowning, the only thing worse than failing to throw them a life preserver is handing them a reason." Yes, Kate. Yes!

YES, EVERYTHING HAPPENS—AND SOMETIMES THERE'S NO REASON

You don't need to find a reason for the bad thing happening. You can name it meaningless. Nora McInerny, host of the *Terrible, Thanks for Asking* podcast, says it perfectly. "I am done trying to reason with it. For now, at least. There is no reason. There is nothing to understand. There is no could-have or should-have because there is only what is."

I agree with Nora. And yet so many of us find it difficult to give ourselves the kind of permission that she gave herself. Our effort to find a reason for this senseless and painful loss is part of how we feel we can stay close to them. If you're not ready to set down your search, that's OK.

I've learned some things from my own seasons of grappling with reasons and from my work with others. First, setting down your search isn't a one-time event. You may feel ready to set it down, and that's great. I suggest adding "at least for now." Chances are you may pick up the search again further down the road. Especially when another hard thing happens, whether it's related to this loss or not. That's OK. That's normal. I've been there, done that.

I've also learned that letting myself off the hook from searching for a reason has made more space in my mind and in my heart to be in search of other things. This includes being on the lookout for shoulds, trying to locate joy, and even seeking a sense of meaning in this shattered life I'm putting back together.

MOVING THROUGH THE WORLD DIFFERENTLY

One way to think of the urge for meaning-making in grief is to consider how the person's life and death have made you a different person in ways that make you better, make the world better, or in how you carry the person's legacy forward.

One of the first guests for my podcast was restaurant entrepreneur Jae Kim. He shared that watching his little sister's illness journey with neurofibromatosis type 2 (NF2) and losing her caused a sea change in how he lives his life—both personally and professionally. Kim told me, "Absolutely. I am a different person today because of her." Soon after her death, he developed a daily practice of gratitude, and today he shows up to work looking for and noticing what's going right instead of what's wrong. Kim explained that, as an entrepreneur, he's always thinking about the future, about what's next. Living in the world without his sister has transformed his life. Now when a new opportunity presents itself, he thinks, "Yes, we could do that, but does this move my heart?"

A TRANSFORMED HEART

Finding meaning in life doesn't need to include big gestures such as starting a nonprofit, being an outspoken advocate, or changing your vocation to try to remedy the cause of your loss. Though I've done all those things, the true reflection of the meaning I find in my life is represented in my transformed heart. I think the same is true for many of us.

When leveled by loss, we can discover meaning in life by allowing the experience to transform our hearts. If we allow it, grief can soften our hard parts. It can help us get clear on what is and isn't important.

When leveled by loss, we can discover meaning in life by allowing the experience to transform our hearts. If we allow it, grief can soften our hard parts. It can help us get clear on what is and isn't important. In a world that primarily exhibits sympathy and pity, expanding our capacity for empathy and compassion is how we make meaning in the wake of these losses. We can carry our hearts, with them in it, into the world with so much more care than ever before. The cohesive narrative we're creating and acting out sees a world that requires and benefits from compassion.

AN APPRECIATION OF TIME

I won't be telling you, "Time heals all wounds." I cover the problem with that expression in "The Messy Middle." I do believe that many of us have a newfound appreciation for time. We have a changed perspective, discovering time's sacred qualities in ways that many who haven't experienced profound loss aren't able to grasp.

As grievers, we're able to shift our narratives of time because we were reminded that our time here isn't limitless, and that everyone and everything we love is temporary. You don't need to move through the world with an appreciation of time and hold sacred every single moment for it to be a sign that you've found meaning. We all get lost in the distractions of the world. I think simply being able to remind yourself with a prompt such as, "Time is precious. Is this how I want to be spending it?" is evidence enough. Or as poet Mary Oliver captures so beautifully in the last stanza of "Summer Days": "Doesn't everything die at last, and too soon? / Tell me, what is it you plan to do / with your one wild and precious life?"

SEEKING ALIVENESS

Many of us move through one or more seasons of our lives in some state of numbness. Sometimes we're aware of it; often we're not. The reasons and circumstances may vary, but in large part, the numbness protects us from the pain and heartache of personal loss. We may be numbing ourselves against the losses we witness as we consume the news of our community or the world.

We may numb to protect ourselves from the lack of safety and security we feel in the wake of trauma. When we lose some aspect of our health or abilities, we may dull our engagement with the world too as an act of self-preservation. Every single person who's had a loved one die knows the sensation of shock and the experience of being dazed and confused.

Again, shock and numbness are appropriate for short periods of our lives. They serve a purpose. It's when they keep us from emerging into a life of meaning that they become a barrier. We often stay in this place longer than needed because the internal protective response is compounded by a culture that reinforces limited attention spans and escapism.

Yet finding meaning in life is impossible from this place of lifelessness. The irony is that while a significant loss can lead us to a place where we're disconnected from our lives, it's also the very experience that can energize us to reconnect and engage with the world with renewed intention and spirit.

We come to understand that sorrow is a part of life, so the goal isn't to avoid it or to seek an everlasting state of happiness. Instead, the invitation is to move forward in grief with meaning and purpose by seeking *aliveness*. I learned this term from podcast guest Cecilie Surasky when she shared the story of her eighteen-year-old son Theo's death from an accidental overdose. Surasky described the meaning she was creating out of this loss: "I used to think that the only continuum that mattered for humans was sad to happy. But now I think that the continuum that matters, especially in this culture, is numbness to aliveness."

Yet finding meaning in life is impossible from this place of lifelessness. The irony is that while a significant loss can lead us to a place where we're disconnected from our lives, it's also the very experience that can energize us to reconnect and engage with the world with renewed intention and spirit.

FIND IT IN THE SPACE BEFORE THE STORY

As I mention throughout this book, the stories we tell of our experiences aren't neutral. Each time we tell a story, we shape and reshape both our memories and how we feel about the past. Not only that, but the repeated stories we tell also influence the possibilities we see (or don't see) in our future. It's in the space before we tell the story that we have a chance to find new meaning.

In the beginning we tell the story of loss repeatedly to try to make sense of it. It's reiterated, adjusted, repeated. That is one of the many important ways in which we can begin to digest the reality of our loss. At some point, and I wish I could tell you when, there's a chance to pause before you tell the story. Not because it doesn't need to be heard, but it's in the space before the story that you can discover what's been hidden from you. With curiosity and compassion, you may find in that space a deep well of values you hold dearest. It's in that quiet space that you may discover the meaning you've been searching for.

In honor of National Poetry Month one year, I wrote "In the Space Before the Story." It's an invitation to discover the space so that we can find meaning in our loss stories.

In the Space Before the Story

There is a space
A quiet, subtle, often unnoticed opening
Between the happening and the story of the happening

An opportunity lies in that alcove
In that quiet, subtle, and unnoticed opening
Look closely and discover a vast vocabulary nestled there

Always in a rush to discover meaning
Before our mind has a chance to curate
Words begin to tumble out, piling into sentences
Sentences scaffold one on top of another forming paragraphs
Paragraphs unknowingly take on unmistakable shapes
The shapes that become the story of the happening

Instead, perhaps we might choose to linger in that space
Between the happening and the story of the happening
Sorting and selecting from the expansive collection of words
Considering the tone and texture of the sentences being built
Carefully evaluating the integrity of the frames taking shape

Then we might see
How the shapes become the story of the happening
How the story of the happening makes its meaning
How the meaning made by the story of the happening
Is the home in which we will reside

☽ AN INVITATION FOR YOU ☾
make space for meaning in your story

Whether it's in the stories we tell out loud to others about our losses or the ones we tell in our head about the how and why of our suffering, each telling reinforces a certain narrative. If you're in a place in your grief where you're ready to make space for meaning in your story, I invite you to explore the prompts below. If you're not ready, that's OK. The prompts will be here when you are.

---

write your story
and make space for something new

step 1

Get out your journal and write the "The Story of My Loss." Write the version you've told recently. Write without editing or judging. Just write as if you were telling someone your story for the first time.

step 2

Walk away from your story for an hour or a day or a week.

step 3

Read your story out loud. Be with the emotions that it brings up.

Then below the story or on the next page, make notes about any new learning, wisdom, or insights you've gained. It can be something you've discovered about your identity or preferences. It might include insights or new perspectives on relationships. It could be something broader, relating to the nature of what it means to be human. It doesn't even have to be something new. It could be something you already knew, but in reflecting, you discover how it was reinforced or amplified in the wake of loss. No knowledge is too small to record.

---

when grief becomes part of the story—but not the whole story

GRIEF IS BECOMING A PART OF YOUR STORY, NOT YOUR WHOLE STORY

If you remember (and it's OK if you don't, because grief brain), I started this book by telling you that we have a problem with our collective story of grief. I said that our grief story is too narrow and singular, causing grief to be needlessly sneaky and for us to suffer unnecessarily. Throughout this book, I've done my best to expand our collective story of grief so that you can see your lived experience reflected in this new, emerging, and expanding story.

I began by sharing what I see as our current collective grief story, starting with the narrow, singular version:

> Grief happens when someone you're close to dies. You feel sad and occasionally angry (but only in moderation). Those feelings can last for a while, maybe months (if the person was someone you were close to). You mostly keep your feelings to yourself. If you must, you see a therapist or find a group of other grievers like you so that you don't get your grief on other people. You keep busy, get back to work—you know, because it's "good for you." Then, as soon as possible, you move neatly and in an orderly fashion through the five stages of grief like some sort of to-do list. And voilà. If you're good enough, tried hard enough, and are strong enough, in about a year, you're done. And now, you can move on.

My hope is that you now hold an expanded grief story. A story that helps you feel seen and supported. A story that perhaps you can share with others so that they won't suffer unnecessarily.

EXPANDED, INCLUSIVE GRIEF STORY

Grief happens when the manuscript of your life is torn to shreds. Your life story includes people, relationships, abilities, dreams, and a sense of home. When you lose one of those things, you grieve. It's a normal response to loss. Grief impacts your physical, cognitive, emotional, spiritual, and relational well-being. While grief is experienced by 100 percent of the population, multiple times in our lives, you will experience grief in your own unique way. There's no timeline or formula for grieving. There are some skills, resources, and supports that will ease your suffering and make grief suck less. You will not move on *from* your grief. You will move forward *with* it. Grieving is learning, and you will integrate the knowledge you're gaining along the way into an emerging story of your life. Your loss and your grief become a part of your story, not the whole story.

ANOTHER CHAPTER EMERGES

In the wake of loss, your whole story was grief (or still is if you're in those early days). In that season, every breath you take, every thought you have of the past, present, and future is grief-related. Every emotion you feel, from worry to sorrow to anger, is about the loss you experienced. That's the nature of grief. In the beginning, it consumes us.

As time passes, as you weep and rage, as you pick yourself up and fall down again, as you reach for support and have moments of joy and new experiences, somehow a new chapter of your story emerges. The storyline of the next chapter will still include your profound losses, but these losses will show up in different ways with new people, events, and experiences. Your loss will appear in every subsequent chapter for the remainder of your story, though the number of pages it takes up will likely decrease over time. Remember, it's not that your grief gets smaller. It's that your life expands around it.

I want to pause here for a moment.

You may have very mixed feelings about all this, and that's OK. If you're not ready to think about living into the next chapters, you may want to pause, too, and be with whatever emotions are coming up for you. Maybe even explore the feelings in your journal. Or you might want to hop over to another chapter, maybe "The World's Still Spinning" or "Start Close In."

As time passes, as you weep and rage, as you pick yourself up and fall down again, as you reach for support and have moments of joy and new experiences, somehow a new chapter of your story emerges.

A (MORE) COHESIVE STORY IS EMERGING

A wise therapist or grief support group leader might say, "The goal of your sessions is ultimately to help you integrate your grief." What might that mean? Early on in grief, that first new chapter that emerges after loss feels like an outlier. It doesn't really fit with the all-consuming story of the grief we've been experiencing for the past weeks and months or more. Over time, and with thoughtful intention, each new chapter we write integrates our identities and experiences into a more cohesive story. Each new chapter we write and rewrite helps make the overarching story of our lives more interrelated.

We don't have to find a reason for or make sense of the loss, but integrating our story means that we're rebuilding our sense of self, purpose, and our place in the world.

In 2022, after devouring *The Healing Power of Storytelling* by physician and researcher Dr. Annie Brewster, I invited her to be a guest on the podcast to explore the subject. In her book, in clinics, and through her work at Health Story Collaboratives, Brewster offers so much guidance and wisdom for writing and rewriting our personal narratives. She works with patients with chronic and terminal illnesses to find a path toward emotional healing using narrative techniques. Her goal is to "inspire you to engage deeply with your own story, to craft a version of the story you are living at this moment, and then to reframe and refine it ... to make it the most authentic and empowering story possible." That's what we're seeking as we live into these next chapters of our lives: a story (a.k.a. a life) that is the most authentic and empowering version of the person we're becoming.

YOU'RE STILL THE MAIN CHARACTER, ONLY DIFFERENT

Maybe someone has said to you, "Why can't you just be like you were before?" Maybe you've even asked that question of yourself, desperately wishing you could be the version of yourself you were before the loss. I think we've all wished that.

The challenge is that people (including ourselves) expect us to play the same character as before. They act as if our character hasn't been permanently altered. They fail to acknowledge that the backstory to our lives has been profoundly changed. So we must adapt. They don't appreciate that we're left to our own devices to begin rewriting the manuscript of our lives with no instructions. Sometimes we get unsolicited feedback from "editors" who want to change our tone, our style, our lines, or how we should feel, just so that we can make sense to them again.

Remember, my friend, you're still the main character of your life story. And in life, as in fiction, characters change. They age, meet new people, have new experiences, face challenges and losses, adapt. They're still them, only different. The same is happening to you.

This can be really disorienting, I know. It's OK if you can't find yourself right now. It might feel as if you're in an overcrowded bar looking for you and you can't find yourself. It's hot, you're sweaty, the music's too loud, and people are shouting. You're desperately looking into their faces to find yourself, but you can't. Even when you look in the mirror, you don't recognize yourself.

It will take time to become familiar with the changing you. When you feel lost like this, I invite you to pause. Take in some deep breaths, place your hand over your heart, and say out loud to yourself, "I'm still here. I'm still in here. I'm not going anywhere. I'm not alone."

YOU'RE STILL THE AUTHOR

Even though these losses happened to you, remember that you're still the author of your story. While you're getting input from others, and that can be helpful sometimes, *you* get to decide how you will adapt and what you want for your main character. As Dr. Atul Gawande so beautifully explains in his book *Being Mortal: Medicine and What Matters in the End*, "You may not control life's circumstances, but getting to be the author of your life means getting to control what you do with them."

One way to think about this in a way that might feel softer or less scary is to consider that writing your story is more about adding than editing. I'm not suggesting that you should edit out the significance, value, or impact of the loss in your life. Instead, I invite you to think about approaching your emerging story as you would read a book. When you read the first chapter, you're in it and have a close-in, immediate view and perspective of the characters, their lives, maybe even a sense of their future.

As you continue reading, new information comes to light and characters endure new experiences, and this often changes how you see them and how you feel about them. This opens new possibilities for their story to unfold. This new information doesn't require you to erase or forget about what happened in that first chapter. It simply invites you to see a fuller, richer version of the characters. I wonder if that helps you see this place in your story in a way that feels less scary and still allows you to honor the significance of your loss.

FINDING HOME IN YOUR STORY

The first chapter of our life in the wake of loss feels so odd. Early in grief, we can't imagine ever feeling that sense of belonging to a place or to the world in any meaningful way. We often feel adrift, without a home—without our loved one. But the *home* we're desperately trying to find is a place in our own lives, in our own story.

As we move forward in grief, as we invest in our physical, emotional, cognitive, spiritual, and relational well-being, we're taking steps back to that place of belonging to ourselves, belonging to our own story. Each time we accept support, share a memory, or create a new memory, we're laying the foundation for our story—a place we can call home.

Before you go, I want to share one more beautiful piece of wisdom from David Whyte. In his epic poem "The House of Belonging," he explores the longing to find home within our own story, within our own lives. The poem closes with this:

> *This is the bright home*
> *in which I live,*
> *[...]*
> *this is where I want*
> *to love all the things*
> *it has taken me so long*
> *to learn to love.*
> —from "The House of Belonging" by David Whyte

TURNING THE PAGE, NOT CLOSING THE BOOK

You've been reading for a while, and now it's your turn to write. This book will always be here for you. You can return to it when you once again need to feel seen and held in your grief. It will be here to suggest you set down the shoulds and be on the lookout for joy. Pick it back up when you need a reminder to care for your whole self. Open the pages when you need an invitation to keep discovering what you need and to help you find courage to ask others for support. This book is here to help you practice all the new skills you're learning and to remind you that wherever you are in your grief journey is where you need to be.

Remember, you've already started, so that's the good news. Keep your focus close in. There's no one destination, no right path to get where you're going. There's simply you: kindly, compassionately, and patiently rewriting the manuscript of your emerging story, one that includes the memories, the values, the love, and the meaning you're making of what you've lost.

I see you. I hear you. I'm holding you in my heart.

With love, your friend and fellow griever,

Lisa

a
little
extra

afterword

I dreamt of bringing this book to you for years. I worked on the manuscript in every coffee shop in Austin, on front porches, in airports, and in my new home in Southern California. Pieces of this book started as voice memos while walking or driving, as Instagram posts, and as scribbles in various notebooks and on sticky notes I carried around. I always believed with my whole heart that I would somehow find a way to bring these grief lessons to you.

What I never imagined during those years is that ten days before the manuscript deadline, I would receive a cancer diagnosis. WTF? Really? A diagnosis, by the way, that was delayed by more than a year, just like what happened to my late husband with his cancer diagnosis.

As I write this, I'm about halfway through my treatment for triple positive breast cancer. I'm grateful to share the news that the prognosis is good, despite surgery, chemotherapy, and radiation that were brutal and utterly humbling. And while I'm not (nor will I likely ever be) ready to declare cancer as a gift, there have been some beautiful moments along the way. I believe this diagnosis gave me something I needed, an opportunity to relearn the most important life lesson I had lost track of along the way: that we all need help sometimes.

Initially I found myself wanting to be busy, independent, and strong. I felt compelled to tell everyone, "I'm fine. It's OK. I can do it on my own." But this book had a message for me. The only chapter I had left to write in those ten days between the diagnosis and submission deadline was the chapter "Your Turn to Buddy-Breathe." OK, I hear you!

I immediately committed to saying "Yes" to offers of support. I found myself saying, "Thank you," instead of, "You don't have to." When people asked for my mailing address or my Venmo, instead of telling them, "You don't need to get me anything," I gave them the information with an attitude of gratitude. When three friends offered to fly across the country to take me to weekly chemotherapy sessions, instead of telling them, "It's too much," I said, "That would be wonderful. Thank you."

It will be a while before I'm healthy enough to get on my scuba gear, dive in, and breathe deeply. In the meantime, I'm grateful that I've had the chance to practice the third part of the life lesson I learned forty years ago. This time around, I discovered a bonus about buddy-breathing that I previously missed: Letting people help deepens a sense of connection and belonging. It enriches relationships. I began to feel deeply in my core that, although no one can go through the treatment for me, I don't have to navigate this alone. None of us do.

appendix a

an alphabet of reminders for your grief journey

*A*ttend to your whole self
*B*e with your emotions
*C*reate, be curious, be compassionate
*D*iscover capacity and resiliency
*E*merge in your story
*F*eel it all
*G*rief-wave surf
*H*eal your body, mind, and soul
*I*nvestigate what matters
*J*oy-detect
*K*eep memories
*L*earn a new language
*M*ap untraveled routes
*N*otice mindfully
*O*bserve the shoulds
*P*ractice patience, patience, patience
*Q*uestion without answers
*R*est, restore, remember
*S*tart close in
*T*ake help
*U*npack grief beliefs
*V*ocabulary expansion
*W*rite and rewrite narratives
*eX*plore new terrain
*Y*es/and your story
*Z*illion and one thoughts and feelings

appendix b

a letter to the grief supporters

---

show up, shut up, and listen—oh, and keep showing up

Dear grief supporter,

I know it can be heartbreaking to witness someone you love grieving a deep loss. You may wonder, "What do I say? What do I do?" And you may search for the right or perfect words. I know: You don't want to get it wrong. Here's the thing, though: You might. Most of us do. The important thing is that you show up anyway.

Below is a quick cheat sheet of things to know about being a grief supporter. If you remember nothing else, remember this: You cannot fix the griever, no matter how hard you try. In fact, the griever doesn't need to be fixed. What the person needs most is your compassionate presence. The best way to support a griever is simple: Show up, shut up, and listen—and keep showing up.

BEFORE YOU SHOW UP TO SUPPORT YOUR PERSON
Know This
Grief looks different for everyone and it's not always visible. The person may be crying, yelling, laughing, silent, or all the above within a matter of minutes. All emotions are valid in grief, including anger. Grief isn't linear and it doesn't follow stages. Grief is messy, comes in waves, and can affect the person's physical, cognitive, emotional, spiritual, and relational well-being. The significant impact of grief lasts months and years, not weeks. People don't move on from grief, they move forward with it.

Assess Your Expectations

It's not your job to fix the griever's pain or to make the person feel better or happy. It's not that person's job to make you feel comfortable or show you gratitude. There is no right thing to say, though there are some things that can be harmful (see below). This interaction isn't about you, so don't expect a two-way conversation. Continue to bring the focus back to the griever.

Check Your Energy

Your energy is contagious. If you're nervous and worried, the griever will feel it. Take a few minutes before you show up in person, pick up the phone, or hop on a video call. Breathe deeply. Remind yourself that it isn't your responsibility to fix the person's pain. Your caring presence and calm energy are the gift of support the griever needs most.

WHEN YOU SHOW UP, ASK—THEN SHUT UP AND LISTEN

The best thing you can do to show that you care and to learn what the griever needs most in the moment is to be present. You might start by asking what the griever needs. Then shut up and listen. The person might not know the answers. Or the answers might not match what you expected or what you were prepared to offer. That's OK. Follow the griever's lead. Even in the long silences. Even if the griever is crying. Use eye contact and hugs or other physical touch (when appropriate) to show you care.

> *DON'T say things such as:*
> *"Everything happens for a reason."*
> *"At least she isn't suffering anymore."*
> *Any sentence that starts with "At least . . ."*
> *"You're so strong. I don't know how you do it."*
> *"You'll find love again."*
> *"You still have/can have children."*
> *"You just need to move on."*
> *"I just can't imagine."*
> *"You need to stop thinking about him."*

"This is like the time when I . . ."
"This reminds me of when . . ."
Any sentence that starts with "You should . . ."

DO say things such as:
"I'm holding you in my heart."
"Whatever you're feeling in your grief is normal."
"There's no right or wrong way to grieve."
"They will always be with you."
"Your [person] was such a loving presence."
*"You can talk to me about your [person] whenever you want. I'm
    here to listen."*
"It's OK to not be OK."
*"I want you to know that you're not alone in carrying their
    memory forward."*
"I promise to keep showing up."
*"You don't have to do or say or be anything other than what
    comes naturally."*
"This is fucking bullshit and it sucks so much."

Help in a Way That Helps the Griever

Think of a time when you were laid low by grief or in pain for some other reason. What did support look or feel like? I'm guessing it didn't involve big gestures. I imagine it was someone's calm, loving presence. No one tried to rush you to get over the pain or talk you out of it. Your supporter was there to acknowledge and affirm how hard it was.

That's the best kind of help you can offer the griever in your life.

It's great to offer practical support or help too. Remember, grief impacts people's cognitive functioning. Little tasks can be overwhelming. So to help ease the griever's burden, offer to help set up automated payments or reminders, take care of household chores, or run errands. It's important to make sure that you're offering help that is useful and doesn't require the person to make big decisions or put in a lot of effort.

KEEP SHOWING UP

Most people stop showing up for the griever after the funeral or memorial. Some continue to show up over the first month or two. Only a few tend to keep checking in after that. Be one of those people who continues to show up. Grievers are often just coming out of the shock of it all after the first few months, only to feel more alone.

Below are a few ways to keep showing up in a meaningful way:

1. Put the death date or other milestone dates (holidays, birthdays, Hallmark holidays such as Father's/Mother's Day) in your calendar. Make sure to reach out on or before that day.
2. Show up in person, call or text, send an audio memo, make a video call, or mail a card. Ask if the griever is open to setting up a regular phone call or video meeting to ensure the person knows that you'll be checking in.
3. When you text or call, remind the person that you don't need a response. You will always hold the person in your mind and in your heart.
4. Ask if it's OK to share a favorite memory of the person who's died. Invite the griever to share a memory too.
5. Continue to offer practical support. Acknowledge that the person might not always know what's needed, and that needs might change. Remind the griever that's OK.

On behalf of your loved one, thanks for being willing to learn how to show up, shut up, and listen—and to keep showing up.

about the author

Lisa Keefauver is a grief activist, writer, and speaker. She began her career as a social worker and narrative therapist in 2004. She expanded her activism in a variety of roles: clinical director, cofounder of a nonprofit, clinical supervisor, facilitator of personal and professional growth and healing, and mentor. Lisa's activism also includes the intimate work of holding space and bearing witness for people as they navigate their grief journey. Lisa's professional insights and wisdom illuminate and dismantle the limited and misleading collective story of grief that leads to unnecessary suffering that causes so much harm. Her wisdom and insights on grief are also embodied from her personal losses, including the death of her husband Eric in 2011.

Lisa's grief advocacy inspired her to found Reimagining Grief to create a more grief-literate world. Best known for her interview skills as host of the top-rated podcast *Grief is a Sneaky Bitch*, Lisa has shared her warmth, wisdom, humor, and compassion by facilitating conversations on stages, as an organizational consultant for companies, in workshops and retreats, and with clients one-on-one. Lisa's unique approach to shifting our grief culture led to an invitation to teach a Loss and Grief course at the University of Texas at Austin.

Lisa's role as a thought leader has also led her to appear across media platforms; write for outlets such as *Thrive Global, SAP, Medicinal Media*, and *Candidly*; serve as a CBS-TV contributor; and appear on stages, including the one where she presented her viral TEDx Talk, "Why Knowing More about Grief Can Make It Suck Less." She was also profiled as a Media Maker by Medicinal Media. Lisa lives in Southern California with her rescue pup, Ms. Frankie.

dedications to my grief supporters

I've been extraordinarily fortunate to have loved and been loved by so many people who have accompanied me through the darkness and the light in my life. This book is a result of their love and unwavering belief in my mission to create a more grief-literate world, and because of their sweet (and often passionate) encouragement, I share my uncensored insights with all of you.

Eric Keefauver: My late husband, for giving me the chance to experience what it truly means to love and to be loved.

Lily Keefauver: My wise, witty, and caring daughter, for inspiring me daily with her courageous, curious, and creative approach to living.

Autumn Campbell: My soul sister, for the countless hours she lovingly and thoughtfully provided me encouragement and for constructive feedback on this book—and for always helping me keep the needs of my readers in the forefront of my mind.

Krissy Teegerstrom: My warm and wise friend, artist, and creative coach, for believing in and guiding me from the first day we met at the beginning of my journey to reimagine grief.

Andy and Joan Nagy, Susan Schreiber, and Robert Nagy: My parents, stepmom, and big brother, for their unwavering love and support in my life, in my grief, and in my quest to bring this book to life.

Susan Martin and all the ladies of the "Take Care of Lisa Crew": My incredible group of girlfriends, for picking me up off the ground (literally and metaphorically) in the wake of Eric's death—and for keeping me company down there when I couldn't get up.

Melissa Gould, J'aime Morrison, Leslie Gray Streeter, and many others: My friends and fellow unlucky members of the Widow Club, for making the journey of navigating this loss so much less lonely and for bringing joy to my days.

Joe Esquibal: My one-of-a-kind friend, for being a grief support role model and for the lessons he gifted me when I had the honor of accompanying him as he took his last breath.

acknowledging my grief guides

Over the past decade, I've had an incredible and at times insatiable appetite for discovering and learning from poets, spiritual leaders, trauma experts, novelists, thinkers, artists, researchers, and scientists. I marvel at the way each one uses language so differently, and from unique perspectives, to teach us about the essentials of what it means to be human—on the nature of being and becoming.

As I meditated on what to share with you in this book, I kept coming back to the varied and profound wisdom that so many of these people have had on the topic of transformation, of crossing thresholds, of emerging. I've found comfort in their experiences, expertise, and wisdom as I continue to grapple with living while grieving. Or is it grieving while living? My hope is that their wisdom brings you comfort too.

Some grief guides referenced in this book include:

All my podcast guests, whose deep vulnerability and unique wisdom inspired me to continue my mission to change the narratives of grief, one conversation at a time.

Chimamanda Ngozi Adichie: award-winning author, whose work, particularly her TED Talk "The Danger of a Single Story" and memoir *Notes on Grief*, amplified my passion for expanded storytelling.

Elizabeth Alexander: poet, scholar, widow, and *New York Times* best-selling author, whose memoir *The Light of the World* spoke deeply to my own experience of widowhood.

Pauline Boss: considered the godmother of "ambiguous loss," whose book of the same title and lifelong research gave language to a more expansive and comprehensive view of grief.

Annie Brewster: physician, podcast guest, and author of the extraordinary book *The Healing Power of Storytelling*, which reignited my passion for the transformational impact of narratives.

Brené Brown: social worker, whose book *Atlas of the Heart* reminds me of the importance of using precise language for my very human experience of grief and grieving.

Susan Cain: best-selling author of *Bittersweet*, whose invitation to find beauty in the "both/and" affirmed my own inner-knowing and quest to invite others to sit with complexity.

Susan David: psychologist and best-selling author of *Emotional Agility*, whose insights on our need for emotional agility and her relentless challenge of toxic positivity inspires me daily.

Megan Devine: social worker and author, whose book *It's Okay That You're Not Okay* was a powerful affirmation of my beliefs that our culture has caused unnecessary suffering for grievers.

Elizabeth Gilbert: award-winning author, whose book *Big Magic* reignited my creativity and whose precious reminder to bow in absolute humility to the force of grief has been lifesaving.

Prentis Hemphill: therapist and somatic teacher, whose wisdom on the embodied self and the beauty of boundaries has been an enormous help in returning to my body in grief.

Dr. Gabor Maté: physician and author, whose book *The Myth of Normal* expanded my understanding of the relationship between Big T and little t traumas, attachment, and grief.

Nora McInerny: author of *Hot Young Widows Club* and podcast host, whose combination of humor and heart helped me reclaim my love of humor and sarcasm to soften the hardness of life.

Resmaa Menakem: healer, social worker, and somatic practitioner, whose book *My Grandmother's Hand* inspired me to feel and embody in a new way the place of culture in navigating trauma.

Emily and Amelia Nagoski: authors of *Burnout: The Secret to Unlocking the Stress Cycle*, whose instruction on connecting our heads and our bodies has helped lessen the stickiness (and sneakiness) of grief.

Kristin Neff: Researcher and podcast guest whose wisdom on the power and practice of self-compassion has eased my journey.

Dario Robleto: artist and materialist poet, whose work has been a constant reminder to see the moral responsibility and beauty of carrying forward the memory of others.

Mary-Frances O'Connor: psychologist, researcher, and podcast guest, whose book *The Grieving Brain* offered me a deeper understanding on why we experience "grief brain."

Mary Oliver: poet, whose profound reflections on life and our connection to nature, best captured in her poem "The Summer Day," is a constant source of grounding for me, especially when life feels heavy.

John O'Donohue: poet and philosopher, who has been a life teacher through the wisdom and poetry found in his books, especially *Anam Cara*, on wide-ranging topics that include the meaning of beauty and love, our connection to the earth, what it means to be human, and, of course, grief.

Ruth Ozeki: author, whose novel *A Tale for Time Being* explored our shared humanity and search for home and so beautifully articulated what the tears of grief represent.

Rainer Maria Rilke: poet, whose work, particularly in *Go to the Limits of Your Longing*, thoughtfully offered the invitation to be with the "both/and" of life.

Krista Tippett: best-selling author of *Becoming Wise* and host of the profound podcast *On Being*, whose sustained meditation on the nature of what it means to be human has taught me so much about this journey of life.

David Whyte: poet and author, whose words in *Start Close In* and whose Three Sunday series offered an invaluable invitation to adjust my gaze when life feels daunting.